D1453598

TREASURES
from Earth's Storehouse

BASED ON THE EDGAR CAYCE READINGS

by Juliet Brooke Ballard

A.R.E. PRESS • VIRGINIA BEACH • VIRGINIA

TO THE MEMORY OF
MARJORIE CHERMSIDE,
MY DEAR AUNT AND FOSTER MOTHER,
WHO FIRST MADE ME AWARE OF THE
TREASURES IN EARTH'S STOREHOUSE

A Note to the Reader

The A.R.E. does not present any of the information in this book as prescription for the treatment of disease. Application of medical information found in the Edgar Cayce readings should be undertaken only under supervision of a physician.

More in-depth information on certain medical problems is available to A.R.E. members in the Circulating Files. For information on the Files or for a list of suppliers of items found in the Cayce readings write to: Membership Services, A.R.E., Box 595, Virginia Beach, VA 23451.

CONTENTS

A DIRECTORY TO THIS BOOK

TREASURES
from Earth's Storehouse

PROLOGUE

The Scope of This Study

In a prior volume, *The Hidden Laws of Earth,* the author undertook to present the salient features in this universe of ours, which according to the Edgar Cayce readings was created entirely "to meet the needs of man, for which there was made all that was made." (3744-4) In that book, the author examined the general features of the framework in which man operates.

This book is a continuation of that one and deals primarily with the kingdoms given into man's care on earth—mineral, vegetable and animal. If man handles these wisely and in accordance with the overall plan, they can be of great help to him in his everyday living and spiritual development. If he uses them poorly, he will find them impediments. It is, therefore, important to know the nature of all three kingdoms, how they should be approached, how they should be utilized. This book presents the viewpoint of the readings on these subjects.

Summation of the Preceding Volume

Since this book is a continuation, it is imperative that it contain a brief summary of its predecessor, in which pertinent references from the Edgar Cayce readings may be found.

According to the readings, God, a motive Force, created souls to be His companions. They were given free will so that they could *voluntarily* attain the position of co-creator. Using free will, many souls fell into matter. God then set up a way by which they could evolve upwards out of the bonds of materiality.

This return to the Father is accomplished slowly during a succession of lives (incarnations) separated by sojourns in the environs of the planets. During a planetary sojourn an entity (or individual) is subjected to the mental influences peculiar to the environs of that planet. Returning to earth in another body, the entity should carry some of these mental characteristics in his make-up to be used in the following earth life as well as in future ones. He is attracted to one planet after another in successive interims between incarnations on earth until finally the benefit of all the necessary mental influences has been acquired.

The other volume explains that it is by vibration that man is given the opportunity to change. Using the same free will by which he plunged into materiality, he can utilize vibrations in the environment around him to advance himself.

The first book deals with the nature of the vibrations stemming from the heavenly bodies on an astrological level and, in the case of the sun and moon, on a more purely physical one as well. It explores the subject of water. It includes the readings' statements on how force emerges from the sun and can be developed in different forms. Three of these—electricity, color and sound—are discussed.

Lastly it explores the matter of cycles, a necessary feature of such a system as ours and one which insures that all of these influences will be available for an entity to handle, but not all simultaneously!

The purpose of these two books is to show the nature of the respective influences and kingdoms provided, all potentials for help or harm, in order that the reader may conduct himself here on earth in a manner that will allow him to *reap the benefits and avoid the hazards* through knowledge of the laws.

For maximum results information from both volumes should be merged.

THE THREE KINGDOMS

What is the nature of the three kingdoms on earth over which man has dominion? The readings tell us that they are expressions of God and that through their creative influence, they themselves seek expression.

God seeks all to be one with Him. And as all things were made by Him, that which is the creative influence in every herb, mineral, vegetable, or individual activity, *is* that same force ye call God—and *seeks* expression!   294-202

. . .whether it is mineral, vegetable or animal, these are spiritualized in that ability of using, doing, being all that the Creator had given them to do.   281-54

In man himself may be found all that is part of the earth plane, including these three kingdoms. In addition man has a soul.

For within the human body—living, not dead—*living* human forces—we find every element, every gas, every mineral, every influence that is outside of the organism itself. For indeed it is one with the whole.   470-22

All those essential forces as are manifest in the Universe are manifest in the living man, and above that the soul of man. The chemical or material, or animated forces as are seen in all animal, vegetable, mineral forces, with their combinations, are found in the combinations in man. . .   900-70

In man there is found—in the living man—that, all of that, which may be found without, in the whole world or earth plane; and other than (in addition to) that, the *soul of man* is that making him above all animal, vegetable, mineral kingdoms of the earth plane.   3744-4

Man as a combination of the other forms in this creation is, therefore, in a position to understand them.

Then man—the creation in itself, that combining all of the forms of creation so far created, that that same force might understand by having passed through that same creation as was necessary to bring up to that dividing point between man and animal and plant, the mineral kingdom—was *given* then the will, and the soul, that it might make itself One with that Creation.   900-340

The kingdoms continue to develop (evolution) as does man, also—all of them growing toward the Spiritual Source from which they originated.

Now, that will, then, is heredity. That environment is the evolution. There you have reincarnation, there you have evolution, there you have the mineral kingdom, the plant kingdom, the animal kingdom, each developing towards its own source, yet all belonging and becoming one in that force as it develops itself to become one with the Creative Energy, and One with the God. The one then surviving in the earth, through mineral, through plant kingdom. . .through the animal kingdom, each as the geological survey shows, held its sway in the earth, passing from one into the other; yet man was given that to be lord over all, and the *only* survivor of that creation.   900-340

How is it that man can be "the only survivor" of this spiritual evolution?
Psychic force is manifested in the various kingdoms.

Hence we see from the lowest to the highest the manifestations of psychic phenomena in the material world. . .[those] of the lower animal kingdom, of the mineral kingdom, of the plant kingdom, of the animal kingdom as advanced, and as then becomes the man's condition, position.   900-19

The role of psychic force in two of the kingdoms and in man's development is made clear. The plant life is one-purpose, the animal life two-purpose, man's life three-purpose and spiritualized man's four-purpose. Each lives upon the other lives of lesser purpose or absorbs them. As a result, only spiritual man survives.

Now, as we have presented in this [manuscript] as read, where there comes the division, or the presentation of psychic force as presented through plant or vegetable life, this should be presented as the one purpose as is set. Where we have the entrance of the animal life the two-purpose life. . .with the entrance of man the three-purpose life. . .with the entrance into the spiritual the fourfold or purpose life. . .

Now as. . .in the spirit forces, again we have this same projection which shows that which modifies the reproductive elements within the spiritual elements, for in each the greater force becomes the spiritual element of its development. Hence the necessity of each living, as it were, upon the other.

. . .there. . .[are] the soul forces to animate and inanimate objects as. . .presented through that of the one-, two-, three- and four-purpose development in earth's plane. . .   900-47

. . .then *all things,* conditions and elements, are subject unto that self! That's a universal law, as may be seen in that as may be demonstrated either in gases that destroy one another by becoming elements of the same, or that in the mineral or the animal kingdom as may be found that destroy, or *become* one *with* the other.   364-7

There are three dimensions governing earth living.

Earth, in this solar system, merely represents three dimensions.   5755-2

It would appear, therefore, that plant, animal and human life in some way represent these three and that when man becomes spiritualized, he moves into another plane or the fourth dimension. The three dimensions are given as time, space and patience.

So man's concept of the Godhead is three-dimensional. . .The communication or the activity or the motivating force. . .is three-dimensional—time, space and patience.   4035-1

Time, space and patience, then, are those channels through which man as a finite mind may become aware of the infinite.   3161-1

If plant, animal and human life do represent these three dimensions, it would seem reasonable that they do so in the same sequence. Plant life because of its cycles of growth and decay is concerned with time. Animal life, in addition to experiencing such cycles, is ambulatory, therefore concerned with space. Man has added to these concerns that of evincing spirituality or love. "Love manifested is patience," says reading 3161-1. Man, therefore, is concerned with patience.

Surely when love is *completely attained,* man goes into another plane or the fourth dimension.

Now let us examine the system of which man is the sole survivor. How can his consciousness be so much more advanced than that shown by the three kingdoms? We find that there is a group mind in each one which returns to the Force that created it. Man, however, because of free will has individual mind accompanying his soul. His destiny can bring him to companionship with God. Mind is the dividing factor.

Mind is. . .both spiritual and physical. In the material world, where we find expressions of the physical and of the spiritual, we find mind. Yet what is known as the group mind—or that of the plant kingdom, the mineral kingdom and the animal kingdom or group—returns (as its destiny) to the Creative Force which is its Author, its Maker. *Man*—the free will agent; man made to become a companion to the Creator through the purification, by manifestation of the love of God as may be manifested in the earth—makes his destiny as to whether his mind (that accompanies his soul) is one with or in opposition to the Creative Forces. For he, for weal or woe, gives expression of same in his activity. And his destiny—his mind's destiny—is in Him if he, man, will but make the mind one with that which is creative in its essence, in its activity, in its flow. For mind is the dividing line between that which is human, that which is man, and that which is animal—or. . .that division of a group soul or consciousness.   262-80

If patience or the third dimension is represented by human life, it is easy to see why mind is the dividing line between the human and the animal. To develop patience one needs mind.

What should be man's role toward the three kingdoms? One of helpfulness so that they may manifest to their own greater purpose in the earth.

Then, give that import as ye supply that which aids the plant, the animal, the tree, nature itself, to better give greater sustenance, greater strength, greater purpose for its material manifestation in the earth.   2627-1

If man fulfills his role in dominion over the earth, he may derive real benefit from it.

Know that man. . .was given dominion over all, and in the understanding of same may use all of the laws. . .pertaining to same for his benefit.   1895-1

THE MINERAL KINGDOM

The Psychic and Mental Effects
of Gems, Stones and Metals

The Breastplate of Judgment

From time immemorial men and women have adorned themselves with jewelry. This has not been done for beautification alone. Students of truth have worn gems, stones and metals in an attempt to intensify clairvoyance. They have hoped that the vibrations of the particular materials would "step up" their sensitivity or psychic ability.

Probably the best known example of this to Westerners is the account in the Holy Bible of the High Priest of the Israelites being girded with a "breastplate of judgment" at the times when he went into the Holy Place and when he sought an answer from the Lord to the questions of the people. (Leviticus 8:8, Numbers 27:21) This breastplate had been fashioned according to express directions given by God to Moses. (Exodus 28:4, 15-30) It was of gold, blue, purple and scarlet linen with four rows of stones set in it. The first row consisted of a sardius, a topaz and a carbuncle; the second of an emerald, a sapphire and a diamond; the third of a ligure, an agate and an amethyst; and the fourth of a beryl, an onyx and a jasper. The gems were set in gold; and the names of the twelve tribes of Israel were engraved on them, the name of a separate tribe to each stone. The breastplate was attached to the ephod, another garment, by a series of gold rings and two gold chains. The Urim and Thummin had been "put in the breastplate of judgment," which was worn over the heart of the High Priest.

Of what the Urim and Thummin consisted has long been a matter of speculation, debated by scholars. *Cruden's Unabridged Concordance*[1] gives the literal meaning of these two words as light and perfection or the shining and the perfect. Somehow the presence of the Urim and Thummin in this garment, which held certain gems in a certain position over the priest's breast, enabled him to become a better channel of psychic force.

The explanation for the phenomenon found in the Edgar Cayce readings is a very satisfying one. Urim and Thummin are vision and dream.

> Again that ever ready guidance, when one allows...[himself] to drift into, or by physical actions to place...[himself] in that condition wherein the voice from within speaks to the individual through Urim.   900-86

> This a dream, or through Thummin, as has been termed...
>   294-136

> As He has spoken through prophet, through sage, through Urim, through Thummin, through dream, through vision...
>   338-3

The readings emphasize that Urim and Thummin are channels for psychic force.

> ...Urim and Thummin, a channel only.   355-1

> These three [Leydigian, pineal and reproductive] are the ducts or glands [directly connected with psychic development] ...They are the *channels* through which the activities have their impulse! though the manifestations may be in sight, in sound, in speech, in vision, in writing, in dreams, in Urim or Thummin, or in *any*. For these represent Urim and Thummin in their essence or in *any* of the *responding* forces in a body; but their impulse arises from or through these sources in much the same manner as the heart and the liver are of the physical body the motivating forces, or impulses, that carry the stream of life itself; or as the brain is that motivating center of impulse or mind.   294-142

How can vision and dream be more readily induced by wearing a garment such as the breastplate, replete with its

---

[1]Alexander Cruden, *Cruden's Unabridged Concordance to the Old and New Testaments and the Apocrypha,* Baker Book House, Grand Rapids, Mich., 1966, pg. 514.

twelve stones? The answer may be found in a reading given for the person who fashioned the original breastplate. It tells us that the setting of the stones and their placement on the garment had to be done in a precise manner. A sensitive was guided to carry this out. When the High Priest, clad in his sacred garments, including the breastplate, officiated in the Holy of Holies, he felt urges to make certain movements. These movements were interpreted by the same sensitive. For her the stones had special significance, and she understood (partially at least) the message conveyed by the effect of the stones on the movements of the priest. She then gave this message to the waiting people from the door of the tabernacle.

. . .mystical signs, mystical numbers, mystical conditions have much to do with the entity at times. And these may come in the *vision* and in the dreams. . .
For, as will be seen, the entity made *for* the priest the Urim and the Thummin!. . .
Before that we find the entity was in that land, that period, when the chosen people were being given upon the holy mount the manner of their exercise in the temple, or in the service before the tabernacle.
The entity then was among the daughters of Levi, and those chosen to make the vestment of the priest. And to the entity, because of its own abilities, there was given the preparation of the settings of the breastplate and the putting of the stones thereon, and the preparation of the Urim and Thummin for the interpretations of the movements that came upon the High Priest in the Holy of Holies to be given to his people in or from the door of the tabernacle.
Then in the name Henriettah, the entity's activities were in a high force *equal to* [those of] the cousin, Miriam.   987-2

The fashioning of the breastplate was man's first attempt to induce a state of psychic sensitivity by means of stones.

Read what was in the first effort that was made, as to all those that used the stones as settings to induce the influences from without that would aid an individual in its contact with the higher sources of activity! [Exodus 28:15-30]   440-2

Later the Urim and Thummin were woven into the robe made for Jesus by Nicodemus' wife. His sensitivity was so great that she did not feel any need to add gems. The purpose for the special garment was, however, the same. The additional channeling of the Higher Forces, induced by it, would aid in

9

creating *balance*. This had been especially needed when the priest passed judgment but could be helpful to anyone, even the Master.

From a reading for Martha, sister of Peter's mother-in-law and also the wife of Nicodemus:

The color of the robe was pearl-gray...with selvage woven around the neck, as well as that upon the edge, as over the shoulder and to the bottom portion of same; no belts [bells?], no pomegranates, but those which are woven in such a manner that into the selvage portion of the bottom was woven the Thummin and the Urim. These were as the balance in which judgments were passed by the priest. But these were woven, not placed upon the top of same. Neither were there jewels set in same.   3175-3

Transmission of Vibration

How do precious stones and metals increase the wearer's psychic sensitivity? The readings explain that the particular vibrations in them work with those in the body. The stones throw off and also draw in through positive and negative vibrations. A person whose vibrations closely resemble those of a gem is affected strongly by it. However, the very nature of the stone makes it effective with any human body. Placing special stones or metals close to one or more of the spiritual centers of the body undoubtedly adds to the potency.

In giving that which may be helpful it is necessary, for this mind or body seeking same, that there be rather the analysis of the composition of the stones as related to their vibrations—as relate then to a human body. . .
Either of these shows a variation of their composition; as to the elements of those influences that make for vibrations in the ether as related to that which may be effective in drawing to or disseminating from—through, of course, the vibrations being those that are of the positive and negative natures in the very stone itself—making for, then, the analysis; knowing same by what is called the constituents of it, through the mineralogy, the activity through those channels themselves. We would then find that the one that is the nearer in accord to the vibrations of the body that may use same would be the more effective with *that* particular body. Yet the very *nature* of the thing makes it effective with any—*any*—human body. . . but the more effective with one that is more in accord, or

whose positive and negative vibrations are according with the stone itself for it throws off as well as draws in...through the positive-negative vibration. This assists, then, in the unison as a relationship. This is as a comparison—don't confuse it and say that it is electricity; it is electrical, of course, in its vibration, but as the stone in its vibration is then in sympathy with a body that is also sympathetic—or may be said to be *sensitive*—it assists in "stepping up" the sensitiveness of the body as would the electrical vibration in an alternating force step up by the addition of influences or forces of electrical vibration being thrown off from other channels in making it more powerful...Towards what? Towards the effectiveness in its sensitiveness (that is, the body) as to what it may be seeking. Hence, as given of old, use such for the abilities to become more of all those influences called in the present psychic, clairaudient, or any of those vibrations that build up or "step up" a body. Also effective, of course, in bringing to the body the abilities to become more effective in giving out of itself for activity in any of these various directions.   440-18

However, the readings warn us not to worship the stone or metal. It has been given man as a help but only that. He may use it to keep more in touch with the Infinite, but he himself must direct his own life.

Q-2. How can I use the...vibrations from metal, from stones which influence me, to advantage in my present life?
A-2. ...these are but lights, but signs in thine experience; they are as but a candle that one stumbles not in the dark. But worship *not* the light of the candle; rather that to which it may guide thee in thy service. So whether [thou art guided] from the vibrations of numbers, of metals, of stones, these are merely to become the necessary influences to make thee in attune, one with the Creative Forces; just as the pitch of a song of praise is not the song nor the message therein, but is a helpmeet for those that would find strength in the service of the Lord. So, use them to attune self. How, ye ask? As ye apply, ye are given the next step.
Q-3. Should I carry these stones on my person, and how may I know through meditation the message they would give me?
A-3. If necessary. And how may ye know? These do not give the messages! They only attune self so that the Christ Consciousness may give the message! Listen to no message of a stone, of a number, even of a star; for they are but servants of the Lord and Master of all—even as thou!   707-2

Forms of Lapis

The gem material most often mentioned in the Edgar Cayce readings is lapis in different forms. Exact identification of these forms is difficult since Edgar Cayce's terminology is sometimes outdated.

Some of his terminology can, however, be clarified by its Latin derivation. This important fact was pointed out to the author some years back by Margaret H. Gammon, a retired Latin teacher and editor of *The Searchlight,* a former A.R.E. publication. She explained the marked similarity in sentence structure between the material found in the readings and Latin prose by the fact that Edgar Cayce's most communicative incarnation depicted in the readings was that of Lucius the Roman, who was active in the early Christian church. (294-192) As a Church Father he must have given many a sermon or exhortation. He was also credited by the readings with being the author of the Gospel according to St. Luke, which was "written...unto those of the faith under the Roman *influence*." (1598-2) Doubtless this activity in a former life made it natural for the sleeping Edgar Cayce to use Latin constructions and, at times, actual Latin words in his sentences. That such are contained in the readings is evident after only a casual examination.

Identification of gems has been furthered by three excellent articles by Ken Carley, a long-time lapidary supply dealer.[2]

Lapis is spoken of in one reading as "copper in its *elemental* form." It can help activate psychic consciousness.

> ...the lapis or copper in its *elemental* form...[brings] great passion, intenseness, the abilities to loose emotions through the very centers of the body for the closer association of the spiritual with the activative influences of the mental self.
>
> 1580-1

Clear Lapis

In a reading, [440] was advised to secure some lapis to assist him in psychic development. He was directed to go to the New York Museum of Natural History and, as an interesting

[2]Ken Carley, "Lapis Lazuli," *The A.R.E. Journal,* July, 1975, pp. 161-169.
------------"Reflections of a Rockhound," *The A.R.E. Journal,* November, 1973, pp. 229-236.
------------"The Stones of Egypt," *The A.R.E. Journal,* September, 1974, pp. 200-211.

experiment, to sit beside a large piece of this type of stone and to listen to it sing.

...[at] Phoenix [Ariz.] and north and west from there, at not great distances, may be found two or three various deposits of the lapis that may be found to be most beneficial in many of the experimentations in which the body is particularly interested ...lapis is not considered a high quality of gem; rather a very low form, but for that indicated in the character of the stone itself, it would be most helpful in creating that vibration which will make for developments of certain characters of demonstrations with any psychic forces or psychic individuals. This may be—will be—a very interesting experiment for the body. Go to the New York Museum of Natural History. Sit by a large quantity of this type of stone and listen...[to] it sing! Do it in the open! Don't let others make a fool of you, or their remarks overcome you—but sit by it and listen...[to] it sing; for it does! It's from Arizona.   440-3

When [440] sought additional information about the particular formation, he was told it was translucent and blue.

...the lapis—not lapis lingua, because that is different but ...comes from the same formation...[The] lapis is there, in the hall—north side—front of the north window, in the mineral divisions here—large blue stone. It weighs nearly a ton and has many facets, in the manner in which it was removed from the mines; is from Arizona, and the color necessary for use as instructed—may be seen by stooping below or getting the light through a portion of the upper part, though—to be sure—it's very much thicker than would be necessary for use. It's there! Not lapis linguis, but *lapis!*
Q-1. *Under what name is it catalogued? Please spell the entire name.*
A-1. L-a-p-i-s.
Q-2. *From what place in Arizona is it listed as having come...?*
A-2. Nearer Tucson.   440-9

The requirements for [440]'s personal stone were to be transmission of light and ability to sing or give off the emanations it had caught from him.

Q-8. *How will I know when I have found this stone that is most useful for my purposes?*
A-8. When there is found that which is sufficiently clear for the transmission of light and that which may be held in the hand for five to ten minutes and then set aside...[after which]

the movements or the vibrations given off from the emanations from self [may be heard].

Q-9. Should it be translucent to light?
A-9. Should be transparent, or sufficient for the light to pass
through.   440-11

The value of clarity in a stone is mentioned in a reading for
another person.

In stones, the whiter, the more crystal the better.   1775-1

[440] was told in a later reading that he had been directed to
the lapis stones to improve his understanding of vibrations as
related to the mineral kingdom.

*Q-12. Why were these stones mentioned to me in the
beginning?*
A-12. They are as those things of old, which if followed. . .
may be used as stepping-stones for the understanding of vibrations as related to the mineral forces and. . .man.   440-18

[816] was advised to keep a lapis about his person to aid or
strengthen him by the vibrations of the higher forces contained
in it. There are emanations of high electrical forces from its
copper base.

. . .the lapis. . .should be as a stone that would be about the
body of the entity; not as an omen, not as a symbol; rather that
the vibrations of the higher forces from these proper
expressions of activities throughout the universal forces in
materiality may be an aid or as a strengthening. . .there are the
emanations of high electrical forces from its copper base.
                                                             816-3

When [440] was originally apprised that he should locate a
lapis, he immediately asked how it should be set and cut. He
found it was to be worn pendant, on wrist or around the waist.
The ordinary method of cutting for precious or semi-precious
stones would be suitable. The mounting was to be white gold or
silver. The stone was to be worn next to the skin. If he wished to
train himself, he would keep it in the hollow above the collar
bone on the left side.

*Q-9. Describe these stones so that the body may be able to
locate them.*
A-9. Go and look at them in the museum!

Q-10. How should. . .[the stones] be set and cut?

A-10. As pendant, either on wrist and worn on body or around the waist.   440-3

Q-10. Should this [stone] touch the skin in wearing it?

A-10. To be sure. Usually worn, of course, around the neck or over the body close to the vibrations from the heart or from the breast itself in its vibrations.

Q-11. Would it not be best over the lyden gland? [Leydigian gland?]

A-11. Not be best over the lyden gland, for too great emanations from its surroundings might influence the body itself. You are used to influence the stone to an effect, either upon those to whom it may be given or to bring for self the ability to aid in its abilities as raising the vibrations for self. Hence would come over this particular portion, or if desired—for the better in training of self—held over that portion of the hollow on the left side above what is commonly called the collar bone.

Q-12. What is the best method of cutting and what metal should be used in mounting?

A-12. Use in cutting the ordinary use for the precious or semi-precious stones, in whatever shapes or forms—that are usually the larger in the center and tapering towards the outer edge. Of course, not too large for the use to be worn. The mounting would be white gold or silver.   440-11

Lapis Lingua, Lapis Lazuli or Lapis Ligurius (Azurite)

In the reference from 440-9 it was noted that in the formation referred to in the New York Museum of Natural History there was lapis lingua along with the clear lapis. Later in the same paragraph this substance was identified as "lapis linguis." The two terms are synonymous. In Latin *lingua* means "tongue," *cum linguā* "with a tongue," *cum linguis* "with tongues." Often the word *cum* ("with") is omitted.

In other places in the readings we find "lapis languis" and "lapis langis." Since the English word "language" comes from the French *langage* and that in turn from the Latin *lingua*,[3] it is apparent that the "i" in "lingua" is easily corrupted to "a." We shall, therefore, consider these four terms as referring to one gem substance, identified as containing a tongue or tongues.

After [440] had located the formation, a reading clarified for

---

[3]*Webster's Collegiate Dictionary*, G. & C. Merriam Co., Springfield, Mass., 1936, pg. 557.

him the application for lapis linguis. A piece of it could be used as a touchstone, to receive and transmit a blessing or a curse. At this time lapis linguis was, also, identified as the present day "azurite."

Q-4. In relation to the lapis, I found a 900-lb. stone enclosed in a glass case, etc. Is this the one referred to?

A-4. This. . .is the one referred to—though it has been moved from its former locations or surroundings, but is in general in the same—*and* the stone as referred to.

. . .there is in the mind of the body, [440], confusion. . . respecting lapis and lapis linguis. . .lapis linguis is that name which was implied to touchstones, or those used by initiates in their various ceremonial activities. . .those that are of a psychic turn may hear the emanations as retained or thrown off by influences about such stones. They are of semi-gem or semi-value. . .the singing or talking stones—as they have been called in places.

. . .there is the ability within this body. . .to hear the singing or the movements, much. . .in the same way and manner as. . .is given to any. . .[one who] will listen for days. . .[to] a growing tree, or as was accredited to. . .those who have so developed in certain portions of this world as to be able to gain much from especially the growing oak, or certain other trees peculiar to those vicinities. [Many of them did hear emanations from trees.] So, in this stone lapis. Lapis linguis is that one that has been in use or in touch with those whose vibrations or emanations or auras are of such natures as to have given those vibrations. . .[of] the nature that any portion of such a stone may give off that which may be heard. . .

Q-5. Will it being in a glass case interfere with my hearing it sing?

A-5. It should not interfere wholly, though it will not be heard. . .through the glass as definitely as were it separated.

Q-6. This stone contains malachite and azurite. Is the lapis linguis either of these?

A-6. The azurite.

. . .Many various characters of this lapis may be found in Arizona. . .but those that are of the greater value as the touchstones or those that may receive (we are putting it in another form or manner) a blessing and transmit same to another, or a curse and transmit same to another, will be found in. . .nature where the greater portion of the azurite is evidenced in the immediate vicinity.   440-11

The readings supply yet another identification, that of "lapis linguis" with "lapis lazuli." (This is *not* the material presently known as the lapis lazuli since the readings specify, as we have noted, that lapis has a copper base; and today's lapis lazuli consists of silicates of sodium and aluminum, with some sulfur, chlorine and calcium.[4])

Q-7. *Is the stone which I found in Alaska last summer the lapis linguis?*
A-7. Lapis langis, lapis lazuli. This. . .might be said to be a part of that same composition referred to, for it carries that vibration which will give strength to the body. Well that this be preserved between thin layers of glass or such composition, else its radiation is too great.   1931-2

Lazuli, also, is a Latin word, meaning "of *lazulum*"[5] the Latin rendering of the Persian *lājuward,* "a blue color."[6] Lapis lazuli can, therefore, be translated into "lapis of a blue color."

It is interesting to note that in using this term Edgar Cayce was harking back to both Roman (Latin) and Persian lives. One of his most important incarnations was that of Uhjltd in ancient Persia. (294-142) A reading for [5294] tells how caravans brought lapis lazuli from Indo-China to Persia.

Before that we find the entity was in the Persian land, among those who carried the goods from one portion of the land to another, or a caravan maker, dealing in the linens of Egypt, the pearls of Persia, in the opal, the firestone, the lapis lazuli in Indo-China, yea the diamonds and rubies of some of the cities of gold.   5294-1

Lapis lazuli is also referred to as "the rays from copper." A tongue (*lingua*) and a ray are certainly similar in formation. (An additional connotation may be found for *lingua.* This tongue of copper, shaped like a ray, also produces sound or emanations, hence its use as a touchstone.)

**. . .it is [in] mineral rather than stone that this entity would find vibrations—the lapis lazuli, or the rays from copper.
1861-16**

Lapis lazuli is described as a "corrosion of copper." This explains the origin of the rays.

. . .the lapis lazuli or the corrosion of copper. . .   5294-1

---

[4]Carley, "Lapis," pp. 162-163.
[5]*American Heritage Dictionary of the English Language,* American Heritage Publishing Co. and Houghton Mifflin Co., Boston, Mass., 1969, pg. 737.
[6]*Webster's Collegiate Dictionary,* pg. 76, reference "azure."

One other name for lapis lingua is offered by the readings. It is "lapis ligurius." That was the "composition referred to" in the excerpt previously cited from 1931-2. The gem had been recommended in [1931]'s first reading. In a later reading he elicited this information about it.

Q-5. Where may I find the stone lapis lazuli or lapis ligurius?
A-5. This is an exuding of copper. Either in the copper mines of the southwest, or about Superior, or in Montana. 1931-3

The word *ligurius* is a Latin one, meaning "licked" in the sense of having been licked with a tongue. It seems particularly appropriate as applied to this stone, which has been licked with tongues of copper. In addition, "licked" could intimate that the object had been touched. A touchstone is touched or affected by the emanations from individuals. (See prior reference, 440-11.)

Now that the names for this gem material have been established, its precise color will be the next subject to investigate: This is a blue-green.

We find that it would be very helpful for the entity to wear upon the body a piece of stone that is of the lapis lazuli variety, but the essence or fusion of copper; not as a charm but as a helpful force in the vibrations that will coordinate with the body. This worn as a locket or the like would be helpful.

Q-1. Describe in more detail the lapis stone suggested for the body to wear.
A-1. As understood, and may be found by the investigating of same, there is a blue-green stone, that is a fusion in copper deposits, that has the same vibration as the body; and thus is a helpful influence, not merely as an omen or good luck charm, but as the vibratory helpful force for health, for strength, for the ability through the mental self to act upon things, conditions, decisions and activities.

Because of its softness, it will necessarily have to be encased in glass—as two crystals and this between same. It may be worn around the neck, the wrist or the like. But wear it, for it will bring health and hope, and—best of all—the ability to *do* that so desired. 1651-2

There are additional references which establish the color of both lapis ligurius and lapis lazuli as green. Apparently Edgar Cayce was emphasizing the green aspect in relation to creativity in the first reading for [1931] and healing in that for [3416].

...the lapis ligurius would bring much that will act in that manner as would be termed a *protective* influence, if kept about the entity. This is the green stone, you see, the crystallization of copper and those influences that are creative within themselves.

...there is the need for not only the copper ore, that is a part of man's *own* development in many fields, but the need for the very combination of its elements as *protection* to not only the material benefits but the bodily forces necessary for the transmission of benefits through its own physical being.

For, the very elements of body—through which spirit and mind manifest—are atomic in their nature. Hence so are the elements of this stone indicated, that partakes of most of the elements that are to man of great influence or power, because of their representation in the body.

Hence the radial activity of radium, as well as the strengthening influences of gold, the stabilizing influence of silver, are all a part of those elements that make for the transmission through the activity of the very vibratory forces themselves, and become to *this* body of great influence. . .   1931-1

Q-8. Please give my. . .stone. . .

A-8. The lapis lazuli, worn close to the body would be well for the general health of the body—and this you will have to be careful of very soon. The lapis lazuli, of course, is an erosion of copper; but this encased in a glass and worn about the body would be well. The color is green. Hence the entity should ever be as a healing influence to others when it comes about them.
3416-1

Green is either the color of the stone or the proper color to be in the proximity of the wearer. However, stones suggested for personal use *are* of the color needed according to a reference about to be cited. See in the ensuing collection of reading references 696-1.

The role of lapis lingua as a touchstone has been explored. Its other uses will now be taken up. As a chrysalis of copper, it acts as a storage of energies of the inner self. Its emanations create an environment in which holy things can more readily be kept holy and material things held in a proper perspective.

The lapis lazuli stone would be well to wear about the body. This is as a chrysalis to be sure of copper; thus the very natures of same produce those emanations for the body in which the environ is made for keeping holy things holy, and material things in their proper relationships. For it acts. . .as a storage of energies of the inner self.   880-2

...the lapis linguis also would bring to the entity much, if it were worn about the body, keeping low the fires of passion—from materiality—that there may be greater mental and spiritual development of *this* entity in the experience. 559-7

...the entity should ever wear about the body the lapis lazuli or the lapis linguis; for these will bring strength to the body through those vibrations that are brought or built in the innate experience of the entity from its sojourn in the Egyptian land.
. . .wear the stone ever about the body, and *touching* the body. 691-1

From a subsequent reading for the same person:

Q-7. If I were to wear the stone, as suggested in a previous reading, would it improve my mental, physical or spiritual condition?
A-7. This naturally is to make. . .the body more sensitive to the higher vibrations. Not so much in the physical health as in the mental and spiritual influences, that would be materially aided. 691-2

...the wearing of the stone lapis linguis would be as an aid in its meditative periods, and would become as a helpful influence. Not as that of "lucky," but rather that as of a helpful influence towards making for the ability to make decisions in dealing with mental attributes. 1058-1

Keep the bloodstone close to thy body, as combined with the lapis lazuli. This if encased and worn upon the breast would bring healing, and decisions for the entity, because of the very vibrations that such create in their activity. 2282-1

Because of the environment created by the lapis lingua, its presence is an aid to spiritual development and to meditation.

Q-4. Any color, stone or symbol for spiritual development?
A-4. The lapis lazuli should be the better, but this should be encased and worn—for this body—about the waist; not around your neck. 3053-3

Q-9. Is there any special jewelry or stone I should wear that would raise my vibration?
A-9. The lapis lazuli would be very good for the body; if it were worn in crystal next to the skin. 2376-1

So may numbers and those vibrations from stones as given, with metals such as come in the lapis lazuli, make for the raising of the attunement in self through meditation. But know these, my child, are but means—and are *not* the God-Force, *not* the Spirit, but the *manifestations* of same. 707-1

The lapis lingua comes from elements giving vitality, virility, strength and self-assurance. It can, therefore, stimulate these qualities. It is interesting to note that the stone should not be cut so that it is slick or polished. The emanations are transmitted more readily when it is in a more natural state.

As to stones, have near to self, wear preferably upon the body, about the neck, the lapis lazuli; this preferably encased in crystal. It will not be merely as an ornament but as strength from the emanation which will be gained by the body always from same. For the stone is itself an emanation of vibrations of the elements that give vitality, virility, strength, and that of assurance in self. 1981-1

Upon thy body wear the lapis lazuli, which bringeth strength to thy weakened and faltering body at times. The vibrations from these emanations, as you so well used in Egypt, may again bring in thy consciousness the awareness that life itself, health itself, cometh from the Creator. 2564-3

Symbols and such activities have always meant something to the entity. Hence certain characters of adornments would be well about the entity. Keep something blue, and especially the color and emanations of the lapis lazuli; not the slick or polished nature, but of that nature that the emanations from same may give life and vitality. 2132-1

A review of the preceding excerpts on lapis lingua, under its various names, brings out some general directions as to how it may be used most effectively. As a touchstone, it is undoubtedly held in the hand. As an aid to personal development, it is worn on the person. It is best to encase a lapis lingua because of its strong radiation and also, because of its softness, between two pieces of crystal. This triplet can be worn as a pendant, around the neck or wrist. It should touch the body if possible. [2282] was advised to wear a bloodstone and lapis lingua, encased together, on the breast. [3053] was to wear a lapis lingua about the waist rather than the neck. This would infer a belt buckle. The author has not found any suggestion in the readings as to lapis lingua being used in a ring.

Present-day Names

The value of the lapis materials is emphasized in the readings. It is, therefore, important to identify them by their present-day names. The readings provide a definite identification—the large block of gem material in the New York Museum of Natural History, catalogued as "lapis" and containing lapis and lapis lingua, which latter stone was subsequently identified as azurite.

From Ken Carley's article on lapis lazuli comes the information that Fay Clark, a well-known gem expert, states that this particular gem formation in the museum is chrysocolla.[7]

Mr. Carley also tells us that an article "Arizona Minerals in Retrospect" (*Lapidary Journal,* April, 1973) mentions a very large block of azurite ore, approximately four feet in each of six directions, owned by the American Museum of Natural History. Although its origin is not given, it is described along with other items from the Bisbee mining area.[8]

Mr. Carley has had experience with Brisbee chrysocolla, which he has found to be very soft.[9] (Would this not necessitate its being encased for any lengthy preservation?)

According to Mr. Carley, chrysocolla is a hydrous, translucent copper silicate, varying in composition. It occurs in the form of a finely crystalline-appearing chalcedony quartz with delicate hues of blue and green. It may be either clear or enamellike. Located in the upper zone of copper deposits, it has been formed by the changes from primary minerals and is actually an infrequent type of copper ore. Azurite and malachite occur along with it. Azurite, a basic carbonate of copper, azure blue in color, translucent to opaque in clarity, is in its pure form too soft to be cut into gems. Azurite in time slowly changes to malachite, a green basic carbonate of copper. (Reference *Popular Gemology,* pp. 193 and 171)[10]

It is very probable that the clear lapis is the crystalline form of chrysocolla, which *is* elemental copper, and that the lapis lingua (linguis, languis, langis, lazuli and ligurius) is the azurite associated with it, while the azurite is in the stage of turning into malachite. The blue-green stage mentioned in reading 1651-2 is further emphasized in the following excerpt,

[7]Carley, "Lapis," pg. 167.
[8]*Ibid.,* pp. 166-167.
[9]*Ibid.,* pg. 168.
[10]*Ibid.,* pp. 168, 167.

which suggests wearing "the blue-green chalcedony." Mr. Carley characterized chrysocolla as a chalcedony quartz.

Also tones, colors, stones of peculiar type or turn, mean much to the entity. And not as an omen, but for its greater vibration, the entity should have upon its body at all periods the blue-green chalcedony.   813-1

The Pearl

While the lapis or the lapis lingua may be the most influential stone for one person to keep about him, the pearl may be that for another. The pearl, likewise, may be protective. Hardships or irritations were overcome in its formation. Hence it fosters the ability to build resistances.

. . .this [the pearl] is among those of the precious stones that indicates in its formation, in its beauty, the hardships overcome by the very source that made the beauty of the stone itself.   2533-1

. . .the pearl—which *has* been produced by irritations. Hence the ability to build resistances is a natural influence that comes about same. . .   1189-1

The vibrations of the pearl are healing.

The pearl should be worn upon the body, or against the flesh of the body; for its vibrations are healing, as well as creative, because of the very irritation. . .[that] produced same, as a defense in the mollusk. . .   951-4

The last reference points out that the pearl is not only healing but creative as well. This seems to stem primarily from its association with water.

From the sojourns of the entity in Neptune we find rather the influences of water, as well as things coming from water, are a part of the entity's experience.
Thus the entity should ever keep a pearl about the self or upon the person, not only for the material vibration but for the ideal expression. For, it will be an omen—not only because of the vibrations that it may give to self but because of keeping the even temperament, yea the temper itself. . .
Before that the entity was in the Persian land, during those

periods when there arose the turmoils between the bedouins or Arabians and those of the Persian land; when the activities of Croesus made for the greater rule through the eastern portion, extending to the great sea.

The entity was an interpreter, and might be called the keeper of the treasury for Croesus. For, the entity analyzed the abilities of the peoples of the various lands, as to how, in what manner, in what form, tax or payments for the upkeep of the land might be best brought from the varied groups.

Thus the entity became an interpreter of signs, as well as of the mysteries and stories of the east; and the entity in that experience *owned* the larger collection of pearls from the Persian Gulf. . .area, which is still the source of the most beautiful of these precious stones.

Keep such an one about the body, not only because of the vibrations but because of the abilities indicated. For. . .this is among those of the precious stones that indicates in its formation, in its beauty, the hardships overcome by the very source that made the beauty of the stone itself. . .

Q-5. What hobbies will benefit me most in developing any latent talent or ability I may possess?

A-5. The study of stones—especially precious stones. Not necessarily the owning of same, but what part they have played, do play—not in the lives of the idle rich, nor of those so begone by carnal forces; rather as that ye may gain by keeping a pearl close about thy body.   2533-1

For one person rose-colored pearls were suggested.

From those influences we find that certain character of pearls, of corals, any jewelry that would be rose-colored or red, may be and would be well to be about the entity, because of the very vibrations of the sea as creative forces, and as activities through which there is the physical evolution. These become a portion of the entity's experience.   1604-1

Pearls and jade together would help [1189] to express what had been aroused in her emotional self by unseen influences or to accomplish what she had visioned.

About the entity we find unusual characters, that may be called hieroglyphics. We find jade as combined with pearls unusual in their effect upon the entity, especially in moods. For the entity finds its experience as being at times with unseen or unusual influence of vibrations about the entity. These would be helpful, then, to be about the entity when seeking to give expression of that which is either felt in the emotional self or for the accomplishing of same. Not as influences that would be called charms, but rather the vibrations of certain characters of stones, or the certain combinations as indicated in the pearl—which *has* been produced by irritations. Hence the ability to build resistances is a natural influence that comes about same, and not as a talisman for preventing this or that—but that the vibrations created make for same.

The entity was among those who came under the periods of destructive forces to the *physical* structure of the school, yet later when there were the establishings of the teachings in the "city in the hills and the plain" the entity gave forth in those activities that make for the influence of the vibrations from jade and pearls in the experience in the present.

For as these brought healing through the very associations and activities, creating in the physical experience and making for the impression upon the inmost forces of the bodily force then, we find these come as a *helpful* influence by the very atmosphere of vibrations created by the emanations.

For each and every atomic force throws off a vibration to which a sensitive soul becomes aware. Not always aware as to its source or its activity; but as both of these in the experience made for an activity or an active force, thus may they bring help not only of a healing nature but in becoming a hopeful, *helpful* force in the experience of the entity.

Q-2. Any other talents that should be developed?

A-2. Anything that pertains to art and art's expression. Those things particularly in those very associations of stones and their vibrations may be as a portion of self; knowing the vibrations, the *effect* of vibrations of stones and their wearing of same upon the bodies of others. This will not only be interesting, but will make for abilities within self to know others.   1189-1

Pearls express purity. They are also emblems of truth.

. . .the purity of the pearl, though under stress it may come into being. . .   1144-2

Q-9. Are there any other suggestions for the better spiritual development of the entity?

A-9. Keep the emblems of truth before thee in the vibrations of color and stones about thee; those of the pearl and of the blue should ever be close to the body.   696-1

A pearl worn close to the body may give it strength.

Q-6. What. . .stones. . .are best for me?

A-6. The stone—the pearl should be worn close to the body; not as an ornament, but rather that which gives strength to the body. 3374-1

Pearls worn next to the body in time take on the vibrations of the body-forces. This makes them an effective influence. To demagnetize them from other influences initially, they may be exposed for one tenth of a second to the ultra-violet ray. It must not touch them, however.

Q-2. My life reading suggested the wearing of pearls next to my skin for the healing vibration. Does the pearl necklace I'm now wearing help or hinder?
A-2. When its vibrations have taken the body-forces, it will be well. Or if the body would demagnetize the necklace as it is, it would be more helpful for the body. Do not touch with same, but expose necklace to the ultra-violet ray for one-tenth of a second, or as a flash. This will demagnetize it and set it for better body vibration for this body. 951-6

Coral

The pearl is not the only precious stone deriving its quality of creativity from the sea. We have noted that [1604] was advised to wear rose-colored or red coral as well as rose-colored pearls "because of the very vibrations of the sea as creative forces, and as activities through which there is the physical evolution." (1604-1) Another reference also stresses the rose-colored coral.

Ever wear about the entity rose coral. The vibrations of same, from same, may aid in the mental as well as vibratory urge to make those influences less of a disturbing nature which might otherwise become disturbing. . .
Q-1. Please give my seal and its interpretation.
A-1. Rather that as has been indicated. Coral. . .in any form, whether as a [life] seal or as that *preferably* to be worn. . .Wear coral; rose color, not red, not white, but rose coral. This is the seal. . .as this is made up of nature's activity attempting to manifest, so—as ye have experienced and will experience—it is the little things in the association one with another that build those that prove to be the real experiences of the life. A word, a look, a sign, may make, may undo, all of the thoughts of many. 2154-1

From the above we learn that coral exemplifies the building up of real experience by little things. [307] was advised to wear coral whether red *or* white because of the creative forces in it.

Q-7. Are there any colors or jewelry that I should wear in order to have better vibrations? If so, what?

A-7. Any. . .jewelry or ornaments that are of coral would be well; for this is—as it represents, as it is in itself of Creative Forces, or from the water itself. Red, white or coral in any form.   307-15

The calming effect of coral, worn on the flesh of neck, waist or wrist, springs from its origin. The tiny creatures brought forth in the turmoils of the "mother-water" bind together in resistance and thus establish a foundation for much of the material world. It is for this reason that the presence of coral on the body may quiet inner turmoils.

Hence we find. . .those things that should be in the form of omens about the body. . .are from those activities and sojourns that will make for variations in the *vibrations* about the entity, hence bringing much more of harmony into the experience of the entity in the present activity: The very red stones; as of coral, that is rather of the deepsea variety, and when this is worn about the neck or about the waist—or upon the arm—let it rest upon the flesh, for it will bring quiet to the body. . .And the body will find that the unquiet and the tumultous conditions will be changed to the harmonious abilities to give out. . .there are those things that make for harmony in their relationships. . .one to another, as do the turmoils of the mother-water that brings forth in its activity about the earth those tiny creatures that in their beginnings make for the establishing of that which is the foundation of much of those in materiality. Hence the red, the deep red coral, upon thine flesh, will bring quietness in those turmoils that have arisen within the inner self. . .

Q-4. Should the coral, as suggested, be [of] any particular shape or carving?

A-4. No particular shape, just so it is mounted so that the coral itself may be upon the flesh of the body.   694-2

There is a relation between the construction of coral and the activity of soul forces.

Coral should be about the entity at all times; worn—not as a charm, not other than [as] the vibrations of the body as related to same. Because of the very nature of its construction, and the very activity of the soul forces of the entity, this would become a helpful influence in the experience of the entity. Hence this we would wear about the body, but against the flesh. . .the

27

wearing of the coral. . .would keep the body in better
attunement.   2073-2

The Ruby and/or Bloodstone

A very beneficent effect may be exerted by the ruby and/or
bloodstone. According to *Webster's Dictionary*[11] the true or
oriental ruby is a red, crystalized variety of corundum.
According to W.B. Crow it is a crimson, transparent stone of the
nature of corundum but colored with particles of chromium
oxide of sub-microscopic size. The stone formerly known as
"spinel" or "balas" ruby (according to color) is actually
composed of magnesium aluminate.[12]

The true ruby, apart from color, has the same physical
properties as sapphire and is found in the same parts of the
world, particularly upper Burma.[13]

In the discussion of lapis lazuli, a reference was given which
mentioned precious stones from Indo-China, then continued,
"yea the diamonds and rubies of some of the cities of gold."
(5294-1) The most important city of gold at this time appears to
have been located in the Gobi, to be mentioned later in this
study. However, [1387] was told of a sojourn in Indo-China as a
princess in another city of gold. (1387-1) The "rubies of the cities
of gold" were doubtless Burmese rubies.

The identity of the bloodstone is in no way clear. Today the
name is applied to heliotrope, a dark green chalcedony, flecked
with small spots of red jasper. However, the name has also been
applied to carnelian, red coral, red agate, red marble and red
jasper.[14] It would seem that it has been used to describe almost
any stone of the color of blood.

The reading references to bloodstone classify it as an
exceedingly red gem (not a green one with red flecks). Can we
puzzle out what Edgar Cayce meant by "bloodstone"? There
are several excerpts from which it could be understood that the
bloodstone *is* the ruby.

Have about the entity stones that are red; as the bloodstone,
the ruby, or everything of that nature—in stone but *not* in
hangings or draperies.   1616-1

[11]*Webster's*, pg. 845.
[12]W.B. Crow, D.Sc., Ph.D., *Precious Stones*, Samuel Weiser, Inc., N.Y.,
N.Y., 1968, pg. 32.
[13]*Ibid.*, pp. 32-33.
[14]Carley, "Stones," pg. 204.

. . .the vibratory forces of color, or those of the mineral as may be crystallized in material forces.

Hence the bloodstone or the ruby is well to ever be about the entity, upon its body; so that the very vibratory forces of same give—with that of thought in constructive force—creative environs or vibrations for the entity in its use or application.

1770-2

The most conclusive evidence for identifying the bloodstone with the ruby lies in a suggestion to [608] to keep about the body a moonstone or a bloodstone. The former is identified by its color, turquoise blue; the latter as "the pigeon-blood ruby."

Keep not as a charm, but as the influences that may bring the greater force about the body, the moonstone or the bloodstone as the ornaments about the body; but those that will be found (that are akin to these [influences]) in the turquoise blue and the pigeon-blood ruby.   608-7

It appears that in the above context Edgar Cayce was identifying the bloodstone with the pigeon-blood ruby. The identity of the turquoise blue moonstone will be taken up in a later section.

The bloodstone combined with the lapis lazuli would bring healing and the ability to make decisions. (Note that the same two colors, red and blue, are involved.)

Keep the bloodstone close to thy body, as combined with the lapis lazuli. This if encased and worn upon the breast would bring healing, and decisions for the entity, because of the very vibrations that such create in their activity.   2282-1

The bloodstone and the clear lapis were recommended for an entity who had dealt with metals in a previous life and who was now in a position to deal with metals *and* stones. The significance of the two gem materials was spelled out—the high electrical forces in the lapis and the purity of high vibration in the bloodstone.

Before that (among those [lives] that influence the entity in the present) we find the entity was in that land now known as the land of the entity's nativity, in those portions that were the place of refuge from Mu and the upper or first activities of the Atlantean land—and in that now known as Arizona and Utah did the entity then become among the first of those that established the cave dwellers, and the use of the metals as a medium of exchange and adornment.

The entity innately from that experience is one who is a respresentative of, or one that may deal in, precious stones or metals, and from the *material* angle be always the gainer. The name then was Gomo.

In the present the innate influences of metals and stones upon the entity will have their influence through those activities of the atomic forces. Hence the bloodstone or the lapis, or both, should be as a stone that would be about the body of the entity; not as an omen, not as a symbol; rather that the vibrations of the higher forces from these proper expressions of activities throughout the universal forces in materiality may be an aid or as a strengthening. From one there are the emanations of high electrical forces from its copper base. From the other there are the high electrical vibrations that emanate from its *pureness* of the higher vibration.   816-3

This higher vibration of the bloodstone brings harmony.

. . .the bloodstone is that which will bring more harmony as to vibrations. . .   3407-1

There are those to whom the bloodstone brings harmony, and less of the tendencies for anger. . .   5294-1

This higher vibration is also attributed to the ruby, which would keep [5322] in better attune with the infinite.

Ye should find the diamond and the ruby close to your body oft, for their vibrations will keep the vibrations of the body in better attune with infinity and not with purely mental or material things of life.   5322-1

It seems very likely that Edgar Cayce's term "bloodstone" was applied to the ruby. Several other effects of the ruby are brought out besides those dealt with so far. It may improve an individual's concentration. It may impart valor and strength, power and might.

Q-5. Is there a stone or ring somewhere waiting for me, that I should wear? What causes the feeling that there is, and what power has such a stone in reference to one's life?

A-5. That has been builded by the knowledge which has come to self oft, as to the influences that are *without* self. That thoughts are things and may be miracles or crimes is true. So, the experiences have brought that; as to how those things in their various emanations of the cosmic or etheric forces in nature gather about them—as in stones—a concentration of a force or power.

The ruby would make for the body that [force], not as something which would be other than the power that self attributes to same, through its actual experience. But the light or reflection from same, worn on hand or body, will enable the body to concentrate in its mental application the greater— through the influences such a stone brings to material expression.

How? Each element, each stone, each variation of stone, has its own atomic movement, held together by the units of energy that in the universe are concentrated in that particular activity. Hence they come under varied activities according to their color, vibration or emanation.

In this particular one (the ruby) there is that fitness with that which has been the experience of *this* soul, this entity, through material expression. Hence it is an aid, a crutch to lean upon. But as has always been given, let it be a stepping-stone; *not* that which thou *standest* only upon!   531-3

. . .the valor and the strength that is imparted in the inner influence of the ruby about the body.   1144-2

However, if the ruby is kept close to the body, it will bring strength, power and might in a manner to the purposes set by the entity, or those choices given.   2571-1

The Opal

The effect of the fire opal may be the same as that of the clear lapis in fostering intenseness and the ability to loose emotions through the body centers so that spiritual and mental influences may more nearly merge.

. . .the fire opal, [and] the lapis or copper in its *elemental* form, bring great passion, intenseness, the abilities to loose emotions through the very centers of the body for the closer association of the spiritual with the activative influences of the mental self.   1580-1

The role of the fire opal arises from the vigor or fire in it, which brings about understanding. That, in turn, leads to purification. As the fires of the flesh are burned out, the entity becomes a clear channel for living truth, shown in this way to others.

The *entity* came into the experience in Egypt but was of the Atlantean peoples, and interpreted in the Temple Beautiful those beauties of the temples in Poseidia; for from there we find those great lights—opaline lights, as it were—about the entity. And these. . .would be those stones that to others may bring. . .mystery yet the fire opal would be of the stones that should be about the entity; for the holding of that fire, that vigor, that *understanding* that makes for purification, even though the fires of the flesh must be *burned out* that the glory of self may be made manifest in being a channel for the glory of the living truths to be known and experienced among others.

1193-1

A young girl who was extremely sensitive to the vibrations of others was advised to wear the fire opal in a locket about her neck. She was told she could trust persons whose auras held light red and green, turning into white, and that association with them would make for spiritual enlightenment, mental understanding and helpful influences. Since those colors are found in the fire opal, it would apparently reinforce such influences.

An interesting point is made in this reading that gems worn on the neck or on the ears bring out the qualities associated with them in other individuals. Therefore, the young girl was advised against wearing on ears or neck gems with those vibrations which were disturbing to her. Their use on the extremities in rings, amulets or anklets would not produce the same effect.

Colors—these become as means in which the entity may, for itself, determine much. But know as to what colors mean. For the entity is not only able and capable to receive the vibrations of individuals about the entity as to their colors but as to their vibrations. And these then make for a sensitiveness that is often disturbing to the entity.

This may be developed or it may be passed over. But those that are as symbols or signs or conditions that may be used constructively, use. . .do not abuse same. For that which is good, to be sure, may be used to one's own undoing.

Then study those influences. And know when such arise in the experience that warnings are ahead, and govern the associations and the activities accordingly.

When these reach those stages as to where there is felt the lighter red, and those that turn to shades of green with the influences that make for shadings into white, then these trust, these hold to; for such individuals, such associations, may bring in the experience of the entity that which will make for spiritual enlightenment, a mental understanding, and the influences that would bring helpful influences in every experience.

Hence the opal that is called the change, with the moonstone, should be stones about the body or entity oft. Wear the fire opal as a locket about the neck. This would be well. Not upon the hands nor upon the wrists, but about the neck.

Wear the others, as of the pearl with moonstone or the like, as rings or amulets or anklets; but never those upon the neck or in the ears—rather upon the extremities; for they will make for the bringing out—in the experiences of those the entity meets—of those very colors and vibrations that have been indicated to which the entity is so sensitive [and which may be disturbing]. 1406-1

Some individuals wearing a fire opal would be difficult to deal with in matters of sex. Could this refer to the burning out of the "fires of the flesh" just mentioned?

There being then individuals who when wearing a fire opal would be hard individuals to deal with when it came to sex. 5294-1

If a person has the correct attitude, the wearing of opals may help to keep the temper in check.

Q-4. Will wearing opals by one who does not have them as [a] birthstone signify ill omens for that person?
A-4. No...opals will be helpful if there is kept the correct attitude for it will enable the entity to hold on to self or to prevent those who would be angry from flying off the handle too much. 4006-1

For a person who is fickle, however, the changing lights in opals may reinforce an undesirable trait.

Q-6. Any special jewelry that I should wear?
A-6. Anything that is jade or green; not opals, however. Though these appear in the seal, they are—as self—sometimes fickle. 2522-1

Opals should not be worn by those who have colors in their auras indicating fire signs. The opals and these colors work against one another. It is better for these persons to wear gems of a more delicate influence to attune themselves to nature.

Persons with these fire-sign colors around them will find that flowers fade when worn on their bodies.

The auras as compared to the stone, these would work in ninety-nine percent of the conditions where these are considered as those things that work with, not against, the colors seen in the auras; that is, those which indicate the fire signs in the auras of such should never wear opals, and they will even fade flowers when worn on their bodies. But the more delicate, as would bring the nature, is preferable. . .

5294-1

The Amethyst

An amethyst, worn on the body, may help a person to be a better channel for healing. It may, also, help to induce visions. Its purple color seems to be significant.

Well that the entity have the stones or minerals about self when in periods of meditation, or in those periods when it may find itself the more easily attuned to the influences that may use the body either in the healing forces that flow through— through its attunements, or through the visions and the associations of the entity; the chrysolite or the amethyst. For the color purple should be close to the body; and the perfumes or odors of lavender have their influence—not as in great quantity, but that which makes for attunements.   688-2

An amethyst pendant will help to control temperament.

In the choice of stones, do wear the amethyst as a pendant about the neck, as a part of the jewelry. This will also work with the colors to control temperament [entity's determination to have its own way].   3806-1

A "white" amethyst helps to bring harmony to both body and mind.

Stones—the entity should have the amethyst (the white) about self often. These vibrations will bring greater harmony, in not only body but in the mental attributes.   1986-1

The Moonstone and the Diamond

According to a recent guide to minerals, gems and rocks, the term "moonstone" is today being applied to albite with a bluish sheen.[15]

In the Edgar Cayce readings, however, this name seems to designate another gem. One of the readings quoted under the section on "The Ruby and/or Bloodstone" describes a turquoise blue moonstone which would bring greater force about the body. (608-7) Another excerpt advises a woman to wear the moonstone, which will give strength and keep what is nearest to her, closer. The moonstone had been to her in a former life such an helpmeet, urge and vibration. She was also told that in this former life she had panned for gold and found diamonds.

W.B. Crow refers to colored diamonds, in particular mentioning the *Hope*, which is sapphire blue in color, and the *Excelsior* of a fine bluish-white tinge.[16] This reference to Margaret Fitzhugh seems to tell us that the moonstone of the readings is a bluish-white diamond.

> . . .the entity was among those who had come from portions of Alabama and settled in what is now Arkansas (or Ar-Kansas as then called); and the entity was among those who panned for gold and found diamonds.
> But the entity learned from those experiences that which would be well for the body. While it should never wear a great deal of jewelry—it doesn't fit the universality of mind of the entity, nor does the vibration of jewelry (cheap or good) mean much to the entity. . .wear the moonstone close to the body, or on your body. It will give strength, and it will keep that which is nearest to you closer to you; not as an omen but as a part of your mental and spiritual consciousness. Have same. . .upon a chain, about your neck; not as an ornament, but rather as a helpmeet, as an urge, as a vibration that will be most helpful— as it was in the experience in that land as Margaret Fitzhugh.
>
> 5125-1

One last reference to the moonstone tells us that it may bring peace, harmony and tendencies toward spiritual things.

> The. . .individual wearing or having in the apparel the moonstone might find that it would bring peace, harmony and those tendencies toward spiritual things.   5294-1

[5322] was advised that the vibration of the diamond would keep the body in better attunement with infinity. This seems to

---

[15]Herbert S. Zim and Paul R. Shaffer, Professor of Geology, University of Illinois, *Rocks and Minerals*, Golden Press, Inc., N.Y., 1957, pg. 88.
[16]Crow, pp. 28-29.

reflect the advice given [5294] about the moonstone, thus
reinforcing the probability that the moonstone is a form of blue-
white diamond.

Ye should find the diamond and the ruby close to your body
oft, for their vibrations will keep the vibrations of the body in
better attune with infinity and not with purely mental or
material things of life.   5322-1

The Crystal or White Stone

Under *Clear Lapis,* we learned "in stones, the whiter, the
more crystal the better." (1775-1) [2285] was advised to carry a
piece of crystal or any white stone about the body as a helpful
influence.

As to the elemental influences having to do with the entity's
experience, we find that the crystal as a stone, or any white
stone, has a helpful influence—if carried about the body; not as
an omen, not merely as a "good luck piece" or "good luck
charm" but these vibrations that are needed as helpful
influences for the entity are well to be kept close about the
body.   2285-1

Yellow Stones and Topaz

Yellow stones, also, have their place. One person was advised
to wear them because of astrological influences.

Stones—those of the yellow tint or nature would be the
better. These bring the vibrations for more harmonious
influence in one who is especially influenced by those from
Mercury, Venus and Mars. For. . .each of these is indicated in
the white, the red, the blue, the yellow [and] harmonizes in
same.   2648-1

Topaz specifically was advised for [2281] because of its
beauty, purity and clarity, which would bring strength.

Then, in choosing the interpretations of the records of those
things that have their influence or urge, keep the topaz as a
stone about thee always. Its beauty, its purity, its clarity, may
bring to thee strength. For this ye have found, and will find oft
needed in thy dealings with thy problems, and with thy fellow
men.   2281-1

Perhaps this topaz was the oriental topaz, which is a type of corundum, of the same chemical nature as sapphire and ruby.[17]

Jade

See reference 1189-1 under the section on "The Pearl" for a combination of opal and jade.

The Beryl and the Agate

A scarab (beetle) made of beryl was advised for a person who had been skilled in the placing of stones in ancient Egypt. It was to be worn as an amulet or ring and would bring safety.

In this [Egyptian] experience the entity rose to power, position, place, fame, through the experiences in that period, as related to the various manners of expression of praise in music, in art, and *especially* in that of placing of stones. In the present, the innate desire to feel precious stones, to compare same, to watch the change in the color in same, is seen from *this* experience. These will make for much *judgment* to the entity, and the beryl and scarab should be a portion of the entity's dress, *ever;* either worn as the amulet, the ring, or such, will make for a safety in the entity's present experience.
1719-1

The beryl is a mineral or gem from which come the aquamarine and the emerald.[18] The beryl and the agate also may bring about receptiveness.

Hence we find the agate, the beryl, should be *stones* with the vibrations and under the influence that the entity may find carrying an incense to the finer self that makes for an awakening, an opening of the inner self for the *receptiveness.* And attunement is made through such vibrations, just as there may be with the tungsten in a portion of a vacuum that may raise those sound waves that through their relativity of activity of the electrical vibration that makes for the activity of the atomic forces in same, give that which is gathered from the ether waves. 707-1

---

[17]Crow, pp. 34-35.
[18]Webster, pg. 98; Zim and Shaffer, pg. 84.

The Sardonyx Stone and Soya Bean

The sardonyx stone, a form of agate, may influence the choices made mentally by the person carrying it. However, many of the same vibrations may be obtained from the soya bean. It is well for a person so influenced to have figures made of sardonyx placed about his sleeping quarters or home.

Well that there be carried on the person the sardonyx stone (that is, in its semi-precious state); either in statuettes, pins, buttons, or a piece of same carried. Not as a protection but rather for the vibratory forces that influence the choices made by the mental forces of the entity itself. Statuettes, frames or the like are well. Much of the same vibrations may be obtained from using those combinations of stone made from the soya bean; that may act in much the same capacity. Figures made of same are well to have about the entity's *sleeping* quarters or abode. **1528-1**

The Sardius

The sardius was recommended for a woman who had helped others with understanding in ancient Egypt. It would again influence understanding of the laws governing man's relationships to the higher forces.

In this experience [Egypt], in the portion the entity gained in the abilities to give to others that understanding as attained from the builders and from those who wrought in fine metals, those who had the understandings of precious stones and their settings, and their colors, and their vibrations, as gave for the influences in peoples. In this the entity gained, and the stone... the entity should have about same, is the sardius—for this gives for an influence. . .to understand those laws as apply to man's relationships to the higher forces. **1714-1**

The identity of the sardius is unclear. Webster suggests it may be a ruby. However a sard is classified by this authority as a brownish red variety of chalcedony.[19]

General Advice on Gems

We have previously noted under *Clear Lapis* the advice given to [440] to have this gem cut by the method ordinarily used for

---

[19]Webster, pg. 857.

precious or semi-precious stones with the gem larger in the center and tapering toward the outer edge. (440-11)

It was suggested to one young woman that she wear the bloodstone in the form of a triangle ovaled on the edges.

. . .wear especially the bloodstone, cut in the form of a triangle, though ovaled on its edges. 2163-1

We have also noted that often the stone advised was to be worn in a pendant on the neck, sometimes on wrist or waist. It was to touch the body. (440-11) If the stone was soft in composition, it was to be encased in crystal for preservation. With reference to the young sensitive it was disclosed that gems worn on the neck or ears bring out in other individuals the qualities associated with these stones. She was, therefore, advised against such use of certain stones. They could be worn on the extremities, however, in rings, amulets or anklets without this effect. (1406-1)

There are several other interesting observations from the readings in this general field. [1532] was advised against the use of pins. It would appear that this suggestion would apply to anyone who had in some past life had a traumatic experience with piercing or cutting instruments. Circles or bands were suggested instead. (It is possible, though, that *they* might not be in order where there had been a past life experience with constriction. However, individual preference or antipathy may well be a guide in this respect.)

And ornaments of circles or bands or wristlets, these are well for the entity—more than pins or brooches. . .anything that is as a band upon the arm, the fingers or the ankle or the neck. But refrain from pins and the like, for these bring the inclinations for disturbing forces in the experience. 1532-1

[1540] was told that when physical changes were in progress, it was best for her not to wear jewelry. Afterwards anything very *old* would be helpful.

Q-9. Is there any special jewelry that I should wear that will raise my vibration?
A-9. We would not wear jewelry during those periods of this change in the vibrations of the body (through using the violet ray in the manner indicated). Afterwards, anything that is very *old* would be aiding to the body. 1540-3

The Study and Collection of Jewels

Several persons were advised to work with precious stones. [2761] had been head of the caravan which had found and rescued the wounded Uhjltd in ancient Persia. He was told that in this experience

...the abilities in carving stones and setting precious stones became the greater part of the entity's activity, some almost to the undoing—until the enlightening of those tenets of that leader in the "city in the hills."
We find that in those fields of precious stones, or of glass or prisms, or in literature or art, the entity may find the outlets for its application of abilities in this present experience.

2761-1

[5294] had been the caravan maker, excerpts from whose reading we have previously noted. The sequence of his life then will now be included, showing what a firm basis had been established for his study and use of stones today in helping others.

In any form...which has to do with color...might the entity bring a great deal of joy, of harmony into the experience of those with whom he might work, or direct such, as a collector of stones that are colored, especially opals, emeralds, moonstone, bloodstone, what may be termed the semi-precious stones.
These not merely as a collector, but as one who might prepare or gather such for not merely setting, for...these have their value in the effect, the vibrations that they...bring about the body.
Study them, then, with the purpose of acquainting individuals as well as preparing same...These are well for the entity to study, as well as considering the physical, as well as mental, auras of individuals.
The auras as compared to the stones, these should work in ninety-nine percent of the conditions where these are considered as those things that work with, not against, the colors seen in the auras...
Before that we find the entity was in the Persian land, among those who carried the goods from one portion of the land to another, or a caravan maker, dealing in the linens of Egypt, the pearls of Persia, in the opal, the firestone, the lapis lazuli in Indo-China, yea the diamonds and rubies of some of the cities of gold. These find an attraction for the entity in the

experience in the present. Be not rather as a hoarder but use such then, of the knowledge of such, in the study as to the helpful force in the experience of thy fellow man.

Before that. . .the entity was in the Holy Land, when there was the entering in of the children of promise to the Holy Land. The entity was then of the sons of Hittites who dealt with the sons of Aaron as they prepared the garments of the priest, and the entity supplied the various stones, especially the carbuncle and the agate of that particular land. [Reference to Breastplate of Judgment]

In the experience the entity was helpful and yet never learned, in that particular period, the value of same in the experience of individuals; not as omens, not as a sign, but, knowing the vibration of the elements that composed such stones and what might be lacking in a body that might bring those changed vibrations.   5294-1

The preceding excerpt emphasizes the importance of acquainting individuals with the effects of various stones. [2522] was told to collect data on the important part jewels had played in history.

Q-5. What should my hobby be?
A-5. The gathering of data of the nature of all characters; how that some have played such a part in the love affairs, in the life and death, and in the home and in the empire building of some lands. Few realize how much part some of these have played in this land, or in England, or in France, or in Persia, India, Hindustan, and the crown jewels in Russia. All of these, and the data of same, would be a lovely hobby—and bring those vibrations good for the body.   2522-1

The famous novelist Bulwer-Lytton had been, it seems, knowledgeable as to precious stones and metals. Incarnated again, he was advised to write a story, a book, incorporating this special information. The magazines publishing his serials would become better known, so obviously the readers would find what he had to say of great interest.

For this one was Bulwer-Lytton! [Edward George Bulwer-Lytton (1803-1873)]

The experience. . .is too well known to be commented upon, except to use the good, discard the bad. . .This has brought to the experience of the entity abilities in creative and constructive lines, yea as a worker with stones, and as to judgments in working with metals—but precious metals and precious stones, not semi-precious ones. These the entity may use, the knowledge of same, as the basis now for its story—first, as serials in not too well-known magazines, and they'll become better known if you'll write a story for them. Then a book, yes—for every man, the story of his own life would make a book, if he would be true and not try to make it something else.   3657-1

Correspondence Between Gems, Minerals and Metals

We have previously noted that wearing stones with vibrations similar to those of one's own stage of development can be a form of reinforcement and help to an individual. Since most gems are derived from minerals, what might be the effect of proximity to the corresponding mineral? The readings tell us that the effect is nearly the same.

Q-6. What are the entity's stone, mineral and metal?
A-6. These are rather the same; for in the kingdom that the influences of an entity have developed with or acted as concerning, that has made for its advancement or retardment and is to be an influence in its experience in the varied activities to which and through which the entity may be influenced by that association in its mental forces. We find near the same, as in *most* individuals. . .   282-7

There is, however, in the readings little matching of stones with minerals or metals except for that of lapis with copper. In fact, a few extracts in this field pose questions. For example, do the vibrations of the pearl correspond to those of zinc?

Q-7. What metal and stones hold the better vibrations for me?
A-7. The pearl as the stone, zinc as the metal.   2746-1

How great is the difference in vibration between coal and a diamond, both variations of carbon, one with water, the other under pressure?

In Mercury also we find the inclinations for definite divisions of application of the mental self to material things—minerals and their attributes; that is, the *emotions* that arise in the experience from individuals in the variations, as might be said, of carbon; in its variations between coal and a diamond—they are the same, but one is under the pressure, the other is with water!   1561-1

Gold and silver apparently pertain to the variations between uranium and radium.

Gold, silver, those things pertaining to the variations between uranium and radium and the effect of the various elements that would prevent the separations—all urges in these directions would arise from those experiences of the entity, *innately,* in the Mercurian sojourn.   1561-1

The exact value of these particular vibrations is pointed out. Gold is strengthening, silver stabilizing.

Hence the radial activity of radium, as well as the strengthening influences of gold, the stabilizing influence of silver, are all a part of those elements that make for the transmission through the activity of the very vibratory forces themselves, and become to *this* body of great influence. . .   1931-1

The Wearing of Metals

There are several suggestions as to how gold should be worn. For one young girl it was to be in the form of circles or many bangles. Her need for gold as a portion of her dress stemmed from a highly advanced life in Egypt and Mongolia.

Yet. . .those things that are. . .of gold. . .should be a portion of the dress or of the environment; whether in the home, in the activity, or in whatever field of expression. These become a portion of the entity for wielding an influence in the manner in which the entity (the soul) gives expression to same in *its* relationships to its fellow man.

And the entity's activities in the Egyptian land, after those periods of. . .consecration of body and mind through the activities and the initiations in the Temple Beautiful, became rather associated with those in the land of the Mongolian—or in the temples that are yet to be uncovered.

For with the entity's missions there, and the entity's activities, the entity became as the leader or the princess of those people to the activities in the Temple of Gold; the temple that was set with the jewels of the land.

From those experiences of the entity, as Isth-She-Both, there comes the desire of self-adornment, the desire for self-expression as in activities before others—and the abilities for leaderships in whatever activity the entity may undertake...

Q-5. *Is there any particular stone or stones I should wear?*

A-5. Gold in the forms of circles or of many bangles, and the like, are greater to the entity than stones; save diamonds.
        852-12

For a mature woman these bangles were at times almost necessary and at others confusing. Plain gold, silver or platinum because of their stability were best for her.

We find here that stones, too, have an influence; lots of bangles at times become confusing and at others almost necessary. Hence those things that are stable—as plain gold, or plain silver, or platinum, with the finishings—are those influences that are strongest about the entity for helpful forces. **2390-1**

From the above reference it appears that the plain gold, silver and platinum were to be finished in such a way that they could be worn on the body.

Influence of Overlays

[1847] had been in Indo-China in a city no longer existent. (Could it have been one of the cities of gold referred to in 5294-1? See section "The Ruby and/or Bloodstone.") Carvings, filigree and overlays of gold, ivory or coral were of great influence to the individual, who had a close relationship to vibratory forces from the mineral, animal or vegetable kingdoms. It is clear that the overlay of gold was tied in to mineral forces, that of ivory and coral to animal.

Before that we find the entity was in the Indo-China land. . . in the activities of the city which has become as nought. . .

In the present experience, things pertaining to the oriental *mind* **become of special interest to the entity; as also especially the intricate work as carvings, filigree, and activities of such a nature that are a part of the entity's experience through that sojourn. Things overlaid with gold or ivory or coral, things of that nature become a part of the entity's experience—these are innate or manifested by a great influence.**

Hence the abilities of the entity in the present to attain or maintain close relationship to vibratory influences and forces, whether they emanate from the mineral, the animal or the vegetable kingdoms. All of these become innately as portions of the entity's experience. **1847-1**

Possible Connection Between Sun Worship and Gold

Sun worship was the religion held in the Mongolian Temple of Gold, previously referred to. (852-12) It dealt with the inner meaning of the sun and emphasized love of God made manifest in the souls of human beings. Perhaps the gold used in the temple construction helped to raise the consciousness of the worshippers. We can only speculate.

. . .the entity was in the Gobi land, in the city of gold—that may one day be discovered.

The entity was one of those who represented the Goddess of the Sun in that period of activity. . .　　　　　　　　2420-1

. . .the entity was in what is now known as the Mongolian or the Gobi land. . .

The entity then was a princess in the Golden Temple of those peoples, aiding—after much persuasion—in the correlating of truths.

Hence we may find the entity's interests in many of the various thoughts that have grown to seed in the varied groups and the varied traditions of groups in their activity or a social order, or a worshipfulness order. Yet to the entity they all lead from the one, the source, the sun—with its *inner* meaning.

　　　　　　　　　　　　　　　　　　　　　　1219-1

. . .the entity was in what is now called the Gobi land, with the children of the Sun.

Then in the name Taoi, the entity was a priestess in the Temple of Gold, that is yet to be unearthed, that there may be more known of those things that are as old as the earth itself. For the love of God as made manifest in the souls of human beings in the earth, is as old as the earth itself.　　2402-2

Physical Effects of Minerals on the Body

We have seen that minerals in the forms of gems, stones and metals, placed either on the body or in close proximity to it, may have a very pronounced effect on mental and spiritual attributes. It is, therefore, not surprising to learn that mineral vibratory forces, when introduced into the body itself, affect its physical make-up and functioning.

There are several ways in which these may be introduced. One method is by means of either of two electrical appliances, the construction of which is carefully noted in the readings. Another is through close proximity to minerals. A third is through oral ingestion of minerals in basic form. The most commonly used method is through ingestion of minerals contained either in food of plant or animal origin or in air or water.

Effects Produced by Certain Electrical Appliances

We will first take up the two electrical devices. The Radio-active (or Radial-active) Appliance is designated for general use. Its effect on the body seems to be based on a mineralized reaction, which *may be* augmented in specific instances by the introduction into its electrical circuit of various mineral solutions, selected to help particular parts of the body. A person desiring to improve his or her health in general might use the Radio-active Appliance in its basic form. One desiring an overall improvement in health plus assistance for a special condition might benefit by using the Radio-active Appliance in conjunction with the solution recommended by the readings for that condition.

The Wet Cell Appliance is designed chiefly for specific conditions. Its circuit includes a solution jar, the contents of which are varied according to need.

The more general nature of the basic Radio-active Appliance is pointed up in the following excerpts.

These [Radio-active Appliances] may be distributed to many peoples and be found very beneficial in any condition as given.
1800-5

. . .the Radio-active Appliance may be given or prepared in a commercial way and manner; while the Wet Cell Appliance is builded in most cases for specific conditions—and for general use at times.
1800-25

The Radio-active Appliance

Many readings relate to the construction and application of the Radio-active Appliance. The first general reading, 1800-4, which gives the principles involved, is now summarized as follows:

The human body is made up of electronic vibration; and every atom and element of the body, every organ and organism of it, has its own electronic vibration necessary for sustaining it and keeping it in balance. Every unit of the body, then, can reproduce itself by division. When the force in any organ or element of the body becomes deficient in its ability to reproduce the balance necessary for sustenance and reproduction of physical existence, that *part* of the body becomes deficient because of the lack of electronic energy. Such a condition may be brought about by injury or disease, arising from external forces, also by lack of eliminations or of other agencies, arising from internal forces.

Metals also produce electronic vibration, which, when applied to the body, makes a form of motion for it. The forces that have slowed down may be revitalized into renewed activity.

The electronic forces of the Radio-active Appliance arise from a formation of carbon steel, "electronized" by ice and ice water. The vibrations of these components are similar to those of which the human body is chiefly constituted.

Iron corresponds to blood and the greater constituents of force it supplies. Cold or ice corresponds to the combination of other elements which act as an aid to man in sustaining life. These together produce an equilibrium and relieve any tension arising from a deficiency or overactivity of any of the electronic forces in the body. This is achieved because the union of electronic agencies may force an excess from one agency to assist where there is a deficiency in another. This application is the same as that arising in the recuperation of the body during sleep.

For [195] the application of the Radio-active Appliance would result in a lowering of vibration in centers where an excess was preventing normal vibration of the auditory system.

In general this appliance would be helpful with any catarrhal condition or one involving poor eliminations in an early stage. Catarrhal conditions are the debilitating ones most often occurring in human beings and may exist in any portion of the organism, including the head, throat, nasal organs, ears, lungs, stomach, liver, kidneys and urinary organs. Conditions stemming from poor eliminations may appear as rheumatism, neuralgia, headache and others. The Radio-active Appliance would in such cases act as an equalizer. Its use would, therefore, be a preventive rather than a curative one. It would put the person in a position, however, to assist himself through mental forces and those normal physical forces of appetite and rebuilding. (End of summary.)

Since this device has been built, apparently very successfully, by persons versed in technical knowledge, its specifications will not be included here. For more information about its application, see the directions in "A Note to the Reader" on the copyright page.

References quoted below describe the use of the Radio-active Appliance with its solution jar for the treatment of some specific ailments.

Q-4. In attaching a container. . .in which is placed tincture of iron, would the application of this cure anemia?

A-4. Cure anemia, even in a virulent or exaggerated state. This would of necessity be rather the preventive than curative forces, though with the application of this we gradually build that condition in the system to overcome, or add iron to the system. . .

Q-5. Would tincture of iodine cure goitre?

A-5. Tincture of iodine cures and prevents goitre. This. . . would reduce any condition that affects the ductless glands. Would also prove preventive. . .in cases first beginning, of appendicitis, or of any condition relating to either thyroid or the appendix.

Q-6. What would spirits of camphor, silver nitrate and gold chloride, each, cure?

A-6. Silver nitrate is a nerve stimulant. . .Any condition pertaining to the nerve system. Chloride of gold—any condition wherein there is any form of the condition bordering on rheumatics, or of the necessity of rejuvenating any organ of the system showing. . .delinquency in action. . .Nitrate. . .is added through the silver solution. . .for those of a neurotic [neuritic] condition, even unto neuritis, or any form of condition pertaining to enlarged joints, muscles, tissue, any protuberance as comes to portions of body. . .

Q-7. What would the spirits of camphor cure?

A-7. Nausea and summer complaints. Any intestinal disturbance.

Q-8. Would the system absorb the tincture of iron, or merely the vibration as given off by the tincture of iron?

A-8. The vibration as given off, which creates that same vibration, giving the action with the elements in the system that create iron, those properties or those actions of same in system. Same as is acquired from that of the other forms that may be applied through same to system.   1800-6

The Wet Cell Appliance

A reading recommending use of the Wet Cell Appliance clarifies somewhat the effect it produces in therapy.

Then, the consideration that is to be given in making any application for corrective forces, that there may be the better coordination in the mental, the superficial, the imaginative and the physical being, would be to create within the system itself that as makes for the proper coordination of atomic forces as control the functioning of, and the changing of, those material conditions as are taken, for sustenance, into the physical body, into such vibratory forces as to create a normal equilibrium between the matter in the body and that of a normal, or near normal functioning of that matter in a material plane and in a material body.

. . .all atomic forces are of an *electrical* nature in their effect and affect upon a physical organism. Not all portions of the system function in the same vibratory rate, as the nerves of the sensory organism are made—as it were—in a series of necessary portions of system for the proper alteration of vibration of atomic forces to create either that of vision, hearing, feeling, tasting, and the like; for these are an alteration of vibration. So also, in the assimilation as for gland functioning—as creates in the system those elements that either add to the nerve energies in their activity those necessary elements for the *coordination* of the muscular forces within the system, [so] as to produce functioning in a nominal or normal manner, or. . .[if the nerve energies] are *overcharged* or undercharged. . .[the elements] *prevent* their functioning in a nominal manner. Hence, the activity of the physical body may be altered by the concerted activity of minds that are directed to the atomic forces of an individual, in raising their vibrations to a nominal or normal manner. Hence we have. . .spiritual healing to a body.

Now, the same vibrations may be raised for a *physical* body in the *physical* sense, as may be raised in a mental or spiritual body by its association or *its* connection with that that creates a necessary element of vibration for corrective forces in a system.

Then, to find the correct vibration for elements that are lacking in their sustaining forces for a living organism, and to create that within the enlivening portion of the system in such a way and manner as for same to be assimilated by, or become effective in, a living organism, is to be able to change that environ of that physical organism [so] as to be creative and evoluting in its activity in that system.

For this body, then, we would find that we would add those vibrations from the low form of the electrical vibration as comes. . .in the Wet Cell vibrations from those atomic forces necessary in the forces of the body itself. These, we will find, it will be necessary to change or alter somewhat in this particular condition: [Instructions follow].   5576-1

Since the Wet Cell Appliance has been constructed, apparently very successfully, by technically trained persons, the author will not include here the specifications for it. For additional information, see "A Note to the Reader" on the copyright page.

Effects of Various Minerals Applied Vibratorially

To correspond to individual ailments the Edgar Cayce readings suggest a number of modifications in the treatments using the Radio-active and Wet Cell Appliances. There are hundreds of reference cards in the A.R.E. Library listing the ailments to be treated by these means. Space does not permit a review of all; but general consideration of the effects of certain minerals applied vibratorially is in order.

Iron

Iron as applied to the body through the Radio-active device has already been taken up. Iron corresponds to *blood* and the greater constituents of *force*. When the carbon steel is "electronized" by ice, the vibrations sent out are said to equalize the sensory system and improve poor eliminations. (1800-4) It is also reported that tincture of iron may be applied by means of the Radio-active Appliance to cure anemia, even in a virulent form. (1800-6)

Gold

Gold has an effect upon the nerves, of which it is a basic metallic principle. (2436-3) It is reported that the nerve forces gain energy from glandular reactions and use this energy to resuscitate nerve impulses. (1905-1) These impulses are directed to brain centers, from which come other impulses—for activity. (2436-3)

Q-3. Has the Wet Cell Appliance treatment [with chloride of gold] been of any help?
A-3. If not, we would not suggest that it still be applied. This has brought changes. It is adding that nerve influence. This is a basic condition: In each element of the body-energies, there are those glandular or cell forces that take from that assimilated the necessary influences for the strengthening of various portions of the body. In blood there must be iron, silicon, calcium, soda and those elements for its constituencies other *than* that influence carried in same. In bone another form of calcium and combinations of other elements. The same in muscle, in skin. Also the same in nerve—nerve along which there may be the functioning of that as may be rightly called the electric system of the human body. . .This is illustrated in all of nature itself.

Hence in this body, the lacking element has been gold; such influences that go to make activities in the sensory system as combined in the responses from brain—which is the nerve head or center through which channels of same respond, or through which reflexes react from elements supplied to the body.

This vibratory activity of the Wet Cell Appliance adds an element for strengthening the nerves of a body, for it—the gold—is a basic metallic principle of the nerve itself.

Hence now, as indicated, there needs to be a guiding of those centers through which impulses are directed to brain centers, from which the optic nerves take their impulse for activity. This may be done osteopathically. It will be seen, by the examinations that will be made, that the lens are there; that the blood flow through the optic socket, the optic itself, is existent. The ability of the nerve to supply that reflex necessary in this nerve plasm is lacking. This may be added in the general system for strength, for resistance in all portions of the system now needing guiding through those ganglia themselves direct to the areas afflicted in these directions. Thus we may find quicker response, and the needed helpfulness for the body.   2436-3

For [1905] the application of gold through the Wet Cell Appliance was recommended to help arrest even a complete breakdown of nerve forces.

. . .the conditions in the present appear *very* serious—as there is the lack of the reaction between the nerve impulse to and from the activities. Hence the languidness, and coma—at times.

Yet this need not *necessarily* be fatal to the better body-forces, if there is the proper application made. [Suggestions follow for calling a neurologist and giving injections of liver extract.]

Then we would make use of the Wet Cell Appliance carrying gold to the body-activity (and in the proportion of. . .chloride of gold to. . .distilled water, carried into the body vibratorially. . .) which will aid in assisting the nerve forces through their activities to take from the glandular reactions the energies necessary for the resuscitating of the nerve *impulse* itself. [Other directions follow.]

Q-1. What has caused this condition?

A-1. A breaking down of the nervous system. This is a multiple of the condition. And these elements added in the manner indicated will prevent the brain adherence, or the liquefying of same.

Q-2. Anything else that can be done to make him comfortable?

A-2. Do *this!* It won't make him very comfortable in the

beginning, but these will begin the resuscitation as well as the hindering of the deterioration which is going on in the present.   1905-1

According to notes following this reading the directions were apparently not followed. The patient died six weeks later.

For [631] the nerve tissue had degenerated to the point that locomotion was impaired and there was a distinct possibility of a breakdown between the cerebrospinal and sympathetic systems. (The cause of this degeneration had been gonorrheal in nature.) Application of gold chloride by means of the Wet Cell was recommended.

In the present we find there is the indication of the breaking down of the impulses through the nerve force itself; thus producing a deteriorating force in nerve tissue, thus softening the impress of the influences of locomotion. . .for activity of mental forces—through the coordinating centers of the body as well as the sensory system.

These. . .may *yet* be aided, *if* there would be a *consistent* and persistent application of influences which would turn the activity of that assimilated through the channels of the glandular forces as relate to nerve building.

Thus the impulses would be stimulated for improvement of the white and gray matter. . .in the nerve and brain centers, or circulation, to replenish rather than allow. . .to become in such a nature that the coordination between cerebrospinal and sympathetic becomes either blocked entirely or becomes atrophied in portions and thus a softening which would become the *lack* of ability to produce coordination through the system!   631-8

The glandular reaction resulting from application of chloride of gold is pointed up by the following reference to the pituitary gland.

With the addition of those elements in the chloride of gold, which act directly upon the pituitary gland, we will make for those necessary influences to coordinate with the rest of the system.   831-1

Silver and Gold

We have previously noted that silver nitrate applied with the Radio-active device is recommended as a nerve stimulant for the relief of neuritis and any condition pertaining to enlarged joints, muscles and tissues. (1800-6)

Gold and silver together are suggested in conjunction with the Wet Cell. Their role in the body is described as that of "the cords of life-expression."

For remember, silver and gold in their elements necessarily are as the cords in life-expression in the physical body. 1029-1

Through the Wet Cell Appliance, then, the vibrations from the gold and silver may be carried into the system. . .
These. . .will carry to the system those radial forces from these elements that—adding to a revivifying force in the bodily functionings—will bring about new life, new energies. 887-4

The solutions for use in this connection are silver nitrate and gold chloride.

Begin then with the use of the low form of electrical vibration carrying the elements that are in their very nature reactory to the glandular forces of the body; that is, gold—in a chloride state, and silver—in a nitrate state. We refer to the Wet Cell Appliance.   1134-1

. . .the chloride of gold, that will make for a change of activity in the blood cellular force as to the creative energies—and the nitrate of silver, that will make for a change in the impulse in the nerve forces themselves; one solution used [with the Wet Cell] one day, the other the next. . .   1242-1

The very nature or type of this disturbance is insidious and subtle. There is the inability to remain conscious of the reaction or response between the brain and sensory forces. Hence there is an attack to the nerve areas lying between the conscious and unconscious, or between the voluntary and involuntary activity. The cerebrospinal system becomes involuntary, and the sympathetic or vegetative system becomes voluntary.

. . .this is a blood disturbance or the lack of the effluvia in the blood to make. . .the proper connections between the positive and negative vibrations in the system.

So. . .for this character or type of disorder—we would apply the radial low electrical forces that would carry the necessary elements in the system to make for positive and negative reactions between these poles in the system. And we find there would be the response.

These would be applied with the Wet Cell or low electrical

forces for thirty minutes each morning, carrying the chloride of gold solution; and for thirty minutes each evening, carrying the silver nitrate solution. [Other directions follow.]   986-1

There are elements in the earth from which, to which, every atom of the body responds. Here we find that silver and gold are those necessary elements that are needed in body when mind has been attuned to Creative Forces for helpful influences. . .

We would use the low Wet Cell Appliance, as this produces that vibration nearer to life energy itself in human experience. For, all life is electrical energy. That produced as life force is from the combinations of the principal elements in the Wet Cell Appliance, preparing. . .[Directions follow, including recommendation of chloride of gold sodium and nitrate of silver solutions.]   3491-1

. . .there is a lacking of elements in the glands that function in a physical body, that supply that necessary element in a living organism for the mental transportation or mental reactions of the physical body, and these are. . .those that will make for the changing of vibrations in the physical functioning of the system, so that—as there are responses in the mental body; that is, impressions that are received by the awakening of the active forces in a physical organism—there are the proper *connections* that will make brain impulses. . .for the imaginative system. . .for the sensory organism, for the locomotary forces of the body, *coordinate* in their responses in the body, so that—as the body *wills* to move in its daily activities, either as to walking, talking, feeling, seeing, hearing—the *responses coordinate* to the centers that will make for a response from the sensory, or sympathetic *and* sensory, system to the cerebrospinal; and there will come more stamina in the activities of the body, in the limbs, in the arms, in the forces of the brain forces themselves, and in the abilities for assimilation.

These. . .may be supplied by. . .that as would *raise* vibrations in the system to a *coordinating* manner, or with the addition of those things being applied. Do not change those in the present, for they have their effect upon the body. Add these:

The chloride of gold with the *carbonate* of soda, in a low electrical vibration. . .These should be charged in the low electrical vibration and given to the body at least twice each week.

We would also, once each week, add the low electrical vibration from a *plain* electrical charge of nitrate of silver.

Silver and gold, then, as metals for the body, enliven the glands of the system that are lax in their physical functioning, supplying to the brain centers even themselves *that* impulse, that incentive, as to make for *proper physical coordination* in the body here.

In the applications, these should be kept in an atmosphere and surroundings that are in keeping with those tenets, those lessons of the body, that are *being* taken for the *spiritual* awakening, as well as the material developments. . .

Q-2. How long should the electrical treatments be given each time?

A-2. The gold, charged in the low electrical vibration, would be for twenty to thirty minutes at a treatment. The silver would be from ten to twenty minutes, when given. The change in time is as this: Remember, there is truth in, "When shall the silver cord be broken, or the golden horn be empty?" The golden activity upon the system is to supply that necessary element in the glands that secrete in the system for the supplying of the assimilated forces of a developing body, and pour their fluids as from the horn into the body. Hence more is necessary. While. . .the silver cord. . .makes for that transmutation of *impulse* from the brain to the organs of the body, *sustaining*. . .that spark of life itself in a material plane.

Here, to be sure, we are dealing with *metaphysical* problems, but they both come from that of material forces to the actual active forces of *living* organisms. [Other directions follow.]

5500-1

This last reading relates that silver is needed for transmutation of impulses from the brain to the organs of the body and gold for glandular secretions to supply assimilated forces.

For an individual whose coordination is poor, both silver and gold might be needed. For an individual whose mental flexes are sufficient but whose body is under par because of improper glandular functioning (with resulting excess of drosses in the system), the gold alone might be needed. In fact, application of silver to this last type of person could presumably result in overstimulation of mental flexes. These conclusions are the author's.

An arresting thought on the role of gold will now be examined. Under *Gold,* this section, we found that "elements in the chloride of gold. . .act directly upon the pituitary gland." (831-1) In the section "Possible Connection Between Sun Worship and Gold" the possibility was brought out that gold raised the consciousness of the sun worshippers in the Mongolian Temple of Gold so that they better understood the inner meaning of the sun or love of God. A conclusion might be drawn that love of God is conveyed in the inner meaning of the sun; that gold heightens perception of this; and that gold in the human body affects the pituitary (the third eye, according to 281-54), the center on a spiritual level embodying consciousness of the Father. So there is a direct link in the readings between the sun, gold and the pituitary, all of service in the development of godly man. The author raises the question: Is this so?

Iodine

A prior reference has told us that tincture of iodine may be applied with the Radio-active Appliance to cure and prevent goitre, to prevent appendicitis at the onset and to reduce any condition affecting the ductless glands. (1800-6)

In the following extract it is indicated that iodine in solution may be applied through the Wet Cell to stimulate bodily functions.

In one application we would use the gold solution [with Wet Cell Appliance]. . .to make for the plasm of strength and resistance. . .

And in the other application we would use the iodine in solution. . .so that it is assimilated by the bodily functionings; not being taken internally but as stimulations to the bodily functions themselves. 1031-1

The next reference states that a lack of thyroid secretion had affected [130]'s lungs, digestion and heart. It was recommended that iodine should be given vibratorially through the Wet Cell, along with oral thyroid medication.

In the throat, bronchi, and lungs, we find the effect of disorders as have affected the circulatory forces in the system, and while the lungs in their whole activity signify the distresses, the *clarification* of the blood supply is carried on above a normal reactory force of conditions. This produced by the reaction in the nerves of the cerebrospinal system being in near a normal reactory force, so that the body—while it may collapse easily at times, from depression or shortness of breath, fast palpitation or activity of the circulation. . .will as easily recover from same, when sufficient *oxygen* is supplied to build for. . .carbonization in the system.

Also in the thyroids we find the lack of sufficient. . . secretions to meet an even balance with potashes in the system, so that the digestive system in same is easily upset, as is the heart's action—especially through the carotid artery.

These are not. . .hardening of arterial circulation, nor. . .an organic heart disorder; [but] a functional [disorder], produced by those depressions, or in the amount of lung *area* proper . . . in the clarification activity of the blood supply; so that, with undue pressure, either from overactivity—by the sudden pressure of gastric juices, or gas in the stomach—these will produce that shortness, that causes a filling or engorging of the heart's activity. [Difficulties in other parts of the body are next taken up.]

In meeting, then, the needs of the conditions. . .for this body, there should be first considered that condition in the respiratory system, to use *all* as is available in the *respiratory* system, especially of the pulmonaries, to increase the characterization of an *even* circulation of the hepatics, the heart, the lungs. These are the first to consider, so that these *pressures* may be relieved, adding in the vibration *to* the body such as will carry *with* the vibrations more of the iodines for the body, as to aid more in those of the thyroid activity, with also the thyroid taken *internally* in small *quantities,* [which] will be helpful in creating *proper* balance in digestive forces. These would be taken in the low form of wet *battery* vibrations—that is, those of the iodine—charged *in* same; these being added only a few minutes in the beginning— twenty to thirty minutes, then increased as the. . .body [is able] to retain same without producing a pressure in the hypo- gastric or the cardiac and hypogastric plexus; attaching same [the wet battery] first to the ankle and to the other ankle, and the opposite pole or the negative *carrying* the iodine to the solar plexus center. This, we will find, will aid materially; the *respiratory* system may be used through the respirator, or through the manipulative forces—*easily* begun—that use the lungs *as* the pumps to *clarify* the whole of the blood supply in its activity, *releasing* those pressures as exist in the lumbar and sacral region. This we would do osteopathically, rather than through the osteopathic adjustments, for these do not *need* the *adjustment* so much *in* the beginning. To be sure, we should equalize same throughout the cerebrospinal centers.

In the matter of diet, not too *much* iodine foods—but those that carry plenty of iron, calcium, silicon, and *especially* those that carry the phosphorus—for these will aid in the bringing about of an equilibrium, *with* the vibrations set up in the system.

Plenty of rest, and a moderate amount of exercise—this measured first, in the beginning—and we will find that in three to five weeks there will be a sudden and a certain change in the physical abilities and forces of body.

130-1

The Triune Effect of the Two Electrical Devices

In this study of the two appliances the physical effects of their use have been dwelt on in some detail. In concluding the study it is paramount to consider the total triune effect, that is the mental and spiritual effects as well as the physical.

We have learned previously from reading 5576-1 that the effect of the Wet Cell is the same as that produced by a group of persons raising the atomic forces of an individual in healing. The effect of the Radio-active Appliance is of the same nature. This is beautifully brought out in the following selection:

Q-10. Is the Radio-active Appliance working properly, and should it be used?

A-10....the Radio-active Appliance that is in position for use is working properly...

This used keeps a normal balance and is most effective for resting, and is a good aid when meditation is desirable.

For as we find, the body is as a triune. As the Father, the Son, the Holy Spirit, so the body, the mind, the soul. If they are as one—body, mind, soul—as the effective activity of a low current of electrical reaction or radiation is created in the active forces of the Radio-active Appliance—it brings to the system just those influences; the tendency to make the body-physical, the body-mental and the mental-spiritual forces more and more in accord by a unison.

Hence in the use of this, use these as the periods of thy meditations, and in thy reading of the Scriptures that refer to thee. Read them not as history, read them not as axioms or as dogmas, but as of thine own being. For in the study of these ye will find that ye draw unto that force from which the writers of same gained their strength, their patience.

And as He hath given, in learning patience as all do in suffering, ye become aware of your soul and its relationships to the Creative Forces that were experienced by the writers of almost all of our history of same; and these are ever this:

He is the same yesterday, today and forever. And as has been their experience, not possibly in the same manner but each to his own calling. For some are ministers, some are healers, some are preachers. But to all is given according to the measure of their faith. [Exodus 28]

And as ye apply this, through a mechanical implement made by man (yet also was the ephod, also was the altar made by man—yet these have brought, these may bring, these do bring even as the vision of the Cross, even as Gethsemane's garden, even as the ordinances...the awakening of the consciousness of the inner being of a soul, of a man) so may this be—not as a rosary, not as a picture, but rather as *uniting* the body, the mind, the soul with that trinity—God, the Father, the Son, the Spirit.

Thus may it bring to thee those experiences that are thine alone. And again He gives, "We have much work for [1173] to do!"   1173-8

Proximity to Minerals

[1842] was told that a piece of carbon steel carried about the person, especially in a pocket adjacent to the groin, will ionize the body so that it may more easily resist cold, congestion and irritation of the mucous membranes of throat and nasal passages.

Do not take this as being a thing of superstition, or as something which would be a good luck charm, but if the entity will wear about its person, or in its pocket, a metal that is carbon steel—preferably in the groin pocket. . .it will ionize the body—by its very vibrations—to resist cold, congestion, and those inclinations for disturbance in the mucous membranes of the throat and nasal passages.   1842-1

Actual contact with soil may have a beneficial effect. At least, the readings pointed out that the vibrations in the soil of Bokhoma, Oklahoma, were a strong deterrent to suicidal impulses. Was this because of the minerals in the soil?

A new vibration! Very good. Quite an interesting fact about people born here (Bokhoma, Okla.). [Only] one out of ten thousand would ever commit suicide. Something in the soil; get it between your toes and you'll never commit suicide.
                                                                                                   5125-1

Sunlight combined with the vibrations of certain types of sand can be beneficial to the nervous system.

. . .take sand and sea baths occasionally, but never overtaxing the body physically or mentally.   4512-1

Q-13. Has her stay at Virginia Beach retarded the attacks?
A-13. [It has!] See, the sands and the radiation upon same are such as to be most beneficial to the general nervous system . . .[of] *any*one; and as for this individual body, these we find are most helpful.   2153-4

For some persons sand packs may benefit the capillary circulation. Directions for such a pack follow.

Keep in the sunshine a great deal; this is helpful to the body. Also sand rubs, sand packs, would be well. This increases capillary circulation. Wet the body in salt water, cover in dry sand for twenty minutes—it's a good treatment!   357-1

When there is the sand and sea bath, it is well that the body be covered with sand afterward—dry sand. Let the body be thoroughly wet in the sea water—this meaning with the bathing suit and the body thoroughly wet and then immediately cover the body in *dry* sand. . .not wet. Cover the entire body except, of course, the head and face—which should be shaded from the sun, while the rest of the body should be in the sun as much as possible—that is, the mound of sand *over* the body should be in the sun. . .Do not let there be such a weight on the body as to cause a great deal of distress by the weight of the sand, but let the body remain covered in this manner for twenty to thirty minutes, if it can be fairly comfortable for that length of time without it being a dread or a burden. The sand in this particular locality is not as efficacious as it might be where there is more radium or gold or other activities in same, but use that in hand for the present. This done once a day should *stimulate* the *capillary* circulation.   849-33

For others because of the heavy heart stimulation the sand pack could be most inadvisable.

Q-1. Would you advise sand packs?
A-1. Too much. . .stimuli to the capillary circulation, for same. May sweat in the *sun,* but wouldn't cover the body with the sand. Too heavy for the heart stimulant.   2504-8

Q-2. Would you advise sand packs for this body?
A-2. No. Now the differentiation between conditions of this kind and sand packs: *Water*—water or salt water baths would be *very* good; not sand packs—for sand packs are to stimulate the capillary circulation, and are more for the *exterior* forces—while we are to *stimulate* a circulation that is *internal!*
        340-12

Oral Ingestion of Minerals

In hundreds of instances oral ingestion of mineral and medicinal substances was suggested. A complete study of this material would comprise a mammoth task. The A.R.E. Clinic, Inc., in Phoenix, Arizona, is attempting to evaluate directions in the physical readings and to measure results obtained; but this can be done only slowly.

For this reason we will take up references concerning oral ingestion of minerals of special interest only.

Arsenic

According to the reference given below, tiny doses of Fowler's solution of arsenic may be used to purify the skin of acne and to improve the circulation. During this regime it would be important to avoid fats and limit exposure to sunshine as well as the amount of meat, potatoes and starches in the diet.

> Then. . .(but be mindful with the use of this that there are not fats, or great quantities of meat taken; though potatoes may be taken, as may other starches, but not too *much* of same—rather a well balance):
> We would begin with taking internally small doses, in the manner as we will indicate, of Fowler's solution of arsenic. This is poison! but if it will be taken as indicated, it will purify or cleanse the skin. . .and set the circulation for a general condition (and do not get too much sunshine while taking this!). [Directions follow.]   1709-2

A young man, 22, improving from treatment suggested by the readings, was advised to take Fowler's solution of arsenic as a precautionary measure. It would eliminate drosses, which might otherwise be left in the system, and would clarify his blood. Again great care was to be exercised as to dosage and accompanying diet. This last would include no meat fats. Meat intake would preferably be limited to seafood and fowl prepared without frying, vegetable intake to those vegetables produced above the ground, except for potatoes. Bodily activity was also to be limited.

> Take Fowler's solution of arsenic. Be careful with the quantity, the dosage, also with the diet and the activities of the body while these are active within the system. [Directions follow.] During this time do not eat meats that are other than the sinew of meats, at all; preferably, however, the diet of the flesh should be only that of the seafoods or of fowl, but not fowl that is fried—for this will not be well with these properties. The vegetables—preferably those *above* ground, though potatoes may be taken in moderation. . .   849-6

Arsenic and Iron

Both arsenic and iron were advised in an instance where the white blood cells were increasing out of all proportion to the red blood corpuscles. The accompanying diet was to consist principally of fruits and vegetables and contain *no* meats. The vegetables were to contain large quantities of iron, silicon and phosphorus.

The metabolism as disturbed, is that variation between the pressures as created in circulation, numbers in the white and red blood supply, and the tendency for the creation of those of the pus-forming variety of the white blood, or the streptococci, as. . .altered or changed by this variation. . .

Then, as arsenic and iron—in its combination—may be used as medicinal properties for the cleansing of the system, provided those pressures in system are used in the same way and manner as to *relieve* pressure. . .

Q-1. What would be the dosage of arsenic and iron?

A-1. In its combination; not one without the other, but in the combination. That combination as may be found in that. . . compounded by Merck. . .[Directions follow.]

The diets, during the period, must consist principally of. . . fruits and vegetables, and *no* meats. The vegetables carrying much of iron, silicon, also. . .a combination of. . .silicon and iron, and phosphorus. 2670-1

Iodine

Iodine was suggested by the readings as helpful to the action of the lungs.

. . .lime, and iodine. . .act on. . .the pulmonary organism.
14-1

. . .taking. . .iodine into the system. . .produces a balm to the cell force of the lungs, which should be carried there by the blood that is going into the system. 62-1

Gold and Soda

Gold and soda were to be given together at times. The combination of the soda, a strong alkaline, and the gold solution, an acid, with the gastric juices of the stomach would stimulate the glands that make new bodily tissues. This combination might be helpful even for a woman of 86 years who had suffered a stroke. Directions are given for taking gold and bicarbonate of soda.

While the soda is a very strong alkaline and the gold [solution] an acid, with these combining with the gastric flow of the stomach we will find they will become active with the reproductive glands in *all* portions of the system. They will make for the flow and stimulation to the flow of the nerve forces in a bettered condition.   742-2

There was a precaution to be observed, however. Ingestion of gold and soda for a period longer than that needed could cause excessive superficial circulation.

This [direction for osteopathic adjustments] combined with a changing of the chemical reactions of the body, by taking internally a few drops occasionally of chloride of gold sodium [?] and bicarbonate of soda should correct the conditions. It will change all the activities of the genital system as well as the tendencies here for the creating [of a fullness] in the areas of the eyes at times, or eyelids, and a fullness in hands and feet at times, if there has been an excess activity or a sitting too long in one position. [Exact directions as to gold and soda solutions follow.]

Take this for three weeks. Then leave off, for it will by then have tended to make the eliminations to be changed entirely and if kept too long will cause an excess superficial circulation.   3669-1

Gold and soda were suggested to stimulate fertility in a woman.

For the condition in the physical that would produce the propagation, we would take those vibrations that will give the organs of gentation [genitation, generation] the power of retaining that semen necessary to become fertile instead of sterile by their lack of becoming in touch with the physical connection between soul and spirit force of the individual or where that cord [Eccl. 12:6] is not cut between life and the soul and spirit world...Life, from the physical, we are speaking of. [Directions follow to make up combination of distilled water, chloride of gold and bicarbonate of soda, to be taken as directed. Then]

...use vibrations electrically driven across the...(sacral) and lumbar regions each evening. Within the second moon the body will become fertile.   470-1

Gold and soda, it was stated, also might stimulate fertility in a man.

This [3818] should take when this correction in that of [the wife]'s condition has been completed:

Chloride of gold. . .added to distilled water. . .with. . . bicarbonate of soda.

Then the semen will be found to contain necessary fertilization for completion of conception, and the body [the wife] will conceive, as we find here, that from such conception the birth would be a son, that may be brought to be a light unto his peoples.

Do that for the betterment of each in their lives to come.

3818-5

Gold and soda were suggested to help correct a hardening of the lymph in the joints of the extremities, a condition causing pain.

We find there is that condition wherein the lymph forces in the system are turned into that of the hardening, rather than giving the elasticity to centers about the extremities' joints. This causes the pain—this causes these destructive forces. This condition produced, primarily, from an improper functioning of the glands as secrete the various cellular forces in the plasm of the system, and that division in assimilation becoming the first destructive force.

Now, in taking the system as we find same—in the addition of gold with bromide of soda, we enliven the glands of the system—all reproductive glands; that is, the necessity of the system to be able to resuscitate vital forces in the lymph, in the capillary circulation, in the arterial circulation, is based first, primarily, on the character of assimilation and the number or the count of the plasm going to make up the various elements. The increasing in the system of this dissolvent, or this energy necessary to produce the proper vibratory forces in the assimilated conditions in the system, increases the amount of destroyed forces that are to be eliminated from the system. The greater character of elimination can be carried on by having the proper coordination between the various *manners* in which poisons of different characters are eliminated from the system. Not having any *one* suffering at the expense of another, for we merely transfer the destructive forces in such measures.

Then, the applications of the various exterior forces, as have been given this body, fill a place in the assistance for the system—but to leave off a portion is to start and not go all the way, but all should coordinate one with another. Do that, and we will find bettered conditions for this body.

120-4

Note from the foregoing that other measures besides ingestion of gold and soda were to be undertaken so that the various poisons once loosened, as it were, could be completely eliminated from the body.

It is of interest that in an earlier reading [120] had been told gold would especially affect the adrenals.

...the adrenals—especially—will be aided by the application of the gold in system. . .   120-2

The preceding extracts from 742-2 and 120-4 both refer to the action of soda and gold on the reproductive glands all over the system. These glands are further designated as ductless glands.

The effect to be created. . .[through chloride of gold and sodium bicarbonate] is to enliven the tissue as goes to make up the forces as supplied through the functioning of the ductless glands. . .   **4096-2**

In one of the earliest readings Edgar Cayce gave—on June 13, 1911, in Hopkinsville, Ky.—soda and gold were advised for a condition which had commenced with a common ailment, grippe or influenza. According to the reading the germs had entered the girl's body when she was a small child in the form of a head cold and had been engulfed by white blood corpuscles. It was reported that the entire mass then had found its way to the vertebrae, had located along the second and third lumbars (in the lower back), and there had formed a lesion in the muscular walls along both inner sides of the spine between it and the sympathetic and cerebrospinal nerves. This had produced a form of paralysis or neurasthenia in the area and after she had reached puberty, affected her nervous system at times of ovulation and menstruation. Spasms and convulsions in this location resulted and the muscles became taut. (It would seem that this girl had severe menstrual cramps.)

According to the reading such a condition, if left unattended, could destroy the body or it could loosen itself, form a floating lesion and eventually a floating kidney.

Soda and gold were recommended to improve the tone and power of the nervous and muscular systems. These would then relax when they had been under excessive strain. The spine was to be relaxed by manipulation. All this would help the body to eliminate the lesion.

This reading is of especial interest in showing how the body attempts to take care of foreign matter, such as microbes, but needs help in eliminating the immobilized invaders.

Edgar Cayce: Now, the trouble in this body of [4250]. . .the seat of the trouble or the beginning of it is from away back. We had first into the body, in the form of microbes, or that to the system, as a child, what is termed, or commonly called now, grippe or la grippe, cold, influenza, cold in the head, in the nostrils, chilly sensation, cold over the spine, up and down, a sort of rigor and a little temperature. When these microbes enter the nostrils here, and find their way through the body with those of the white blood corpuscles, forming themselves, or being carried by the circulation through the body, the white blood forming themselves around these, finally locate along in the spine or around the vertebrae, or as we have in this case, in the second and third lumbars, produce, or form a lesion in the muscular walls, on the inside, along the side of the circulation, down either side of the spine, between that of the sympathetic nerves or the cerebrospinal nerves, or branch ends of the cerebrospinal nerves, here just above the celiac plexus and these in the pelvis, or at least one of the ganglia of this branch end. These having formed a thick coat there where nature has thrown out to provide against these, in some status, would form a kind of paralysis or neurasthenia in the system. In this body of [4250], we form a lesion of a character whereby in natural action on to the sex, which is woman here, we produce a form of lesion that has induced the circulation to vary from that of normal at the time of secreting to or for the generatory system, or that to the ovaries themselves, which in turn, form at the time of the flow of blood or at other times, we have through the muscular force, or through the nervous system, excitement to the whole body. (We have it either through one of the forms, through the physical body, through the mental, or through the action of the body in itself). . .we form a flow of the blood upward. Or, as it were, a pushed back of the circulation flowing around to the other form. Now. . .we have the condition in the system, whereby. . .that producing the circulation abnormally in the condition of the body. . .rights itself, and comes from the other side, especially along the spine, in this region. Here above at the other plexus—the solar plexus, cardiac plexus, or some through the circulation, some parts of the hepatics and those of the lungs in the same nature and form.

This condition we have here in this body, at the second lumbar produced this condition. This was the formation. It gradually, as the walls thickened, as nature provides or tries to throw out to alleviate the trouble, trying to eliminate it through absorption through the system in a normal way, produces more and harder of these convulsions or spasms to the body. Flow of the blood to the head becomes rigid; the muscles all become taut—an abnormal condition of the muscular nervous forces in the body. It is not always that way. The rest of the body is normal, except some little conditions we have at the present time, with the digestion or the intestinal tracts in themselves. Because nature has thrown the wall, or that of the forces of the leukocytes or white blood in the body around these particles being carried in the system, the condition—[its] position—only at times tends to increase the forces. If left as it is, it is able to destroy the body, or loosen itself and form a floating lesion and come to the portion of the system where it will produce a floating kidney, because we come in contact with all of these forces supplying. . .these, the Fallopian tube and. . .the forces of the excretory tubes of. . .the kidneys themselves, in the body.

To remove these conditions from the system, would be first to introduce that into the system whereby we give a better tone, or a better property and power to the nervous system, and to the muscular forces in the system. . .whereby we strengthen the forces of the nervous system and the muscular system to relax at the times of strain to these special portions, or these special properties in the system.

We form that into these forms of matter that would be taken into the system through the mouth or in the form of phosphate of soda with chloride of gold, or soda and gold. It forms a force to that of the nervous condition, to that of the forces acted on by the cerebrospinal nerve itself, toning the condition to the muscular system, especially through the pelvis and brain, whereby we act to the muscular system, through the sympathetics, between the nervous system and the muscular system. Relax the condition of the spine by manipulation of the hands or with that of applied force of the hand, through heat or animal heat along the spine, until we form these into the matter to produce an elimination through absorption.

[It is not good to] overtax the condition through the muscular force of the lower part of the spine (or through those of the lumbars, where we have had a relaxed condition at times, not of a formation acted on by that of a muscular nervous relaxation with that, but a relaxing of the circulatory system) through these parts acting in unison, as we would have in this condition applied. We have had treatments in the system. We have had those into the intestines, produced from this form of potash. We have had electrical appliances, and we have had forms of applications. We need to form a unison between the muscular nerves—the circulatory system acting in unison to eliminate or produce a condition we can eliminate through absorption in the system, of these conditions formed here at the second lumbar.

These conditions will be formed at times, with changes along as we find these absorptions, and this will produce a condition in the stomach that will have to be watched, through the form of matter we take in as matter to be digested to act in unison with these we are giving into the body. Not too much stimulation along the cervicals, nor along the solar plexus at the time, but enough of elimination or action of the muscular force at the time, using vibration to the lower part of the body, of the lower limbs, upward. Bent down here, straight, pull forward and up, the body lying flat on the back.

Q-1. Any other treatment for the present?
A-1. Do this.   4250-1

[5449] was advised of dietary restrictions while taking chloride of gold and bromide of soda. (5449-1) These mineral forces were to act with the digestive, assimilative and eliminative systems. In such a case not too many meats and no fried foods were advisable.

The form of soda to be combined with the gold varied for different persons. Although bicarbonate of soda was recommended in most of the preceding extracts, we find bromide of soda suggested in 606-1, 120-4 and 5449-1 and phosphate of soda in 4250-1.

Gold with Silver

A toxic condition of the blood, caused chiefly by the condition of the colon was to be treated with B complex or riboflavin and gold and silver. These latter two were to be administered through the Wet Cell; in addition, a gold solution was to be given orally along with a bicarbonate of soda solution.

...the blood supply...is in a toxic condition, as much or more from the conditions which exist in the colon as from other disturbances. Here there are two areas where spastic conditions exist, or a condition wherein the caecum area is very much disturbed. This is from the lack of the ability, because of the stricture area, for that digested to be properly eliminated.

...the conditions have become so as to weaken the red blood cellular forces to that which is not abnormal, yet not normal for this body. This portion, then, needs strengthening. . .

In making administrations to supply these glandular centers which supply to these patches [Peyer's Patches], or the emunctories, add these in the B complex or the riboflavin—the necessary elements in each portion of the B vitamin forces. There will be found most through the supplying of elements in gold and nitrate of silver—the sodium [?] gold chloride and the nitrate of silver. These should be added to the body, then, vibratorially, as well as through the alimentary canal—or by mouth. . .[Directions follow to ingest gold solution with bicarbonate of soda solution] to equalize same for the activity in the stomach itself. [Other directions follow for Wet Cell with gold and nitrate of silver solutions.]   294-212

The role of gold and silver in longevity is stressed in the readings.

The ordinary conclusions of the activity of gold, when assimilated, is incorrect—for these [vibrations] feed directly to the tissues of the brain *itself,* and—given properly—silver and gold may almost lengthen life to its double, of its present endurance.   120-5

Oral vs. Vibratory Application of Minerals

As we have seen, some persons were advised to take these mineral forces vibratorially and others orally. At times a person was advised definitely against one of these methods.

[1065] was to follow plain Wet Cell treatment with chloride of gold, combined with bicarbonate (not bromide) of soda, taken internally rather than vibratorially.

After the end of the electrical treatment [*plain* Wet Cell Appliance] period. . .begin with the properties internally (not through the vibratory forces of the Appliance, but internally) of chloride of gold with bicarbonate of soda. Not bromide of soda, but bicarbonate of soda. [Directions follow.]   1065-1

[915] was advised that it would be preferable for him to ingest gold rather than derive its benefits vibratorially by means of the Radio-active Appliance although, if selected, the latter method would also be beneficial.

. . .the application of the Radio-active Appliance in the experience in the present would be most helpful for this body; also those vibrations through the same activity carrying the chloride of gold into the system.

Or the gold may be taken internally in very minute doses, for the stimulation of those gland secretions that make for creative energies and forces through the activity of all the glands in the body; thus making coordination between the reproductive forces or glands and the pineal and the adrenal. These would be the more helpful in the present. . .

Q-1. Which would be the better way to take the gold, internally or through the battery appliance?

A-1. Internally. . .   915-2

On the other hand, [701] was explicitly told to take chloride of gold through the Radio-active Appliance rather than orally. The gold in concrete form would be disturbing to the "reproductive" tissues previously mentioned. The vibratory form of the gold would stimulate the glandular centers themselves into initiating resuscitation.

Also add *to* the system those vibrations that will be found in the chloride of gold, taken into the system through the low form of the Radio-active forces; not taken internally, to disturb the vibrations of the system as related to the activity in the creative energy through the glands in the reproductive forces, but taken in the form of the vibration that will add to the gland center itself that necessary for the resuscitation created by the correction. [Adjustments and manipulations had been previously advised as well as massage with a rotary motion.]   701-1

It would appear that those persons needing vibratory rather than oral mineral applications might be ones who function more in the sympathetic nervous system than in the cerebrospinal one. See reference in *The Hidden Laws of Earth* under "The Moon's Effects on Man," relating to Cyril Scott's book, *Music, Its Secret Influence Throughout the Ages.*

Ingestion of Food, Air and Water Containing Mineral Forces

Although many persons were advised to secure needed mineral forces through application of either or both of the two electrical appliances previously considered or through oral ingestion of these minerals alone and not in food, it is evident from the readings that a better way, and one advised for persons whose deterioration was not very advanced, is to eat food containing the minerals. This, of course, is the natural way. Moreover, man assimilates the minerals more readily when they are presented in such a form. This point is made clear with regard to fish, fowl, nuts, fruits and vegetables.

Well that sufficient calcium be taken, whether this is in small quantities of the calcium itself—as a mineral, or whether from the minerals of the fruits or vegetables that make for the assimilating and activity of same. These. . .are preferable ...through the food values as in the fish and fowl, and especially in nuts such as the filberts and almonds and the like.   480-46

It would seem that the assimilation from vegetable sources is the easiest of all.

...in the system that has long been lacking in sufficient of the phosphorus, silicon, iron and iodine. Hence all the vegetables that carry these properties should be included in the meals from day to day; for they are more easily assimilated by the body or system from vegetable matter than from any other source or character.   521-1

...and not too much of that of any of medicinal natures, other than of vegetables, and not minerals; for nothing as would pertain to those influences that have to do with the lower vibrations—as are seen in minerals—are aiding, or an addition to the vibratory influences of the body, whether developments as come to the mental or the physical forces of the body. 1730-1

For a child about a year old minerals were to be secured *only* from vegetable matter.

Also, during this period of the formation of the teeth, keep sufficient quantities of iodine in the food values for the body as well as calcium, and so forth. . .Keep the body well balanced with the diets that make sufficient amounts of silicon, calcium, iron, and the like, in the *vegetable* forces; for these should not be given as separate forces for this body in the present. . .314-2

One person who needed mineral forces not in vegetable form was told that this was unusual.

We find in this. . .body. . .rather the unusual force, that is mineral forces needed in the system where ordinarily it is vegetable forces needed. . .especially in the blood supply forces to produce the perfect elimination throughout the whole body.
                                                          5710-1

Cereals, which are also recommended (see following material), are of plant origin. Liver, tripe, pig knuckles are body and blood building. (578-5) Beef juice is recommended (578-5) and eggs are, also. (1523-3) Gristle, pig's feet and souse are given as being among the best sources of calcium (1158-31), as are seafoods (see following text). It is apparent that minerals from animal sources are readily assimilated, too, although perhaps not quite as readily as those from vegetable sources. This inference is based on advice in reading 1010-1 for the individual to eat vegetable forces alone and "not lower the plane of development by animal vibrations."

Calcium

One of the most important minerals in human nutrition is calcium. Its role was emphasized in one of the extracts quoted previously, but it would be well to restudy this information.

In each element of the body-energies, there are those glandular or cell forces that take from that assimilated the necessary influences for the strengthening of various portions of the body. In blood there must be iron, silicon, calcium, soda and those elements for its constituencies other *than* that influence carried in same. In bone another form of calcium and combinations of other elements. The same in muscle, in skin. Also the same in nerve—nerve along which there may be the functioning of that as may be rightly called the electric system of the human body. . .This is illustrated in all of nature itself.
2436-3

The foregoing brings out that calcium is needed in different forms for blood, bone, muscle, skin and nerve.

Calcium combined with sand can produce a salutary effect on the walls of the small intestines and of the stomach. (Are our digestive processes so very different, after all, from those of birds, who need sand or grit as a regular addition to their diet?)

He, also, needs along with this a little calcium and sand in this system to produce an action on the small intestines: this will expend [expand] the walls of the intestines and of the stomach itself and thoroughly relax the system; this followed by plenty of rest and as much exercise as possible without overexercising the body, then it ought to improve. 134-2

There is a reference to the need for more calcium, iron and dirt to help the stomach function.

The condition of the whole body is brought about by the whole system being run down, worn out, from lack of nutriment. Supply to the rest of the system from the stomach itself. Lack of the stomach in itself to supply the quantity needed by the system; the building material for the bone, muscle, nerve, for the blood, brain, for each different organism in itself. Supply from what is taken in by the digestion carried on in the stomach itself. Here we lack the amount of nutriment to carry all this. Calcium, iron, dirt—need more. . .   134-1

The readings specify foods the calcium in which may be easily assimilated. These include juices and broths from the bony pieces of fowl, wild game, gristle, pig's feet, pig knuckle, souse, milk, eggs, egg yolk, fish, seafoods, turnips, parsnips, salsify or oyster plant, carrots raw or cooked, radishes, onions, potato peelings, the jackets of Irish potatoes, cereals, beans, peas, lentils, red cabbage, sweet potatoes, lettuce, celery, cabbage, spinach, turnip greens, watercress, mustard greens, parsley, tomatoes, squash, butterbeans, watermelon, limes, grapefruit, oranges, almonds and filberts.

In the matter of diet for the body—keep plenty of seafoods of all characters about three times a week; also fowl, and especially the bony pieces, preferably prepare such pieces as the neck, the head, the wing, the feet, and the bony pieces, so that the small bones may be very well masticated by the body, or the juice chewed out of these. For, the juices from these carry more of the calcium that is needed. This, the calcium, may not be supplied as well in other ways as it may be by taking the extra quantities of seafoods (which carry a great deal of the iodines as well as the calcium) and the bony pieces of fowl or chicken.   3076-1

Calcium is now needed, in a manner that it may be assimilated, and gradually take the place of that which has been crystallized in the bursa [bursae] and portions of the structural body. This we would add in the form which we have indicated as the *best*—the chewing of bones or ends of bones of the fowl.   849-53

. . .the broths of fowl; *especially* those portions of the neck, the feet, the back or the like, cooked for a *long* period and broths made from same. From *these* portions we find that calcium, in an assimilated form, would aid in strengthening the blood stream through the assimilation of this for further assisting in purifying the blood force and alleviating those inclinations for that to be carried through the system *from* the hepatics to be eliminated. 1885-1

Q-31. What are the best sources of calcium in foods?
A-31. The ends of bony pieces of fowl or the like, gristle, pig's feet, souse and the like. Vegetables such as turnips, parsnips and all of those that grow under the ground. 1158-31

Q-10. Suggest diet beneficial to preserving teeth.
A-10. Eggs, potato peelings, seafoods—all of these are particularly given to preserving the teeth; or anything that carries quantities of calcium or aids to the thyroids in its production would be beneficial—so it is not overbalanced. . .
Q-11. Is calcium taken in pills advisable?
A-11. That taken from vegetable matter is much more easily assimilated or from fish *and* seafoods. 1523-3

In the general physical condition we find there is a deficiency of calcium. . .This. . .may be best materially aided by the supplying of this element in the foods, and especially in those that carry sufficient quantity of such as may be easily assimilated by the body [11-year-old male]. . .
The principal foods should be—if they are meats—fish and fowl, and especially this cooked in such a manner that the ends of the small bones in same may be chewed by the body. . .Then such as beans, lentils, red cabbage and sweet potatoes should form a part of the diet. Green vegetables should be a portion of the meal each day; lettuce, celery, cabbage, spinach, tomatoes, carrots—any and all of of these with an oil dressing or mayonnaise.
Q-4. What drinks should be taken at meals?
A-4. Cereal drinks, or milk. Cereal drinks such as cocoa or cocoa-malt, or malted milk; or straight milk. 1785-1

Keep plenty of those foods that supply calcium to the body. These we would find especially in raw carrots, cooked turnips and turnip greens, all characters of salads, especially. . .water-cress, mustard and the like; these especially taken raw, though turnips cooked—but cooked in their own juices and *not* with fat meats. 1968-6

Q-7. How are my teeth, and should any be extracted?
A-7. Only local attention. . .is particularly needed at this time; especially if there is included plenty of calcium either in the treatment of same or in the diets—which is included specifically, of course, in the oyster plant, carrots, salsify, the

jackets of Irish potatoes, and the like; and of course in the almond and filbert. 480-13

For a female who had conceived 29¾ days before:

Keep a well-balance between the diets for sufficient calcium and lime; as in watermelon, squash, butterbeans, onions. Things of that nature carry these in such quantities that they may be easily assimilated. So let the foods that are prepared occasionally have more and more of these. Limes, especially limeades, would be well to be taken. 540-6

For the same female later:

There should be those precautions that there be plenty of calcium in the system for developing of bone and muscle tissue. Most of this, of course, may be had from raw milk or those vegetables that carry calcium and silicon and iron in the ways and manners that may be assimilated—as we would find from carrots, salsify especially, and certain characters of seafoods; though those that are of other natures...[make] for irritations. Those of the bi-valves of the seafoods are preferable for the body [540]. These...will make for developments and produce assimilations better for the body. 540-7

...and in the diet there should be supplied more often those elements needed, as in fish, raw carrots and the like.
Thus we would have sufficient calcium for body functionings. 808-14

Q-7. What is the cause of the wearing away of the front tooth and the crumbling of the jaw tooth? What can be done to save these teeth?
A-7. Drink more of lime and orange juice, and make correction locally of those conditions existent there. Lack of proper amount calcidin [calcium?] in the system.
Q-18. Please give in full a blood building diet for my body.
A-18. Those as indicated that have a quantity or an excess of the calcium, and those that will make for a balance in the iodines with the potassiums of the system itself...
Quantities, then, of the orange, the lime, the lemon, the grapefruit. These should form a portion of the diet at most *all* times. *Do not* combine cereals or starches of a great nature with the citrus fruit juices.
Liver, tripe, pig knuckle. Such are those that will be body and blood building...
Seafoods in moderation, but sufficient to keep a balance.

Beef juices. Wine taken as a *food,* not as a drink. An ounce and a half to two ounces of red wine in the afternoon after the body has *worn* itself out; that is, two, three, four o'clock in the afternoon—or cocktail time. Take it as a food, with brown bread. Not beer or ale, nor any of the hard drinks—but *red wine!*

These. . .taken in combination with the regular foods—and have three leafy vegetables to two of the pod nature, or that ratio. 578-5

The lack of calcium in the system has its effect especially to the supplying of elements in the lymph circulation, as well as for the better or more normal activity in the expressions of structural portions in creating the cellular force for the blood supply. . .

Q-3. Are the lungs in good shape?

A-3. Lungs are in very good shape. The lack of the supply of calcium causes the ribs—from which. . .[many] of the red blood cells emerge, of course—to produce a fullness in the pleura and the lungs.

Q-5. Is the body getting the right sort of food elements and food combinations?

A-5. These are very well. As indicated, there is the need only to supply that element which is lacking. Of course, as the body is gradually built up, we will find it possible to get much of this from such things as turnips, turnip greens, onions and all forms of vegetables of such natures; radishes, carrots and all of these—cooked and raw. Don't overdo it, but take those things as would be the normal diet. 816-12

We find that the *blood supply* indicates a lack of those elements that give stamina and stability in the manner of *organic* functionings; that is, a lack of the natures that arise from calcium as it affects the system. This we would change through the diet considerably, or by adding such elements to the diet.

So, at least once each day we would have a meal consisting only of raw vegetables; particularly turnips, carrots, parsley, and these things that make for a quantity of such elements as may be assimilated in the system. These will aid materially in the general welfare. 1008-1

. . .it would be well to have a great deal of those foods that carry an abundant supply (though not an overabundance) of calcium, also phosphorus.

Hence to eat the shellfish (*provided* these are very fresh) will be most helpful. Use salsify; which may be prepared already, of course, at this special season [reading given Aug. 9, 1935], and the vegetables that are of the early *spring* nature; such as onions (the smaller kind), radishes, peas. Of course, necessarily, most of these will have to be canned; and are all right, provided not canned with benzoate of soda. These should be a great portion of the diet.   243-19

It will be necessary to supply more calcium either in foods or in supplementary ways, to aid quicker with the osteopathic corrections.

In the supplying of elements for the body increase the amounts of seafoods in the diet, also the raw foods or vegetables. These should include every character of raw vegetables, that may be prepared, either with gelatin or in salads at times.   3696-1

For a 36-year-old woman with tuberculosis:

Have fish once or twice or three times a week; and preferably this also baked or broiled. Do not have it altogether as seafood nor altogether as fresh fish but have quite a variation in same. And those that are the larger the better. And when this is eaten, especially the larger bone in the back of the fish—baked—should be eaten for the calcium that is in same.   1560-1

Q-3. What causes the deep ridges in thumb nail and what treatments should be followed?
A-3. These are the activities of the glandular force, and the addition of those foods which carry large quantities of calcium will make for bettered conditions in this direction. Take often chicken neck, chew it. Cook this well, the feet and those portions of the fowl and we will find it will add calcium to the body. Also eat bones of fish, as in canned fish. Also parsnips and oyster plant; all of these, of course, in their regular season. Wild game of any kind, but chew the bones of same.

                                      5192-1

Also we would in the meantime take foods or values in foods that would increase the amount of the calcium for the body, *without* producing excess acidity in same. Add this in. . .the diet, as well as in [other] forms. . .

We would have plenty of the orange juice with a little lemon in same—each day. And nearly every day we would have milk and the yolk of an egg (not the white of the egg). . .Do not have cereals within several hours of taking the citrus fruit juices.
                                      1610-1

Ingestion of calcium, we are told, can repair old structural deficiencies and also restore glandular deficiencies, particularly of the thyroid.

With the continued use of the more calciums and iodines, the chalkiness—or the tendency of brittleness in the structural [skeletal] portions—will bc eliminated.   275-16

There is a lack of proper glandular activity. Portions of this have been caused by the lack of the proper amount of calcium in the system. And this affects the circulation, especially as related to those glands particularly of the thyroid—or portions of same; those as related in part to the digestive system, and parts of those glands that cause these disturbances between the liver and the kidneys; the glands that destroy or that use sugars in the body.

While these are not excessive in the present, those tendencies for irritation cause a form of acidity that upsets the circulation through alimentary canal.   1727-2

References from 540-6 and 540-7, given previously, show the need for a pregnant woman to take plenty of calcium into her body to aid development of bone and muscle tissue in the embryo.

It would seem that the readings endorse the mother's nursing the child—if necessary for quite a while. [608] was a female, one year old, whose teeth were coming through very slowly. Her mother was advised to continue nursing the baby until the baby's stomach and eye teeth showed better development.

Q-3. Should the mother continue to nurse the baby?
A-3. Continue through the better part of the summer [reading given June 9, 1927]...until the stomach and eye teeth show better development.   608-1

Since the teeth change in the second year of each [7-year?] cycle, according to the readings, it is wise at these times to ingest calcium-rich foods.

Cycles change for the teeth during the second year of each cycle. During that year take at least 3 to 4 series of Calcios doses or its equivalent, to supply calcium, and it will aid not only the teeth but all the activities of the thyroid gland.
                    3051-3

Dirt

In references from 134-1 and 134-2, previously cited in *Calcium,* this section, we note an individual need for calcium, iron, dirt and sand. The reason for this need of dirt and sand was brought out in greater detail for [134] and also in other readings for other persons. The references emphasize the useful role of very small quantities of clean dirt and sand in supplying needed elements. The vibration or radiation from the ground is required for balance.

We have not expanded the stomach enough with the water, we have had no dirt and we need both.

Q-4. What form of dirt should there be?

A-4. Dirt. . .speaking now of the digestive system of the body of [134], into this stomach we have had a straining, purging, from excitement until we have rolled the walls up until they have contracted hunger all the time; he wants to eat, he cannot eat; it hurts, produces pains to the head, sick all over; produces all this nauseating and dizzy in the head and pains in the back, in the limbs and all over the whole system, at times, until we have drawn the whole system up. We need dross into the stomach so it passes off with these articles or particles of the system. We are of earth; we need dirt to have a normal condition of the stomach. We need something to tone up the stomach, without excitement or stimulation. If we put a stimulant there it would be better if we had claret [Clary?] water after thoroughly washing the stomach, also a little dirt—a little sand—not enough sand to produce a stopping of the secretions along the smaller intestines—dirt—earth— sand. [These] produce a drawing, which will expand the walls of the intestines, of the stomach itself and thoroughly relax the system. . .[Take] plenty of rest and as much exercise as possible, without overexercising the body, and it ought to improve. 134-2

Q-4. When about 3 or 4 years old, I used to eat dirt. Why did I do this, and does it have any bearing on my state of health today?

A-4. It is only recalled for the supplying of those elements necessary, that were lacking in the bodily forces themselves. 1597-2

In the dirt do add to the body those foods especially that grow under the ground. For this particular body peanuts would be very good—as would the oyster plant or such vegetables as the rutabaga, potatoes of all kinds, beets, onions and all that grow under the ground, these cooked as well as those that may be taken raw. What is needed is the vibration or the radiation from ground, earth, soil in the body—even a little sand or dirt taken would be well for this body...there should not be used that which is soiled by any excesses, but that which is in the sunlight, sand close to the riverways. Just three to four to five grains—that means by weight [apothecary grams?], not just grains of sand. It would be well for this to be eaten with the food, or on the food.   3608-1

Don't be afraid to get a little dirt on you once in a while. You know you must eat a certain amount of dirt, else you'll never get well balanced. For this is that from which all conditions arise. For of dust man is made, and to dust he returns.

                                                    3352-1

After this has been done [osteopathic manipulation and massage treatment] some two or three weeks we will take into the system small quantities of earth; just dirt so that we give weight and an action to the stomach itself and the inner linings and *those* properties needed for this body. The quantity to be taken, three to four grains every day. This we would use, that is the kind and quality which shall be used, to be obtained from the bottom of creek of fresh water and then dried and used. When the body is taking the dirt alone, do not take the osteopathic treatment. Alternate each week, after one week of the taking of dirt osteopathic treatment will begin. Eat what the body calls for, no more nor less—as often as the body wishes to, not large quantities.

Q-2. *How is the best way to take this dirt, Mr. Cayce?*
A-2. The only sensible way. Put it in the mouth and swallow it. It is not unpalatable. The body needs it—will call for it—will like it after three or four days.   4740-1

Gold
The role of gold in the body has been touched on previously in the section "Effects of Various Minerals Applied Vibratorially," under *Gold*. The two following excerpts list food sources from which gold may be assimilated. These include cabbage, especially red cabbage, carrots, eggplant, salsify, squash, the rind of Irish potatoes, okra, lettuce, celery, fruits, nuts, egg yolks, fish, oysters, clams and particularly southern conch.

Reading 1000-2 points out that the amount of mineral content depends largely upon the conditions under which the vegetables, fish and seafoods have been brought to maturity. (A discussion of optimum conditions for plants will be found later in this book.)

In the matter of the diets, follow those closely as has been outlined. Those. . .should be alternated. . .the creation with the chlorine foods carry [carries] the gold in its combination. . .

Q-3. What foods contain gold, silicon and phosphorus?

A-3. Look 'em up and see! Ain't that funny! These are contained more in those of the vegetable, of the fish, and of those varieties that are given as same. Cabbage, carrots, lettuce, celery—all such. Fish, oysters, eggplants at times— parts of those depend upon where the vegetation is grown, as to the character of forces that are carried in same. Yolks of eggs—not the white, or the whole may be taken at times—but when taken should be raw—it may be, of course, burnt with spirits frumenti when taken in that manner. Raw cabbage at times carries these properties—especially the red cabbage. Those of the fruits or the nuts—these should be the character of the diet. . .   1000-2

In the diet keep much of that which will add more phosphorus and gold to the system; as we will find in certain of the vegetables—as carrots, salsify, squash, the rind of Irish potatoes (not the pulp), okra, and the like.

Q-5. Should he be given any iron?

A-5. Rather would we change, now to the silicon and phosphorus. . .*only* through the vegetable forces, and the seafoods.

Q-6. You wouldn't give him anything for anemia?

A-6. There is nothing better for anemia than phosphorus, with these conditions! Conch soup would be the *more* effective. *Nothing* more effective in the blood supply than gold, that we obtain from the seafoods: such as oysters, clams—but not crabs, not such natures as these. Certain elements as. . .in the *lobster* would be well, but not the Maine lobster; preferably those of southern waters. But the conch would be excellent. This is best obtained from Miami or Bimini.   698-1

Iodine

Seafoods and vegetables are a good source not only of gold but also of iodine. The latter is found especially in oysters, which should be eaten roasted or raw but not cooked with milk or grease, and also in shellfish, lobsters, crabs and crayfish. Iodine occurs in deep-sea fish such as mackerel and jackfish in larger amounts than in freshwater fish. Vegetables the edible portions of which are above ground contain iodine, as well as some root vegetables. Vegetables mentioned include tomatoes, potatoes, lettuce, celery, spinach, lentils, beans, peas, radishes, salsify, onions and turnips. Fruits include oranges and especially pears. Apparently the iodine, iron and silicon in the pears produce glandular activity of an electrical nature.

Q-1. Are oysters supplying enough iodine for the body?
A-1. Oysters supply [a] considerable amount of iodine.
275-17

Not meats, but those that carry iodine and iron, and the mineral salts. As seafood, and as those that are of the vegetable nature—in tomatoes, potatoes, lettuce, celery, spinach—or any of those that are of the vegetable nature that grow above ground. . .
201-1

Q-1. What is causing the itching sensation in various parts of the body. . .?
A-1. An excess of a chemical reaction that arises from some characters of the fruits and vegetables that have been taken. Too much potash in the system. Thus. . .not too much but a little iodine in the form that may be soluble so as to be assimilated by the body will keep or make a counterbalance—once a week, or some two or three times a week take those foods that carry quantities of iodine.
Q-2. How is the best way to take the iodine?
A-2. . . .it may be taken in those foods rich in iodine—as in seafoods—or it may be taken in the form of. . .soluble iodine. Preferably the foods, for this is the better manner, of course, of assimilating same.
257-243

Shellfish well for the body. Lobster, clam—clam chowders, soups, or such. *These* carry iodine. Taken occasionally. . .In season, oysters are well. These are better in the roast, or the raw, than in milk or grease.
304-12

. . .there should be more *often* taken those [foods] that carry iodine in the system; such as the oyster, or the shellfish, or those of especially certain characters of fish that are of the deep-sea nature, but not those of the nature that carry only certain portions or quantities—but as the mackerel, or as the plummet [?], or jackfish [pike], or the like—these are very good. Those that are of the freshwater, or of coarse flesh, not so good—but principally shellfish, oyster, lobster, or crab or the like. As for vegetables those that carry the iodine—as. . . lentils, beans, peas, radish, salsify, onions and salads of lettuce, celery, and those activities that make for a *cleansing* of the blood stream. . .Not overeating but keeping an even balance.
313-4

Then we may begin with foods that carry the iodine, as much as can be assimilated. Spinach. . .lentils. . .crayfish or the mollusk family. 337-1

In the matter of the diet. . .Occasionally use a great deal of those things that carry quantities of iodine, for this the body requires. But for this body it will be most soluble from vegetables; turnips, salsify and the like; shellfish; oranges; especially pears. Two or three pears each day will be *most* helpful in the manner of furnishing iron, silicon; and especially considering the influences such would have with the electrical forces—that is, the pear's activity to produce an activity to the gland forces of the body. 1049-1

Q-27. Does age only cause change of hair and its color and thinning?
A-27. Color of hair and the change comes from the glandular conditions, but these are natural causes. And these, of course, may be stimulated or helped with that which adds to the activity of the glands that are exercised in the activity in same—which is a portion of the thyroid; and the addition of foods, vegetables that carry that stimuli [stimulus] and activity—all those of the iodine content, leaving off the potashes that cause such irritations. 257-252

This last reference makes it plain that the addition to the diet of foods containing iodine may arrest changes in the condition of the hair generally ascribed to old age.
Iodine, as well as calcium, is needed for the formation of healthy teeth.

Also, during this period of the formation of the teeth, keep sufficient quantities of iodine in the food values for the body, as well as calcium and so forth. 314-2

Iron

How much iron may be secured from eating meat? The readings give valuable insights into the picture.
Meats themselves contain little iron, but their juices contain more though this varies according to the freshness of the meat and the method of cooking.

Q-7. Does beef contain iron?
A-7. Depends upon how soon it is used after being slaughtered. Depends upon the characterization of the preparations. The juices contain iron. The meats contain little. 488-3

Directions for rendering beef juice will be found in a later section.

[4834], who needed more red blood, was advised to eat wild game, nothing that had been killed with blood in it, goat rather than mutton. This person had stomach trouble, caused by lack of assimilation, and could not tolerate anything actively acid.

The body. . .needs more red blood. . .Diet should be of iron such as found in a pear, and that of iron itself, it will be hard to assimilate iron, should be taken in small quantities to begin with, such as we find in Beef, Iron and Wine [a tonic], not in doses as says on the bottle but about half. Meats should be wild game, nothing that has been killed with blood in it.

Q-2. Would mutton be good?

A-2. No, goat would be better. Nothing that is actively acid should be taken. . .

Should be careful about diet, eat wild game which eats from nature; tame game eats what it is fed. 4834-1

However, sources of iron other than meat were stressed for this same person, notably apples and pears. Because of the stomach condition, apples were to be tree-ripened. Thus they would be less acid. Apparently apples of certain varieties are less acid than others anyway.

Pear, which is acid, forms into iron and loses its acid, certain apples are acid, others are not. This body should take apples that have ripened on the tree. 4834-1

The iron in pears and apples directly affects the blood.

. . .we would take. . .into the system. . .fruits, especially apples and pears, which contain. . .an iron condition. . .which we need. . .[in] the blood or what produces blood. . . 4841-1

Other sources of iron include whole grains, yellow foods, whether vegetable or fruit, and berries.

In the diets—keep to those things that add a great amount of the vitamins B and B-1 and iron. These should be preferably found in whole grains or the yellow foods, whether vegetables or fruits. 480-55

So keep an excess of foods that carry especially vitamin B, iron and such. Not the concentrated form, you see, but obtain these from the foods. These would include all fruits, all vegetables that are yellow in their nature. Thus—lemon and orange juice combined, all citrus fruit juices; pineapple as well as grapefruit. Some of these should be a part of the diet each day.

Squash—especially the yellow; carrots, cooked and raw; yellow peaches; yellow apples (preferably the apples cooked, however).

All of these carry an excess or the greater quantity of necessary elements for supplying energies for the body, and... are much more easily assimilated by the body.

Yellow corn, yellow corn meal, buckwheat—all of these are especially needed by the body [of 1968].   1968-7

...those food values carrying an easy assimilation of iron, silicon, and those elements or chemicals—as all forms of berries, most all forms of vegetables that grow under the ground, most of the vegetables of a leafy nature. Fruits and vegetables, nuts and the like, should form a greater part of the regular diet in the present...Keep closer to the alkaline diets; using fruits, berries, vegetables particularly that carry iron, silicon, phosphorus and the like.   480-19

A suggested diet for [255], who needed iron, included spinach, cabbage, turnips, salsify, radishes, pears, apples, lemons and oranges.

Q-2. Specify foods containing iron.
A-2. These may be had from any of those classifications as make for such. These are they...as would respond with this body...spinach...cabbage...turnips...salsify...radish, and ...such natures. These add to the system. In the fruits, and for *this* body—well that pears be eaten. These add a characterization in iron that is well for any condition where there is improper fermentation. Some character of apples...lemons... oranges—*especially* those grown in certain localities. . . Florida oranges carry more iron than those grown in California, while those of the southern states, or. . .the Rio Grande valley, carry more than those even in Florida. 255-3

If the iron from vegetables is added to the vitamins from sunlight, the violet ray effect will be increased on the nerve and assimilating systems.

Q-5. Should beef juice be given again, or Beef, Iron and Wine [a tonic]?
A-5. Beef juice in preference to Beef, Iron and Wine. Let the iron be rather taken in the foods, as it is more easily

assimilated from the vegetable forces; and combining with the vitamins from the sun will add to the violet ray effect upon the nerve and assimilating systems.   1187-9

Iron and Phosphorus

Iron and phosphorus in combination work as recuperative forces.

In the strength of the muscular forces of the body, [it is] necessary that iron be a vital element in the proper replenishing of system. Make a habit of eating at least two pears every day, and of citrus fruits—not too much of the oranges; more of the lemon and grapefruit—but in apples, beware. The fruits are well, but only those that will furnish lots of *iron*—and especially of that *necessary* element in recuperative forces of phosphorus, which comes and will be found *most*—in conch soup.

Q-5. Is it advisable to eat fish, oysters, or shellfish?

A-5. The conch is shell, and this alone we would use in any quantity. Won't like it at first, but it will be well when this is taken as a carrier for that necessary amount of phosphorus in the system. It will change the vibratory forces of the body...
                                                                348-12

For the same person:

Q-2. Is conch soup still needed for the body?

A-2. Whatever will supply the greater amount of phosphorus for the system would be the best. The best that this may be assimilated from is the conch broth or soup, but under the existent conditions those things that carry more of the phosphorus will be well for the body. To be sure in any seafood this is apparent—but not *all* seafoods carry such in such a *way* and manner that it is assimilated, on account of the activities of other properties with it. There may be taken this [phosphorus] in some vegetables, as in parsnips, as in...the oyster plant...carrots—especially if grated and taken raw—and the peel of the Irish potato. These...vegetables carry the correct amount, especially...parsnips.   348-15

The dietary recommendation above calls attention to lemons and grapefruit as a substitute for oranges; cites parsnips, salsify, carrots (especially when raw) and Irish potato peelings as sources of phosphorus; and stresses the phosphorus content of conch soup.

For those who cannot easily obtain conch soup, it is

heartening to know that almonds may be a good substitute to provide iron and phosphorus.

Q-12. In what minerals is the body deficient?
A-12. As indicated from the type of foods suggested; iron, calcium, and phosphorus—these are the ones deficient.
Q-13. Please give the foods that would supply these.
A-13. We have given them; cereals that carry the heart of the grain; vegetables of the leafy kind; fruit and nuts as indicated [almonds, English walnuts, pecans; not Black Walnuts or Brazil Nuts for this particular body; all fruits, canned or fresh except jenneting variety of apples if baked]. The almond carries more phosphorus *and* iron in a combination easily assimilated than any other nut.   1131-2

Again there is a recommendation for leafy vegetables, cereals and fruit.

Iron and Silicon

Iron and silicon build blood and nerves. Reading 478-3 tells us that these may be secured from fresh *raw* vegetables. According to 201-1, previously cited under *Iodine,* this section, iron may be found in tomatoes, potatoes, lettuce, celery, spinach or any vegetables growing above ground.

As to the matter of diet, keep those things that are the more easily assimilated by the body; that is, not merely the liquid diet of such nature but that which carries with same the iron, the silicon, the blood and nerve building influences. And let at least one meal each day, whether the noon or the evening meal, be entirely of green fresh *raw* vegetables. . .   478-3

[275] was advised to eat leafy vegetables grown locally in order to achieve the proper balance of iron and silicon in the system. Cabbage, beans, lentils, broccoli, tomatoes and carrots were mentioned specifically. Spinach juice was to be taken only occasionally—especially if canned. However, leafy vegetable juices were suggested (raw presumably).

Q-4. How many ounces of spinach juice should body have per day?
A-4. During this specific season, when there are so many more activities outside, these may not be adhered to so strictly, but use more of the leafy vegetables that grow in the vicinity and about where the body resides, that make for the proper balancing of the iron and silicon in system. . .Any of these that

grow on the farm would be well. As cabbage, and all its kindred. Beans, lentils, and the like. Spinach we would take occasionally, but this may wear out in the effects with the system, especially when there's the necessity of resorting to the canned.   275-27

Any of the leafy vegetable juices or leafy vegetables may be taken; as lentils, broccoli, and such that carry sufficient iron and silicon for assimilation in system.   275-28

Provided there is the addition of other properties—as in tomatoes, carrots, or large quantities of other vegetable forces that carry iron and silicon—then this [spinach juice in summer months] may be discontinued. . .   275-32

Iron and silicon are needed for healthy teeth.

Q-5. Any special suggestions regarding diet in relation to teeth?
A-5. See that there is the proper amount of iron and silicon, that comes from vegetables—not from minerals, but vegetable minerals for the body.   457-3

Vegetables growing under the ground during the winter carry a great deal of iron and silicon. Turnips, parsnips, carrots, beets and oyster plant (salsify) are noted. For [538] Jerusalem artichokes could be eaten occasionally and then only when cooked. (See later section on the effects of this vegetable.)

All of those [foods] that carry a great deal of iron and silicon, and things of that nature; that is, turnips, turnip greens, all of those that grow under the ground through the winter—as parsnips and carrots and beets and the like. . .oyster plant—all of these are beneficial. Artichoke occasionally should be among them—Jerusalem artichoke, though cooked rather than raw.   538-66

Raw carrots and parsnips were to be used as a teething aid for a one-year-old child who lacked iron and silicon. The parents were to make sure that the baby did not cut off too many pieces while biting on the vegetable.

Well for the body to cut teeth on carrots, or parsnips (raw, see?)—these may be given, just so chunks are not cut off and swallowed too much.   608-1

In reading 1049-1 previously cited under *Iodine,* this section, we noted that iron and silicon are found in pears. This fruit has a real effect on the glandular forces. Two or three pears a day were to be eaten by [1049]. The following excerpt shows that berries also contain the two minerals.

. . .also those food values carrying an easy assimilation of **iron, silicon, and those elements or chemicals—as all forms of berries, most all forms of vegetables that grow under the ground, most of the vegetables of a leafy nature.** 480-19

Iron, Silicon and Lithium

Iron, silicon and lithium may all be found in fruits and vegetables. [4244] was advised to take at least two green vegetables at every meal to help insure the proper building of the blood supply.

Q-1. What mineral elements are lacking in the system?
A-1. Those of the proper building for the blood supply; iron, silicon, and. . .lithium—and these will be added with the diet (preferably fruits and vegetables, and at least two green vegetables taken each meal) and with. . .[electrical medicinal aids and osteopathic adjustments]. 4244-1

Phosphorus

Sources are given for phosphorus alone. These include: carrots, leaf lettuce, shellfish, salsify, the peelings of small Irish potatoes, citrus fruit juices, Bulgarian milk (buttermilk), fresh *warm* raw milk, egg yolk, celery, turnips, artichokes, rutabagas and parsnips.

The phosphorus-forming foods are principally carrots, lettuce (rather the leaf lettuce, which has more soporific activity than the head lettuce), shellfish, salsify, the *peelings* of Irish potatoes (if they are not too large), and things of such natures; these. . .are the most helpful. Not quantities of *any* meats, even though the fowl and wild game may be *at times* included, but not quantities of same. Citrus fruit juices, plenty of milk—the Bulgarian [buttermilk] the better, or the fresh milk that is warm with the animal heat which carries more of the phosphorus and more of those activities that are less constipating, or acting more with the lacteals and the ducts of the liver, the kidneys and the bowels themselves. 560-2

Q-3. Specify foods containing phosphorus.

A-3. The yolk of egg, none of the white. . .carrots, celery, turnips, *all* carry a form of phosphorus that. . .[is] soluble to the system. Milk also, if warm with the animal heat. That which has been pasteurized does not carry same. 255-3

. . .phosphorus. . .is a necessary element, but its assimilation from synthetic concoctions is oft hard upon the body. The assimilation of the same from food values then becomes much more not only palatable but activative with the influences of the body.

Those [values] then. . .of the artichoke [Note—this is *not* the Jerusalem arthichoke.], the lowly rutabaga or turnip—these taken at least once to twice a week for a portion of the meal— will be the better manner for this to be assimilated by this body at the present time. 1173-8

. . .those foods which will carry the most phosphorus in same—especially those of the tubular natures, as. . .carrots, salsify, turnips, parsnips, and the like. . .Also it will be found that any of the mollusks. . .will be most helpful, *especially* those. . .of the *larger*. . .nature. . .those in the waters of the more semi-tropical region. . . 2214-1

One reading tells us that a greater quantity of phosphorus may be assimilated by man from conch broth than from any other food.

. . .the broth of the conch. . .carries. . .greater quantity of phosphorus than any [other] food that may be assimilated by man. 1065-1

One of the functions of phosphorus is to supply force to the cells in the generative system.

. . .phosphorus which is life or cellular force in the make up of the genetory [generative?] system. 3973-1

The role of phosphorus with regard to the glands is one of regeneration.

. . .those [foods] that will carry the more *stabilizing* condition for the system. . .silicon, gold, and those [foods] that regenerate the whole of the system as related to the *glands*— those that carry phosphorus. 1000-1

Phosphorus and Gold
Under *Gold*, this section, references have been given naming

vegetable or animal sources for the combination of these two minerals and in some cases silicon also: namely carrots, salsify, squash, the rind of Irish potatoes, okra, cabbage, especially red cabbage, eggplant, lettuce, celery, fruits, nuts, egg yolks, fish, oysters, clams and particularly southern conch.

Silicon

A proper food-intake of silicon can result in greater staying power for the muscles and especially tendons. Leafy vegetables are good sources.

Take plenty of those foods that carry silicon and those elements that create more stamen [stamina] in the muscle, and especially the tendons of the body. Let's remember that these activities should be in such a nature as to be assimilated and distributed for the system. . .the greater amounts of the leafy vegetables and those properties that carry more silicon and the elements in phosphorus, and in that nature, are well.

275-28

Lack of silicon can result in teeth coming through slowly.

Q-2. Why are the teeth long in coming through?
A-2. Nothing wrong! They're coming all right! Lack of silicon in the body making it drawn out in this. . .   608-1

Silicon is good for the eyes. Celery and tomatoes are among the foods carrying it. Jerusalem artichokes and salsify are also, but should be used sparingly during pregnancy.

Q-5. What foods should be stressed or avoided during pregnancy?
A-5. Those carrying silicon, calcium, those good for the eyes: all of these should be stressed; that is, the salads with carrots, watercress, celery, lettuce and occasionally tomatoes—though not too much of these for they will be ripened indoors and not as good, but use these occasionally. All of these vegetables may be served with oils or mayonnaise. These should be stressed and occasionally [Jerusalem] artichokes, the oyster plant—these are good.   2803-6

(See excerpt from 538-66 under *Iron and Silicon,* this section, for type of artichoke.)
Silicon may also be found in potatoes and yams.

Add all of the foods that carry silicon and the salts that may

...vibrate with the application of the gold to the nerve centers for assimilation; as foods of the tuberous nature of every character—the oyster plant, every form of turnip or potatoes or yams of [or?] the ground artichoke.   3694-1

Beets, carrots and spinach are good sources of silicon.

Q-4. Those [foods] containing silicon.
A-4. . . .beets, carrots, spinach.   255-3

Rolled, crushed or cracked whole wheat will add silicon as well as iron to the body.

. . .rolled or crushed or cracked whole wheat, that is not cooked too long so as to destroy the whole vitamin force. . .will add to the body the proper proportions of iron, silicon and the vitamins necessary to build up the blood supply that makes for resistance in the system. . .   840-1

Under *Gold,* this section, we learned that gold, silicon and phosphorus were to be found in fish, oysters, eggplants at times, yolks of eggs, fruits and nuts.

However, according to the following reference, too much protein-derived silicon can be bad for the body. [333] was told this was causing head pains.

Q-1. What is causing pains in head, particularly at base of brain?
A-1. The unbalanced condition in the blood supply, as we have indicated by those things that have been forming in portions of the system, where too much silicon has been carried into the body from too much protein. . .assimilated by the body.   333-4

We have previously taken up foods containing iron and silicon, also iron, silicon and lithium.

Mineral Balance

There are a number of minerals needed in varying amounts for use in a normal body. This is brought out strikingly in a reading for [924], who had nineteen mineral deficiencies.

Q-3. In what minerals am I deficient?
A-3. Nineteen! Gold, silver, platinum, silicon, iron and the like.
Q-4. Why do I have such a ravenous appetite?

A-4. The desire to supply, or the desire of the body-functionings to supply the elements lacking.   924-1

Diet can bring about mineral balance, the main constituents in which are potash and iodine. Again the point is made that minerals are best secured from vegetable sources.

Q-2. In what minerals is the body lacking and how may they be supplied?

A-2. These may be named as various numbers or names, but if the diet is followed as has been indicated and the acidity reduced, we will find all the mineral salts of the body becoming more and more perfectly balanced. There is a very good balance between the *main* minerals, which are—of course—the iodine and the potassiums, or potash and iodine. These are very well balanced, though some of the elements as a portion in calcium are changed a great deal. The mineral salts as in the sodium, calcium, these make for the better through the vegetable forces as indicated.   1236-1

Avoidance of Minerals Proceeding from Kitchen Utensils

We have learned that it is desirable for the body to ingest minerals derived from vegetable and animal sources rather than minerals *per se*. The readings also tell us that the composition of kitchen utensils should be such that during the cooking process mineral particles cannot be released from these utensils into the food.

The readings are very specific about aluminum utensils. While they are satisfactory for preparing some foods, they are not for others. Some persons can overcome the ill effects, others find it difficult.

Q-5. Is food cooked in aluminum utensils bad for this system?

A-5. Certain characters of food cooked in aluminum are bad for *any* system, and where a systemic condition exists—or a disturbed hepatic circulation or assimilating force, a disturbed hepatic eliminating force—they are naturally so. Cook rather in granite [enameled ironware], or better still in Patapar paper.   1196-7

Q-6. Do I have aluminum or arsenate of lead poisoning?

A-6. Neither of these; though the effect of aluminum...upon the body [made] by foods cooked in same—adds to rather than detracts from the activities in the system.

Hence, as we have indicated for many who are affected by nervous digestion or an overactivity of the nerve forces during the state of digestion taking place, the body should be warned about using or having foods cooked in aluminum. For this naturally produces a hardship upon the activities of the kidneys as related to the lower hepatic circulation, or [affects] the uric acid that is a part of the activity of the kidneys in eliminating same from the system.   843-7

Q-2. Is food cooked in aluminum detrimental to his health?
A-2. Better were they cooked in the *enamel*.   361-2

So with the manner in which foods are processed, these bring allergies to the body which activate through the sympathetic nervous system. . .
Some [foods] it will never hurt to have prepared in aluminum, but in most people it gradually builds something not compatible with the better conditions in the body-forces. This is with certain types of food. Those which are acid will take particles of aluminum into the body.   5211-1

. . .there are some foods that are affected in their activity by aluminum—especially in the preparation of certain fruits, or tomatoes, or cabbage.   1852-1

Q-4. Is there any trace in the body of deposits of elements from aluminum, due to cooking the food in aluminum?
A-4. Where aluminum is used as the cooking vessels, and the food is directly in contact with same, there are produced those elements ever in the human system that become detrimental; unless there are certain characters of vitamins that make for the activity of certain glands in the body. In this body. . .there are certain traces; yet these having been changed or altered do not leave other than indications in the eliminating areas. . .
           445-2

Cooking utensils of enamel or glassware, followed by those of stainless steel, were recommended by the readings as being the most satisfactory. In the case of enamelware, the finish must not be broken or scraped, however.

. . .cooked. . .only, though, in enamel or glassware.   556-8

. . .let this boil slowly, keeping it covered but not in aluminum, either in glass or enamel that is not broken. . .
           5178-1

Q-14. Is stainless steel harmless?
A-14. This is the best, except enamel.   379-10

However, Patapar paper for cooking was deemed the ultimate for securing and preserving food values. This is a parchment-like paper, procurable in sheets at health stores. "Patapar" is the trade name of the Paterson Parchment Co. of Bristol, Penn. The food should be placed on a sheet of this, which is then drawn up around the food to form a bag. The bag should be tied tightly with a string or other closure which will not exude dye or other harmful substances during the cooking. The bag should then be placed in a steamer or pressure cooker (with the proper amount of water below its tray) to be processed. Be sure the loose ends of the top of the bag are not close to the center of the pressure cooker where they could block escaping steam and cause undue pressure. Afterwards when the cooked food and its juices have been removed from the bag, the parchment should be rinsed and dried for storage. These sheets can be reused a number of times.

. . .*preferably* Patapar paper is the better manner for preparing food. . .   1852-1

. . .vegetable juices. And the preferable way to prepare such juices would be through cooking the vegetables after tying them in Patapar paper; not putting them in water to boil, but cooking either in the Patapar paper or in a. . .steamer, so that only the juices from the vegetables may be obtained—and no water added in the cooking at all. . .Even. . .vegetables and the chicken or fish would be better cooked in the Patapar paper or a steam cooker.   133-4

. . .vegetable *juices;* preferably of vegetables cooked within their *own* juices, not in water but in Patapar paper and the juices used, with a portion of the vegetables. . .the salts and juices of these are to be taken as much or more than the *body* of the vegetables themselves. . .   849-27

Ingestion of Air Containing Mineral Forces

The role of air in supplying minerals is pointed up in the following reference. This person needed to be outdoors more in order to secure enough carbon, which was in short supply in the air inside.

The diet shall be those foods only that carry much carbon for the system. . .It is best for the body to be in the air as much as possible. . .We do not get enough carbon in the house. 246-1

Ingestion of Water Containing Mineral Forces

Water found in a state of nature—i.e., not distilled—contains various minerals.

The addition of slaked lime in a certain proportion to [480]'s normal drinking water would provide increased calcium.

In the diets, keep to those things that add a great amount of the vitamins B and B-1 and iron. . .*and* calcium—which. . .may be best supplied in the water (if these foods as indicated are taken). To each gallon of water used, put a level teaspoonful of slaked lime. Boil same and allow this to settle, and then filter or draw off from same—siphoned.   480-55

Calciums and excessive amounts of sodas occur in chalybeate waters, which were recommended for [1297], who needed a stepping-down of high vibratory forces. These waters bring about eliminations from the body in a natural way. Eliminations secured by the use of medicines for [1297] would be unnatural and upsetting.

However. . .that needed instead of *re*-ionizing is rather a *de*-ionizing of the vibratory forces of the body. . .these [effects come from]. . .the high vibratory forces by the emotions, by the activities, to the whole of the system.

. . .then, in making for the better corrections. . .

Being in the open, in such an activity as of chalybeate waters. . .where the activities of same make for an outdoors activity. . .with the better eliminations and with food activities that make for a cleansing and purifying of the bodily forces. . .

To dose by medicine, or to make for activities other than that of nature's or of natural forces would be only. . .to *upset* other activities.

So, we would choose rather those surroundings, those activities, for a week to ten days; and. . .with those actions and activities of the body as indicated, we should bring a near to normal activity of the body. . .

Q-1. What particular foods. . .during this period, for the better eliminations?

A-1. Vegetables of the leafy rather than the tuberous nature; fish or fowl or the like. . .plenty [of] activity.

And the eliminations would be from the use of the waters. . . where the waters are of a chalybeate nature; calciums and excess of the sodas. . .   1297-2

Some healing waters contain soluble iron and magnesia with sulphur. These affect blood and intestinal disorders.

The waters. . .in other parts of these lands of the curative powers, have basis, or the medicinal powers lies in the soluble iron and magnesia with sulphur in this, as a body. . .It is a direct active principle to the human system. . .[where] blood and intestinal disorders are concerned.   3940-1

A pregnant woman was advised to be mindful of the water she was drinking and for the sake of her own body and also that of the embryo to be sure that a normal amount of calcium, chlorines and iodines were in it.

Rather be mindful of the activities, the quality or quantity of waters as are taken, and the manner in which the diets are followed to keep a *normal* amount of calcium, chlorines, iodines and such as will keep normalcy—not only for the mother body but. . .the body developing also.   301-4

In the preceding volume, *The Hidden Laws of Earth,* there is an entire section entitled "Water," which includes a discussion of minerals to be found in pure and healing waters. The reader is referred to this study, from which one conclusion is now quoted: ". . .several references. . .seem to indicate that an ideal water might be of the freestone variety and contain a medium amount of lime, also silica, lithia, magnesia, soda, iron, sulphur and iodine."

THE PLANT KINGDOM

Flowers

The introductory material dealing with the kingdoms of the earth furnished for man's needs brings out the point that there is creative influence or God in every herb, vegetable or individual activity (294-202) and that each is "spiritualized in that ability of using, doing, being all that the Creator has given. . .[it] to do." (281-54)

This spiritualization is especially apparent in flowers. Their lives are an expression of praise to the Creator. In filling their appointed lots they manifest acceptance of God's Will. They seek to live as fully as may be in the role assigned to them. In striving for the greatest perfection they point a way for man to follow.

Get close to nature and *learn* from the lowliest of that which manifests in nature, in the earth; in the birds, in the trees, in the grass, in the flowers, in the bees; that the life of each is a manifesting, is a song of glory to its Maker. And do thou *likewise.*   1089-3

. . .in the way and manner as life and life's development spiritually are being presented through that of the lily. As is seen, in the seemingly uncouth and uncomely herb in the muck, the root puts forth itself to obtain from this muck that which the entity sees burst forth in its beauty and fragrance. From whence cometh this? From that spirit force as has made the lily for the pleasure of the man sense, when used and applied in the manner to better understand and comprehend the Giver's *pleasure* in man, *when* man does coincide with His laws. . .
                                                              137-63

Q-8. Any spiritual advice?

A-8. Would you tell a rose to be beautiful, or a lily to be sweet? As to these—just keep that attitude, and don't let *little* things upset you! 2336-1

Then who may tell the rose where or when to bloom? For it takes from whatever may be its surroundings, and when encompassed even by man it does the best possible to be the beauty, the joy, and to give out that which is pleasing in the service to God. 2778-2

The seal [for 3374] would be:

A square, possibly fourteen inches or such. In the center of same put the open book, the Holy Bible. Upon same put the lily. For the experience of the entity that has meant the most was in that period when it heard the Master say, "Consider the lilies of the field, how they grow; they toil not, neither do they spin; yet Solomon in all his glory was not arrayed like one of these." This is the type, then, the field lily with all its beauty, its whiteness, and yet its center of gold. On same put three bees— these representing the mind, the body and soul. One upon the center of the flower, the lily; one in the air; the other upon the open book. They may add to, they may take from, but he that taketh from, from him shall be taken the promises that are given in the book. To those that add to, shall be added the hardships, the sorrows that are recorded there.

These will ever remind the entity, then, not merely to walk in the straight and narrow way but to teach and live so that others also may know the way in which ye should go.

In giving the appearances of the entity in the earth, there is much beauty to be drawn from the life. One may never tell a rose to be beautiful nor a violet to give off its fragrance, nor yet a sunset or the storm or the wind to add their voice to the songs of nature. Yet music and nature, and beauty of all kinds, appeal much to this entity. Have you wondered why? Have you used or abused such? These you must answer within self, as you may in viewing the words of truth, the whiteness of the lily and the voice of Him—who was attempting to give the lesson that our whole trust is in God and not in the material things of the earth.

Ever be a worker, as the bee, yes—but in that way in which it is ever a contribution to making thy portion of the earth a more beautiful place for men to live in.

For the smile of a baby, the fragrance of the rose, is but a reflection of God's care for man. Would he but learn the lesson of these little things! For it is the foolishness of man that is the wisdom of God, and the wisdom of man that is the foolishness of his Maker. 3374-1

The next [person] may see. . .[love] in the rose, as it seeks—with that it has to do with—to make manifest that beauty in expression that may *glorify* its Maker.   262-45

. . .just as many an individual soul may in a song find God and never in a flower—yet in both are the color, the tone, those influences which apply to the nature, to the inmost expression of the soul—and then finding same.   5398-1

This awoke within the entity that as may be found in the present, how all nature—the face in the water, the dew upon the grass, the tint and the beauty of the rose, the song of the stars, the mourn of the wind, all proclaim—*now*—the mighty words of a merciful, a loving God.   587-6

One that fills the mind, the very being, with an expectancy of God will see His movement, His manifestation, in the wind, the sun, the earth, the flowers, the inhabitants of the earth. . .
                    341-31

Ye love nature, and the things that partake of same; the out of doors, the blossom of the rose, and the sunset, the fall of the water. All of these bring to thee the voice of that which has *almost* persuaded thee as to how close He is to thee. 1809-1

The entity is especially one who appreciates nature's beauty—the snow, the rain, the sleet, the sunshine, the flowers, the green in the springtime, the color in the fall. All these mean much to the entity, for it is sensitive to God's own expression in nature.   3356-1

One capable of seeing beauty depicted in all expressions in nature, whether the bug about its lowly activity of cleansing the conditions about man, or the beauty of song in music, whether reed or string, or the beauty in the rose, the sunset, the stream, or in the awakening of nature as it illustrates to man the new birth into another experience in the material conditions.   539-2

The lesson presented to man by the flowers is not the only way in which they may affect him. There is an interrelationship between people and flowers, a give-and-take by which both may benefit. Flowers may draw vitality from a person. A person attuning to flowers may tap into creativity.

Thus flowers and things of that nature mean much to the entity at certain periods; at others they are soon forgotten.

And there are periods when flowers worn by the entity fade easily—there are others when they seem to draw upon the entity's very emotions to add to their influence.   2700-1

The abilities of the entity are in those fields that pertain to that innate general manner of applied arts. But this may be as much artistic in creating a home as in arranging a bowl of flowers. For each should be seeking to give, as would flowers, the whole of itself in glory to the Creative Forces or God.

3576-1

Flowers—no matter whether they be in or out of season—are well to be oft about the body. The beauty, the aroma, the aliveness of same will make for vibrations that are most helpful, most beneficial.   1877-1

Thus may there again be the effect and the beauty of those things wrought during that period of activity, through the efforts of the entity in following those things in nature.

As there is the music of the spheres, there is indeed the music of the growing things in nature. There is then the music of *nature* itself! There is the music of the growth of the rose, of *every* plant that bears color, of every one that opens its blossom for the edification, for the sanctification even of the environs thereabout!

In the study and in the meditation of such, then, as it unfolds itself to the spiritual awareness of the influences that may bear upon man in the present, the entity may bring help to the many—individually oft; yea, to masses and to the groups of many natures, through help of the very nature that was given during that experience.

How, you ask then, may the entity so attune self?

By looking on the beauty of a sunset, of a rose, of a lily, or any of those things in nature, and—by the very nature of the mood that these create in self—arouse or bring forth those melodies upon the instruments of the day; the piano, the organ, the reed or even the stringed instruments; to express the nature of these as they express themselves in their unfoldment.

And gradually may the entity so enter into the accord with same as to in self *attune* self to that unfoldment, that beauty, that nature to which it adapts itself for the healing forces necessary for man's awakening to his relationships to the Creative Forces.   949-12

Spiritualize the ideals; that is, as the entity sees in the emotions in relationships with others, let them find expression in the visions that might be expressed in nature, in the activities of nature, the unfolding of the bud, the motherhood of the bird, the strength of the storm, the powers and beauty of the sea, any of that in nature. The outlines and symmetrical beauty of an orange, an apple, a lily, a tree, yea a vine as it may cling. Or the expression in music. Yet the art should find the greater expression in this present entity, called [3664].

3664-1

For to fulfill that purpose for which an entity, a being, has manifested in matter is the greater service that can possibly be rendered.

Is the oak the lord over the vine? Is the Jimson [weed] beset before the tomato? Are the grassy roots ashamed of their flower beside the rose?

All those forces in nature are fulfilling rather those purposes to which their Maker, their Creator, has called them into being.

Man—as the entity taught, as the entity gave—is in that position where he may gain the greater lesson from nature, and the creatures in the natural world; they each fulfilling their purpose, singing their song, filling the air with their perfume, that they—too—may honor and praise their Creator ...they each in their *own* humble way are fulfilling that for which they were called into being, reflecting—as each soul, as each man and each woman should do in their particular sphere—their concept of their Maker!

This is the purpose—as the entity taught; this is the purpose the entity may find in giving its comfort, in giving the cheery word, in giving the lessons to those in all walks of life.

Fulfill thy purpose in thy relationship to thy Maker, not to any individual, not to any group, not to any organization, not to any activity outside of self [other] than to thy Creator!

For it is the reflection of Him.

1391-1

We find in Neptune the power of water, or of the influences about same; the creative expression, the ability to aid in reviving or in giving life to things. And most anything that would be planted in the earth by the entity would live. And flowers and those things that are cut from nature blossom or give off *better* perfume by being about or on the body of the entity (and there are few of which this could be said).

2641-1

There is one reading which deals almost entirely with flowers and how they may be used to enhance human lives. This follows in its entirety.

Edgar Cayce: [after repeating suggestions in an undertone] Yes, a very lovely person!

In giving the interpretation of the records as we find them, while we would magnify the virtues and minimize the faults, this is not in any way an attempt to so minimize the faults that the things wherein corrections are needed would not be advised the entity.

But in choosing from the records here, both from the astrological and the material sojourns, there is so much of the good compared to the bad that there is little use in the attempt to minimize the faults too much.

Those activities of the entity should be in or around flowers. For this entity has so oft been the music and the flower lady, until it becomes second nature to work in or with those either in arranging bouquets or corsages, or even the very "foolish" way of sending to those who have passed on. They need the flowers when they are here, not when they are in God's other room!

In this manner, though, and in this work, may the entity not only minister to others, but it may do so in such a way and manner as for the beauty and the color, even the voice and tone of flowers to come to mean so much to people whom the entity would and could interest in such.

Music and flowers, then, should be the entity's work through this experience. These have not altogether been, and yet do work with such. For flowers will love the entity, as the entity loves flowers. Very few would ever find it in themselves to wither while about or on this body.

In giving the interpretations of the records as we find from Venus and Jupiter, and Venus with Uranus and Saturn (and the astrological environs, not aspects), beauty, harmony, flowers and music are those things in which, through which, by which, the entity may attain to whatever it may set [as] its desires, provided that desire is: *"Ever let me be helpful to others, Lord, to others. Let me help them find more love, more beauty, more joy."*

May we indeed inculcate in the lives of others that like the rose, that like the baby's-breath, like every flower that blooms. For it does its best with what has been given it by man, to glorify its Maker with all its beauty, its color, with all of its love for the appreciation of spring, of the rain, the sunshine, the shadows. And so the man in like manner, with the worries, the troubles, heartaches, the disappointments, may draw closer and closer to God, knowing that this may be done as in the Son. He gave Himself that man might know that appreciation, that love, and how that in meting it to others we come to learn, to know the meaning of disappointments, of little hates, little jealousies, and of how they may grow by entertaining them, and how that the joys may grow also just by entertaining them, as do the flowers that God hath given, that man might see His face in the beautiful flowers. Consider the color, the beauty of the lily as it grows from its ugly muck, or the shrinking violet as it sends out its color, its odor to enrich even the very heart of God. Consider the rose as to how it unfolds with the color of the day, and with the opening itself to the sunshine, into the rain.

To the toils that come with same, then, may the entity find greater outlet, for it loves and appreciates beauty. And in these may this entity find that manner in which it may give to others an appreciation of so much beauty, so much loveliness as may come from muck and mud. And the spoilings of things make beauty in life, as. . .in flowers, if they are used in the manner as the flower uses same, in giving its thanks to its Maker for the opportunity of giving glory to the Creator.

As to the appearances in the earth:

Before this we find the entity was in the land when there were those first preparations made, in the land of the entity's present activity, for the study of flowers, of the activity of same.

The entity was then in the name of Maggie Vaughn and was one of those who loved flowers so much as to cause even the government to prepare greater and greater places in the capital for the various types of study and the growth and the development of same.

Thus the entity should in this present experience give some portion of its time to the culture and preparation and the putting together of such. The flowers will love it, and so will you! And what they may bring to those who are sick or "shut in" or those who are happy! That they are to see their loved ones that day, that evening.

For it is. . .[on] such occasions that flowers should be the companionship of those who are lonely. For they may speak to the "shut in." They may bring color again to the cheeks of those who are ill. They may bring to the bride the hope of love, of beauty, of a home. For flowers love the places where there is peace and rest. Sunshine and shadows, yes. There. . .[is] the varied variety from those [in] open fields to those which grow in the bog, but they grow.

Why won't people learn the lesson from them and grow, in love and in beauty, in whatever may be their environ? Learn also from the flower that where thou art, ye, too, may make that place more beautiful for your being there, whether it is in this or that or whatever place. Whether in the hovel or in the home of the mighty, make it beautiful as do the flowers.

Before that we find the entity was in those periods when the holy women brought spices and those things to anoint the body. The entity was not able to bring spices because of the value, so brought flowers of the field which were just as acceptable as was the widow's mite, she of whom the Lord said, "She hath given more than. . .all."

So in thy ministry to others through the beauties of nature, and that for God's companionship to those who love, those who are sick. . .those who are happy, work thou with those things to bring new life and hope to the many. In the name then Tilda.

Before that we find the entity was in the Egyptian land when individuals were being prepared for the various activities. The entity it was who chose the two-toned flowers which grew in the mire and bog of the Nile Valley, for their beauty. Thus came the entity first. But, because of unkind things said, the entity brought those disturbing factors in that experience.

But lose not the opportunity now to again set flowers, yes, all flowers in their proper relationship to man in the various phases of his moods and his tenses in the experience with his fellow man.

As to the abilities, then: These are limited only by the sincerity and the application, and the preparation. Study to show thyself approved unto God, a workman not ashamed, rightly divining the words of truth, keeping self from condemning any. Like as the orchid we crushed underfoot, or by hand, or worn upon the breast of the fair lady, it finds and gives the best that it has. Do thou likewise.

We are through.   5122-1

In keeping with the interrelationship between man and flowers, we find that every person has some flower to which he responds the most. Its development represents his own. Flowers he has known in other lives may hold significance for him, also.

Q-7. What is the entity's tree and flower?
A-7. The flower is the snowdrop, for its purity, for its struggling with the chilling blast and yet carrying within it the heart of the summer light in the spirit of its beauty and freshness. The tree is that *we* call in this land the dogwood, yet in that particular land it bore quite a different blossom. Just as the white and the pink make for the harmonies of the colors in the entity's experience, so do these in their activity represent the activity of the entity.

Some may ask, from what source—*why* is it given to this entity or to another for some particular tree or flower to be its tree or flower? Because their lives, in the use of same in the period of. . .development, that meant the most to others, are represented or presented by that the flower or tree represents in the experience of those that have looked into the heart of the flower, or that have harkened to the position the tree occupies among its fellows; for do they not speak one to another in their manifestations of the spirit they represent to fulfill a place in the experience of the sons of men? If they will but harken to the voice even from nature as represented in the flower or the tree. . .   276-6

Q-5. What are the entity's flower and tree?
A-5. The flower is the rose called, or that has been called, the Rose of Sharon, which—as seen—is of certain color and of certain sizes. The tree is the apple.   282-7

Q-8. What is my flower. . .my tree?
A-8. The Egyptian rose and the elm. The one that is seen in each case is from the varied experiences in the activities of the mental and physical body, in its experience through material sojourn.
The Egyptian rose is that *between* what may be commonly termed the long bud and the single blossom. . .   275-37

Q-5. What. . .[is] my. . .flower. . .?
A-5. The crabapple as the flower. . .   1532-1

As to flowers—the pansy, in its reproduction of its vibrations from the earth, is active in such manners as to become centralizing for the entity in its meditation.   1037-1

. . .arbutus flowers should be about the entity.   963-1

As to the flowers these would be the star of the field—or the pointed star in the field.   379-3

Peculiar—the odor of orris root is about the entity oft, and should be kept close; as the iris, as well as a white flower of some kind always.   1799-1

For a person seeking to uncover relics of a past American Indian life:

For when the flowers bloom again, when the jack-in-the-pulpit, when the blossom of the eagle flower comes again, then

106

ye may sing the song not only of the moon in its glory but thou wilt be shown the way, the manner, if thou wilt but dedicate thyself, thy substance, thy strength, to Him. 707-2

For some individuals it is the color of the flower that is important. We found this was true for [1799], who needed to have a white blossom close at hand. For [1397] flowers of deep, rich hues were indicated.

But in flowers—those colors that are deep and rich should be oft about the body. 1397-1

At times flowers may have too great an influence—when their pollens cause "rose fever." The readings suggest a recourse: Keep away from pollens, especially the heavy ones.

Keep in the open, but away from pollens of any nature, especially flowers that are heavy-pollened, as any of the wild flowers or cosmos or the like. Roses are different.
Do this. . .and we may relieve those conditions so that they will not become constitutional; as is ordinarily indicated from this type of rose fever or pollen fever. [An antiseptic inhalant and osteopathic manipulations were also recommended.]
795-3

Odors

In the excerpt from 1877-1, given previously, it was emphasized that the beauty, *aroma* and aliveness of flowers bring helpful vibrations. What is the nature of aroma and what is its effect? To answer these questions we need to explore the field of odor. The material following will deal with the subject as a whole and include not only the fragrances of flowers but also odors emanating from animal and other sources.

In reading 274-7 it is stated that there is no greater influence in a physical body than the effect of odors upon the olfactory nerves. Obviously odors affect us all whether we realize this or not. Some persons have developed a greater sensitivity to odors than others. Such a person was [274]; and it is fortunate that we can turn to his readings to find out more about this important subject.

[274] was told in his first reading that he might join an archaeological group because of his abilities in testing peculiar types of materials. In his seventh reading he was informed that by examining the feet of a mummified body taken from a

sarcophagus and by analyzing the odors still attached to them, he could indicate what the activities of the dead person had been and what foods the person had chiefly eaten. Where a tomb was opened in which temple or religious ceremonies had been performed, he would be able to tell whether or not there had been human or animal sacrifices attached to these and whether the incense used in them had been derived from flowers, trees, buds or a combination.

Also there lies the ability within the entity for the seeking out, through associations with groups or individuals who may act in the capacity of research in a particular field of archaeology. The entity may join with such a group, through the abilities for testing peculiar types of materials or associations. 274-1

How many of those that usually open an egg that's been buried for five to ten million years can, by its analysis, tell you what its composition is, or what the fowl or animal fed upon that laid it? This body can! . . .
If there were opened a sarcophagus in the form of an activity where the feet of such an animal or man or body were chemically analyzed, as related to the odors and their active influences upon the body itself, would it not be possible to indicate as to what had been the means or activities of such a body during that experience in the earth? and as to what were the principal food values? Such abilities would lend much to many of these. In opening a tomb wherein there had been the form of classifications or activities in a temple service, it would be able to tell whether there had been such sacrifices required as the destruction of animal life or of man, or whether there. . .[were] used the odors of flowers, trees, buds, or a combination. 274-7

It was brought out to [274] that individuals have affinities for different odors (just as we have found they do for different minerals). He himself was to search out a kind of ivy. Synthetic odors cannot duplicate the real thing. The parent stock was given the ability to make its own essence by the Creator Himself. This odor or essence sets in motion olfactory influences in the mucous membranes of man's body. These influences lead to certain activities. Since odor is a gas and not of denser matter, "a sweet savor" may stimulate man to remember his former estate in which he had not fallen into materiality and was of less dense matter himself. However, incense may be contaminated by earthly misdeeds. Certain odors have apparently been developed by the activities of man himself. Mace, allspice and the various peppers arouse a feeling of vengeance.

Odors! . . .there's a kind of ivy. . .The leaf of this the body should study in its associations, for it would make an odor that would be so unusual and effective and worthwhile, as well as being that which he should use as his omen or have about him often. . .

Does the odor of an orris compound affect every individual alike? Or does the attar of roses or the essence of clover or of honeysuckle or crabapple or the like affect [in] the same way and manner? No. To some it would bring repellent influences; to others it would bring experiences that have been builded in the inner self. . .

For, there is no greater influence in a physical body (and this means animal or man. . .) than the effect of odors upon the olfactory nerves of the body. They have made much of the developments for the body. Look at the difference in your New Englander that smells of earth and certain characters, the ringing of the nose, and those in other climes where they have smelt hot peppers and swamps. Watch the difference in the characterizations of the individuals, or the temperament of same. Nothing has had much more influence than such in the *material* life.

. . .from certain characterizations of soil and climatic conditions, as well as other influences. . .not an ivy, and it is an ivy; its bloom is purple, its leaf is shaped round instead of oblong. . .as the strawberry, but it's not poisonous. . .and it should be sought by the body.

While the fleur-de-lis may have been as a pathological symbol, the scientific would be more from the blossom and leaf of this particular flower—as an interest for this body.

274-7

Study *all* of those of the ivy family, including what has been called the geranium. For this is of *that* family. . .

In much of thy seeking (as thy advanced thought is so determined, or accepted by many), the synthetic odors, synthetic reactions from varied forms of vegetation or grasses have been accepted; yet these are much like accepting shadows. . .for the *real* thing! . . .

Follow the stock from which there has been the propagation of those various plants, with all their *varied* odors.

From what did the plant *obtain* its ability to produce in the one that of lemon, in another orange, in another lavender, in another violet?

Its parent stock was given, not by man but by the very Creative Forces, the *ability* to take and make that which becomes as an essence that *responds* to or sets in vibration the olfactory influences in the mucous membranes of the body of man; determining it to be *setting* in motion that which has such an influence!

For as has been indicated, and as may be or should be worked upon or classified by man, there is the ability to make odors that will respond, and do respond, to certain individuals or groups; and many hundreds *are* responding to odors that *produce* the *effect* within their systems for activities that the psychoanalyst and the psychologist have long since discarded ...much as they have the manner in which the Creative Forces or God *may* manifest in an individual!

What meaneth they of old when saying: "This hath ascended to the throne of grace as a sweet savor, a sweet incense before the Maker, the Creator," but that that within the individual is made aware of that estate which he had before he entered into flesh and became contaminated by the forms of matter in such a manner? For odor is gas, and not of the denser matter that makes for such activity in individuals' lives as to make for the degrading things.

Again, what meaneth He when He gave, "I am loath to thy sacrifices and to thy incense, for thou hast contaminated same with the blood of thy sons and daughters in the manner in which thou hast led them astray."

The mixing of those things, then, became as stumbling blocks. What did Jeroboam, that he made the children of Israel to sin, but to offer rather the sandalwoods of the nations or the Egyptians that made for the arousing of the passions in man for the gratifications of the seeking for the activities that would satisfy his own indulgence, rather than the offering of those things that would make for the *glory* of the Lord's entrance into the activities of the individual?

What bringeth the varied odors into the experience of man? Did lavender ever make for bodily associations? Rather has it ever been that upon which the angels of light and mercy would bear the souls of men to a place of mercy and peace, in which there might be experienced more the glory of the Father.

Yet what bringeth mace and allspice and the various peppers but that which would arouse within man that of vengeance? Why?

These are of those influences that build such *in* the experience...Hast thou ever known the odor from a flesh body of a babe to be the same as the odor from a body that has been steeped in the sins of the world, and has become as dross that is fit only to be cast upon the dunghill to become again that through which there may be gained those activities in a sphere of opportunity for a soul expression?

Then, just as these may answer for the varied stages of an individual development, there should be those things that make for such an activity.

Look about thee; and thou may understand how that one of the canine [dog] or cat family may. . .through the very spoor of its master or one of its kind. . .determine not only the days of its passage but the state of its being, interpreted as to its ability for procreation within its own self. This ye see and have taken little thought of.

How much more, then, may there be brought into the experience of individuals that which may answer in their preparations (body and mind), through the varied effects that may be obtained in the entity or individual entering into an activity that becometh it as a son of a living God?

Dost thou put upon the body of the harlot the same that thou findest upon the altar of thy Lord? Dost thou find upon those entering at birth the same as upon those passing at death? Far apart be these, yet it is as in every law. . .*just* the reverse side of the same thing!

Q-4. Could you give some information on the relation of the sense of smell to the other senses?

A-4. These apply as has been indicated in that just given. Study these, not only from the manner in which they affect the body in the various stages of its development but from that they have reflected and do reflect in the activity of that kingdom just below thee. . .yet so often with the appearance of being far above many of those that have made themselves beneath the animal kingdom!   274-10

Various passages in the readings point out the role of incense and perfumes in preparing the body for meditation. Again different individuals respond to different ones.

To some it is necessary. . .that certain or definite odors produce those conditions (or are conducive to producing of conditions) that allay or stimulate the activity of portions of the system, that the more carnal or more material sources are laid aside, or the whole of the body is *purified,* so that the purity of thought as it rises has less to work against in its dissemination of that it brings to the whole of the system, in its rising through the whole of these centers, stations or places along the body.   281-13

First in cleanliness, in purifying of the body...that ye may be purified before thy self first and then before others. The anointing with the incense, making for the raising of that ye know as thine senses or perception or consciousness of the activities to all the faults, by comparison, as arose among others. 281-25

Also the odors which would make for the raising of the vibrations would be lavender and orris root. For these were those of thy choice in the Temple of Sacrifice. They were also thy choice when thou didst walk with those who carried the spices to the tomb. 379-3

And lavender, odors that come from sandalwood have a peculiar influence upon the body in the present; for these bespeak of something innate within self that bespeaks of the abilities of the soul, mind and body to revivify and rejuvenate itself as to an ideal. 578-2

The odors of sandalwood or orris and violet are well; for these, when the entity meditates, create an environment for the entity. 1616-1

Hence...the wearing of the stone lapis linguis would be as an aid in its meditative periods. . .Also the odor of the peach blossom, or of those natures partaking of the sandalwood as combined with same. 1058-1

Q-11. What kind of incense should I use during meditation?
A-11. Cedar. And hyssop. 275-39

For the entity who was Moses' sister in Egypt:

And it is well that self, when contemplating or meditating, surround self with the environs of an oriental nature. . .with the perfumes of the East. 355-1

For this body—not for everybody—odors would have much to do with the ability of the entity to meditate. For the entity in the experiences through the Temple of Sacrifice became greatly attuned through the sense of smell, for the activities were upon the olfactory nerves and muscles of the body itself. For there protuberances were taken away.
As to the manner of meditation, then: Begin with that which is oriental in its nature—oriental incense. Let the mind become, as it were, attuned to such by the humming, producing those sounds of o-o-o-ah-ah-umm-oo-o; not as to become

monotonous, but "feel" the essence of the incense through the body-force in its motion of body. This will open the kundaline forces of the body. Then direct same to be a blessing to others.
2823-3

In the one before this we find in that land known as in the French period, or during those of the Louis's—the fifteenth, and during that period when Richelieu ruled with the greater strength. The entity one to whom Richelieu oft went as one seeking counsel from the incenses burned during that period ...and the entity gained and lost through this experience; gaining in the *understanding* of the influences of incense, or of odors, or of such as are cleansed by fire, and lost in the *application* of same as respecting the influence over men. In the present, much of that as is to be met in a karmic influence is the *proper* application of these same *influences,* as may be used for the *development* of peoples, individuals, men, women, children. In these may the entity meet, overcome, understand, excel; for especially are *some* of those of the aloe, or of the myrrh, those influences innate to the entity for weal or woe...
Q-1. *What should the entity study to develop mysticism?*
A-1. The effect of odor, color, harmony, upon individuals. Individual study and personal application greater than books, though the books of the mystics may be read—but *develop* same in *personal* experience *and* application.   1714-1

Hence the entity should ever be as a healing influence to others when it comes about them. Odors—have the life everlasting about thee often, and ye will find whether as a sachet or as a liquid—it will bring strengthening vibrations to the body.   3416-1

Odors were also suggested for general use to help individuals.

...the odors. . .the body should keep about self. . .orris and lavender.   259-8

Peculiar—the odor of orris root is about the entity oft, and should be kept close; as the iris, as well as a white flower of some kind always.   1799-1

Violet and violet scent with orris are the odors for the entity.
1489-1

Odors—the essence of the red clover should be that chosen.
1981-1

...cedar surrounding the entity will bring a satisfaction; and in the burning of same, in the odors of same, may the entity harken back to much of the developed mental activities.

346-1

[1849] was advised to perfect perfumes for individual use. Doubtless response to such perfumes would determine the buyer's choice.

The making of a specific or definite perfume or the like for the individual would be most advisable to consider.

Choose the individual—make something that would be expressive of the individual. . .Then this will only needs be developed and expanded to meet the needs of various individuals. . .And the remunerations for these would be not exorbitant, but so much variation from that ordinarily indicated, and still so little of that as has been seriously considered from a metaphysical or spiritual angle in this country.

1849-3

The role of odor is beautifully summed up in the following passage.

For odors *are* necessary, else would they have been given to the rose, to the violet, to the lilac, to the clover, to those things that show the beauty of a loving heavenly Father? 1402-1

The effect of odor has not been widely explored as yet in this present age. However, one instance of the use of odor was related in a news item from *The Virginian-Pilot,* Norfolk, Va., in 1965. Dr. H.M. Cathey of the Department of Agriculture reported that tiny amounts of gas coming from ripe apples stimulate blossoms in a great variety of plants. The plant and the ripe apple should be encased in a bag and left for four days. With usual care afterwards the plant will bloom within one to six months, depending on its species, even though it may not ordinarily flower. Roses and carnations are among varieties not responding; in fact, they should be kept away from apples.[20]

There is reference in the July 30, 1965, issue of *Time* to the new science of odor detection or olfactronics, which was then being studied by researchers at Illinois Institute of Technology. It has already been ascertained that human odors show age, sex, race, diet, health and general locality of residence.[21] This,

---

[20]"Apple Gas Causes Plant Blossoms," *The Virginian-Pilot,* Norfolk, Va., August 11, 1965, pg. 24.
[21]"To Catch a Thief," *Time,* Chicago, Ill., Vol. 86, July 30, 1965, pg. 59.

of course, is in keeping with what the readings told [274].

In the Jan. 2, 1977, issue of *Parade,* it was reported that Dr. Orville Chapman, a professor of chemistry at the University of California, Los Angeles, had become interested in odor perception as a result of work undertaken by himself and a student entomologist. According to this account man's sense of smell is one thousand times less sensitive than that of dogs and dogs' is one thousand times less sensitive than that of insects.[22]

Trees

The readings tell us that the spiritual quality found in flowers also occurs in trees. Likewise, there may be a relationship between trees and humans.

*The garden called Eden. . .*The entity. . .sought to know the meaning. . .for it saw then the fruit, the leaves, trees, which had their spiritual meaning in people's lives.   5373-1

Get close to nature and *learn* from the lowliest of that which manifests in nature, in the earth; in the birds, in the trees, in the grass, in the flowers, in the bees; that the life of each is a manifesting, is a song of glory to its Maker. And do thou *likewise.*   1089-3

Is the oak the lord over the vine?. . .
All those forces in nature are fulfilling rather those purposes to which their Maker, their Creator, has called them into being.   1391-1

Listen. . .[to] the birds. Watch the blush of the rose. Listen. . . [to] the life rising in the tree. These serve their Maker. Through what? That psychic force, that is Life itself, in their respective spheres—that were put for the service of man. Learn thine lesson, O man, from that about thee!   364-10

Thinkest thou that the grain of corn has forgotten what manner of expression it has given? Think you that *any* of the influences in nature that you see about you—the acorn, the oak, the elm, or the vine, or *any*thing—has forgotten what manner of expression? Only man forgets!   294-189

Aid others in appreciating the beauty—even of mud, of snow, of nature, of trees. . .   2404-1

---

[22]Charity Hopkins, "Your Nose Knows More than You Know," *Parade,* January 2, 1977, pg. 10.

Know something of nature. How many kinds of trees do you know? and yet you work in wood! How many kinds of birds do you know? and yet you use them as part of that worked in wood! . . .Interest self in all nature!   257-204

An individual entity, from the combination of these, in which there are the psychic and the occult forces. The experiences of the spirit of a rainfall, a sunset, a river, a tree, a herd, a flock, a school of fish—from these the entity may gain, as in the aura from same, much that to others would be imagination, but to the entity may be used as emblems of those things that may be constructive in creating, even in a mechanical manner, that which would control, would affect, would direct such things.

And the entity, with the very words or the blessings in planting even a nut, may insure the next generation a nut-bearing tree! The entity with its very abilities of the magnetic forces within self, may circle one with its hands and it'll bear no more fruit, though it may be bearing nuts in the present.

These are indications, then, of how the entity may use the energies or vibrations, even of the body, constructively or destructively Do not use these for self in either direction. For, as just indicated, if you plant one, be sure it is for the next generation and not for this one. It is others ye must think of, as should every soul. "Others, Lord, others—that I may know thee the better."   3657-1

In the section under "Flowers" we learned that a special tree as well as flower represents the spiritual development of every individual. He or she is, therefore, in tune with it. The dogwood, apple tree and elm were discussed or mentioned in the references cited then.

In the section "The Psychic and Mental Effects of Gems, Stones and Metals" under *Clear Lapis,* we found that when a lapis stone is cut and set in a certain way, the emanations thrown off from it to the active forces in a body may induce psychic sensitivity. The reference elaborated further: "the same thing may be done with an oak tree, or with a persimmon tree." (440-3) We also learned in this section that if [440] would go to the New York Museum of Natural History and sit by the large lapis formation to which he was directed by the readings, he would hear the stone sing. (440-3) In a later reading this singing was discussed more fully and the parallel concerning trees developed.

. . .as has been indicated for this body. . .there is—the ability within this body, [440]. . .to hear the singing or the movements [of certain stones], much. . .in the same way and manner as. . .is given to any. . .[one who] will listen for days. . .[to] a growing tree, or as was accredited to. . .those who have so developed in certain portions of this world as to be able to gain much from especially the growing oak, or certain other trees peculiar to those vicinities. [Many of them did hear emanations from trees.] 440-11

From the foregoing it is evident that sitting under a growing tree regularly over a period of time may attune a person to psychic receptivity. The oak is an especially suitable subject. However, the phrase "other trees peculiar to those vicinities" furnishes additional scope. The persimmon is doubtless one of those peculiar to this country.

According to that famous book of mythology Bulfinch's *The Age of Fable,* the oldest Greek oracle was that of Zeus at Dodona. Here the rustling of the branches in a grove of oak trees was interpreted for the inquirer by priests connected with the shrine.[23] Perhaps the priests *had* developed sensitivity under circumstances similar to those mentioned by the readings.

Biblical reference (Exodus 34:13) to the sacred groves of the heathen indicates that trees played a part in the religious observances of those nations occupying Palestine at the time of the Israelite invasion.

Such emphases on trees as the two discussed apparently stemmed from the teachings of the sage Asdod or Ashdod, who lived some thirty-two thousand years ago. It may be that this seer discovered for himself the value of sitting under a growing tree.

. . .that period just before the prophet or seer or sage that was. . .known as Asdod [Ashdod?], the beginner of that that became *later*. . .the sage of trees; or. . .as measured in years. . . *now,* twenty *thousand* years before the *Chaldean* message, or flood [10,000 B.C.?]. . . 311-3

Vegetables

In the section "Ingestion of Food, Air and Water Containing Mineral Forces," it was made abundantly clear that the food values in vegetables are especially valuable to the human

---

[23]Thomas Bulfinch, *The Age of Fable,* A Mentor Classic, The New American Library, Inc., New York and Toronto, 1962, pp. 336-337.

organism. The various references recommended a number of vegetables, of which some are apparently not in general cultivation at the present time. (One does not usually see them offered for sale or growing in the fields.) A good example is salsify or oyster plant, which can supply calcium, gold, iodine, iron, phosphorus, silicon (all according to previous references) and nicotinic acid or niacin. (1158-31) The author has tried growing this vegetable in her own garden (in Virginia Beach, Virginia) and found it a good fresh vegetable to be kept in the ground for winter use. Except for exceptionally cold weather it will continue to grow very slowly under the ground, provided a light litter is placed around the tops above ground. It may be added that the same culture can be undertaken in the same area for carrots. These then furnish two different kinds of fresh vegetables to be obtained in winter in the more southern parts of the country.

That vegetables grown in one's immediate vicinity are best for a body is brought out clearly in the readings.

For in the consideration of the whole, it will be found that products grown in individual localities are best suited to the needs of individuals living or dwelling within those same localities. 1797-3

Do not have large quantities of any fruits, vegetables, meats, that are not grown in or come to the area where the body is at the time it partakes of such foods. This will be found to be a good rule to be followed by all. This prepares the system to acclimate itself to any given territory. 3542-1

Q-2. Is a diet composed mainly of fruits, vegetables, eggs, and milk the best diet for me?
A-2. We indicated, use more of the products of the soil that are grown in the immediate vicinity. These are better for the body than any special set of fruits, vegetables, grasses or whatnot. 4047-1

. . .as the body of the physical forces in man becomes more easily adjusted to environmental forces or the environments of the activities physically and mentally; *physically* the bodily-forces adjust themselves more readily by activities of the vegetables, fruits, and the viands for the body from that portion of the land in which the body resides. 1029-1

The proportion to be kept in the diet of vegetables growing

above the ground to those below varies with individual needs. [5031], who was suffering from multiple sclerosis, was advised to take three of those underground to one on top.

Have more of the vegetables growing under the ground than those growing above the ground, for this body; such as the tuberous natures—potatoes, carrots, the oyster plant; all characters of vegetables that are grown under the ground. These should form the chief amount. To be sure some leafy vegetables should be taken, but have at least three of those under the ground to one of those on top of the ground, for this body. Rutabaga, turnips, all such are well for this body; not in too large quantities, but they form the salts and the characters of vitamins in the right combinations to make for the strengthening of this body.   5031-1

On the other hand, it was suggested that [2602], who was suffering from excess acidity, have one vegetable below the ground to three above the ground, also at least one leafy vegetable to every one of the pod variety.

Do have plenty of vegetables above the ground; at least three of these to one below the ground. Have at least one leafy vegetable to every one of the pod vegetables taken.   2602-1

[1236], who also had excess acidity, was told to take one vegetable below the ground to two or three above and one of leafy type to two of bulbular or pod.

Have one vegetable below the ground to two or three above the ground, and one of leafy to two of bulbular or pod.
1236-1

[578] was to have three leafy vegetables to two of the pod variety to help supply calcium and balance iodines with potassiums in the system.

. . .and have three leafy vegetables to two of the pod nature, or that ratio.   578-5

The proportion of two or three vegetables above ground to one below was characterized as a good division for someone with toxemia.

. . .vegetables that are well divided as with two or three above the ground to one below ground.   463-1

119

Three vegetables above the ground to one below were advised as a good combination for a 6-year-old child.

> *Evenings:* A fairly well-coordinated vegetable diet, with three vegetables above the ground to.one below the ground.
>
> 3224-2

However, [4293], who was suffering from bronchitis and poor eliminations, was advised to eat no vegetables growing below the ground because of the resulting starches.

> Well-cooked vegetables that grow *above* the ground; none that grow below the ground—none! Those that are of the activity. . .to make for tuberous forces and heavy starches (as all of these are) make for heaviness that is hard to eliminate.
>
> 4293-1

Leafy vegetables would help elimination from the body.

> . . .leafy vegetables will make for the better eliminations. . .
>
> 480-24

> Liver torpid in action, showing the effect of conditions produced about the bile ducts. . .
> The diet would be much of the rougher foods, as bran, whole wheat and bread of that nature. Principally green vegetable foods, seasonable at the present time. Much of that of greens, spinach, celery, lettuce, and those of that nature. Fruits—and these as much green as possible.
>
> 5738-1

These green, leafy vegetables were, however, not to be treated for preservation or color.

> Vegetables that are of the leafy nature are. . .preferable to any dried foods or beans [for 1206]. The green vegetables are well, so long as they are not treated with any chemical for preserving of same or for the color of same.
>
> 1206-9

> Do not use *any* vegetables, however, that have been colored by the use of *any* coloring matter for their preservation or for their color.
>
> 1564-3

The value of salads of fresh green vegetables was repeatedly emphasized. It was also brought out that the term "fresh green vegetable" may be applied to one that is naturally of another color than green, provided it has been freshly gathered. Fresh vegetable juices were also recommended.

[The] raw fresh vegetables. . .would consist of tomatoes, lettuce, celery, spinach, carrots, mustard, onions or the like (not cucumbers) that make for purifying of the humor in the lymph blood as this is absorbed by the lacteal ducts as it is digested.   840-1

Noons—whole green vegetables. . .should be taken raw, in the form of a salad; such as celery, lettuce, onions, leeks, tomatoes, peppers, radish, carrots and the like—raw cabbage, especially the sprouts or the like. An oil or salad dressing may be used that will make it more palatable for the body. . .3823-2

Q-16. How about. . .tablets to supplement green foods?
A-16. There is no supplementary to green foods in the real way or manner; though if there are the periods when there is not the ability to obtain. . .the green foods. . .these others may be used, but rather as extremities than as a regular activity in same. . .   1158-11

Q-3. It is difficult for me to arrange one daily meal of salad only; therefore, might I supplement my diet by tablets recommended by Dr. Black, taking one tablet daily. . .
A-3. These may be taken if there is a lack of those activities from the raw salad; but they do not, *will* not, supply the energies as well or as efficaciously for the *body* as if there were the efforts made to have at least one meal each day altogether of raw vegetables, or two meals carrying a raw salad as a portion of same—each day.   1158-18

Q-3. Should I take Dermetic's Vegetable Tablets?
A-3. Not necessary with one meal of raw fresh vegetables. For although compounds are well, these in their natural state are better. Lettuce, celery, onions, tomatoes, peppers, carrots, spinach, mustard—*any* of these are. . .preferable *green,* fresh, than prepared in a preservative of any kind.
Q-4. What about fresh vegetable juices?
A-4. These are all very good.   1158-1

Once or twice a week take vegetable juices [of the type] that would be prepared by using a vegetable juicer, but only using the vegetables for same that would combine well. They may be combined or taken separately; the juices from such [vegetables] as lettuce, celery, beets, spinach, mustard, carrots, radishes, and a tiny bit of leek or onion—not more than one very small onion, if it is desired that this be mixed with same. All these may be combined or used according to the taste of the body.
                                                                                                        1968-3

At least once each day take an ounce of raw carrot juice. Use a juicer to extract the juice from fresh raw carrots.   243-33

The addition of gelatin to raw vegetables and vegetable juices is highly recommended in the readings. The gelatin works with the glands, causing them to utilize vitamins which would not otherwise be active. This process results in the creation of corpuscle tissue. The gelatin, grated vegetables and juice may be combined to make a jelly, to be eaten after it has set. However, [5031], previously referred to, who suffered from multiple sclerosis, was advised to take the mixture before it had set so that it might act "in and with the gastric flows of digestion."

In the diet keep plenty of raw vegetables, such as watercress, celery, lettuce, tomatoes, carrots. Change these in their manner of preparation, but do have some of these each day. They may be prepared rather often with gelatin, as with lime or lemon gelatin—or Jello. These will not only taste good but be good for you.   3429-1

Include in the diet often raw vegetables prepared in various ways, not merely as a salad but scraped or grated and combined with gelatin or with oils or mayonnaise or in various ways and manners. Include in these watercress, celery, lettuce, carrots, all of those that may be eaten in or with such preparations. Of course, not all of these are to be taken at once necessarily, but let these be a part of the diet almost daily.
    3445-1

In building up the body with foods, preferably have a great deal of raw vegetables for this body—as lettuce, celery, carrots, watercress. All we would take raw, with dressing, and oft with gelatin. These should be grated, or cut very fine, or even ground, but do preserve all of the juices with them when these are prepared in this manner in the gelatin.
    5394-1

Do keep plenty of raw vegetables, having some of these each day. These may be prepared more often with gelatin; such as watercress, lettuce, celery, mustard greens, onions, carrots, all types of foods that may be prepared in a salad.   3642-1

If gelatin will be taken with raw foods rather often (that is, prepare raw vegetables such as carrots often with same)— grate them, eat them raw, we will help the vision.   5148-1

Do add to the diet about twice as many oranges, lemons and limes as. . .[are] a part of the diet in the present. These also supplement with a great deal of carrots, especially as combined with gelatin, if we would aid and strengthen the optic nerves and the tensions between sympathetic and cerebrospinal systems. 5401-1

Q-4. Please explain the vitamin content of gelatin. There is no reference to vitamin content on the package.
A-4. It isn't the vitamin content but its ability to work with the activities of the glands, causing the glands to take from that absorbed or digested the vitamins that would not be active if there is not sufficient gelatin in the body. See, there may be mixed with any chemical that which makes the rest of the system susceptible or able to call from the system that needed. It becomes, then. . ."sensitive" to conditions. Without it there is not that sensitivity. 849-75

Also every day we would take gelatin as an aid to the quick pick-up for energy, aiding the system—from the assimilation of this, with the chemical changes in the body—in creating those activities through the assimilating and glandular force for the energies that create corpuscle tissue in body. 2737-1

In the diet there should be a great deal of raw vegetables, especially mixed with gelatin. Even vegetable juices taken with gelatin would be well; not set, however, but taken as soon as the gelatin is stirred in same, to act in and with the gastric flows of digestion. 5031-1

We have just noted how gelatin works with the glands, causing them to utilize vitamins which would not otherwise be activated. This seems a good spot to emphasize that too great ingestion of vitamins is not in the interest of the body.

Vitamins in a body are elements that are combative with, or in opposition to, the various activities of a living organism, and may be termed—and well termed—as those of bacilli of any nature within a human or physical organism. . .Now, when these are taken into the system, if they are not put to work by the activities of the system—either physical or mental—they become destructive tissue, for they affect the plasm of the blood supply or the emunctory and lymph—which is another name for a portion of a blood supply in a system. Then, in the meeting of the diet—be sure the activities, physically and mentally, are in keeping with; and do not do these spasmodically, but be consistent. . . 341-31

The above reference tells us that we should not take more vitamins into our bodies than those needed to match our mental and physical activities. If we take too many, they will be left as drosses in the system and become destructive to the emunctory and lymph portion of the blood.

The proper amount of vitamins is, however, very needful as it is through them that the glands supply energies to enable the various organs of the body to reproduce themselves.

Vitamins are that from which the glands take those necessary influences to supply the energies to enable the varied organs of the body to reproduce themselves.   2072-9

Even though it is so important to eat plenty of raw vegetables in salad or juice form, at times vegetables and their juices, cooked in Patapar paper, can be assimilated more readily. In the following reference it is also made clear that the juice close to the skin of carrots carries the most vitamin B. It may well be true that many food values in other vegetables are carried in the same way (in the juice) and position (close to the skin).

Q-46. Do carrots carry this vitamin B? Does it make any difference whether they are raw or cooked?
A-46. They do. If cooked, be sure they are cooked in their own juices to preserve the greater portion of same, but there's quite a variation as to that that is released for digestive forces by being cooked. There are periods when they are better assimilated cooked than raw, but the juices are the source of the vitamin—and that, of course, close to the skin.   457-9

Beet and carrot juice, prepared in Patapar paper and given alternately, were suggested for [462]. The tops of beets were to be included but the tops of carrots discarded. All cutting of the vegetables was to be done just prior to preparation to insure the greatest freshness.

The inclinations for a hardening or a filling of portions of the digestive tract becomes the greater disturbance to the body, in hindering the eliminations through the activity of the excretory functionings of the liver as well as the kidneys.
. . .the combination of two juices taken alternately would be preferable for this body, and for this particular body both should be cooked—but in Patapar paper.
One day take about an ounce of beet juice; this means the tops also.

The next day take an ounce of carrot juice; this does not include the tops. . .

The juices from these are to be prepared fresh each day. Do not attempt to keep them from one day to the next—it would be injurious rather than helpful; but the activities of this combination upon the system, with the general activities of the body, will be *most* beneficial.

Preferably take these before retiring, or at the evening meal; one taken one day, the other the next.

Take them for at least a month. Leave off then for a few days, and then take them again; but the beneficial effects from these will make the body desire to keep them pretty regularly.

In the preparation of these, of course, it would be very well that they be cut just before they are wrapped in Patapar paper, instead of remaining cut very long beforehand.   462-13

[1158] was to drink juices prepared in this way from all the cooked vegetables in the diet.

Be well that the cooked vegetables that may be prepared as a portion of the meals be cooked in their own juices, and such juices taken as a stimulant or as a tonic would be very good.
1158-1

Vegetables cooked in their own juices should each be cooked alone and combined later if so desired. However, placing packets of separate vegetables, each *tied up* in its *own* piece of Patapar paper, in a pressure cooker for steaming (with the proper allowance of water in the cooker) would seem to be allowable. Vegetables with approximately the same steaming time would have to be chosen.

Vegetables that are cooked in their *own* juices. . .each cooked ·alone, then combined together afterward if so desired...   3823-3

Q-1. Is cauliflower good for this body?
A-1. Depends upon the manner of preparation, as with most foods. This is very good if it is prepared alone and cooked in its *own* juice, and not in either water or other seasonings. Season same only with salt and butter.   357-7

Note the advice to use only salt and butter as seasonings. The seasoning should be added *after* cooking as cooking with salt destroys much vitamin content.

The cooking of condiments, even salt, *destroys* much of the vitamins of foods.   906-1

Cooking vegetables in their own juices preserves their salts.

Evenings—well-cooked vegetables of all characters, but not too large quantities of those that grow below the ground. And these well-cooked in their *own* juices, that the salts of each vegetable may be preserved in same.   862-2

There is a certain value found in the liquid left from the cooking of vegetables in water, but this should be kept cool and drunk within 24 hours after preparation.

Q-3. Should cooking water from potatoes in jackets and broccoli and asparagus be chilled and drunk?
A-3. This depends upon what they are being taken for. There are properties of course, in each of these ingredients that constitute a helpful experience or helpful application, from those things about the fruits and vegetables, but these kept haphazardly, there is not much good to be obtained. But if these are cared for in the general way, using these specifically at times, it would be much better.
Q-4. How long may they be kept in ice box before using?
A-4. As either of these are strained off, or kept, use them in the next twenty-four hours.   1158-38

Vegetables should not be cooked with meats to flavor them. (See later section *Beef* for vegetable soup made with beef bone.)

Do not cook vegetables with meats to season them...1586-1

Vegetables such as celery, English (or garden) peas and butter beans, which carry dissolving fluids, should be included in the diet.

We would keep at all times sufficient quantities of a vegetable nature carrying a great amount of the dissolving fluids in the system, such as we find in...some of the vegetables that grow above the ground...celery, English peas, butter beans—vegetables of this character...   228-1

For many persons it is advisable that the salt intake be of the kelp variety, derived from sea vegetables, or of the deep-sea variety, rather than of the purified sort.

Do use only the health salt or kelp salt or deep sea salt. All of these are of the same characters. But they are better than just that which has been purified, for the general health of many and this body in particular.   2084-16

Intake of salt of any variety should, however, be limited.

Q-7a. *Is salt harmful?*
A-7a. In excess, harmful. That there is salt in the blood, in the tears, in every secretion of the body, indicates that it becomes a necessary element—in moderation; unless those properties are taken that *produce* same in its activity through the system.   404-6

Beet sugar or unclarified cane sugar, both derived from plants, are the best sort for everyone.

Q-15. *Suggest best sugars for body.*
A-15. Beet sugars are the better for *all,* or the cane sugars that are not clarified [turbinado sugar?].   1131-2

Yellow vegetables, as well as yellow fruits, contain vitamins B and B-1. A daily intake of these vitamins is vital to the body since they are not stored as are vitamins A, C, D and G. Food sources are better than those of tablets or capsules.

Q-32. *What foods are the best sources of vitamin B?*
A-32. And B-1. All of those that are of the yellow variety, in fruits and vegetables. Also in many of those are the acids that go with same.
Q-33. *How often should these foods be used weekly?*
A-33. Have rather regular days or periods in which these foods or fruits are taken, or take some portion of them every day. This is a vitamin that is not stored as is A, D, C or G but needs to be supplied each day.
So keep an excess of foods that carry vitamin B, iron and such. Not the concentrated form. . .but obtain these from the foods. These would include all fruit, all vegetables that are yellow in their nature. Thus lemon and orange juice combined, all citrus fruit juices; pineapple as well as grapefruit. Some of these should be part of the diet each day.
Squash—especially the yellow; carrots, cooked and raw; yellow peaches; yellow apples (preferably the apples cooked, however).
All of these carry an excess or the greater quantity of necessary elements for supplying energies for the body, and... are much more easily assimilated by the body.
Yellow corn, yellow corn meal, buckwheat—all of these are

especially good.

Red cabbage. Such vegetables, such fruits, are especially needed by the body [of this individual]. 1968-7

All of those fruits and vegetables then that are yellow in color should be taken; oranges, lemons, grapefruit, yellow squash, yellow corn, yellow peaches—all of these and such as these; beets—but all of the vegetables cooked in their own juices, and the body eating the juices with same. 2529-1

Note that red cabbage and beets are recommended along with the yellow fruits and vegetables.

Q-13. Should B-1 be taken at the same time?
A-13. This depends upon whether the foods taken carry sufficient quantity of B-1. B-1 is a vitamin not stored in body, but it is necessary that there be the consumption of such each day. While A, C, D and G at times attempt to take the place of same, the B-1 activity is much better taken in foods than in the segregated pellets or capsules. When it is impractical for obtaining the foods with sufficient quantities for the daily needs, very well to take B-1. But to overstress same may at times cause the reaction of the *very* distress that is attempting to be aided!

All foods yellow in their nature, that are naturally yellow, carry B-1. Re-enforced flour, and especially whole wheat, corn flakes, most cereals—if re-enforced with same. So, a normal helping of such each day is about a *fifth* of that necessary. Also it is found in orange juice, citrus fruit juices, the juice and the pulp of grapefruit and the like, and in *all* cereals, and in bread; and especially the *green* leaves of lettuce—not so much in the beautiful white pieces. The green pieces are usually thrown away, and the hearts of lettuce kept that aren't worth very much as food for individuals. Hence lettuce of the leafy variety is really better for the body, carrying the greater source of the nicotinic acid.

Q-14. Yellow peaches in the can?
A-14. All good. Yellow corn meal, squash and every food that is naturally yellow in color. Carrots, raw and cooked—all of these. 257-236

The B-1 should be rich in the foods which are taken. We would find this from all foods which are yellow in color, not as greens that would turn yellow, but as the yellow variety of squash, carrots, wax beans, peaches, all these are well. 5319-1

The actions in the body of some specific vegetables are noted

128

in the readings. Asparagus carries a high percentage of carbons. It is blood building and nerve building and acts as a diuretic. Only fresh asparagus should be used, and this should be cooked.

...vegetables that carry a high percentage of carbons such as asparagus. 4439-1

Cooked vegetables...those that are...blood building...as... asparagus. 5515-1

Take those that are not just *fat* building, but *nerve* building, and those that carry some, as may be termed, *just fodder* in the system; as will be seen in. . .asparagus, and such—that are taken as *green* vegetables. 102-2

...such as asparagus, very little, but this has a diuretic that is good for the system. This, of course, cooked (the asparagus). 4605-1

Beets and beet tops are cited as being healing within and without and should be used plentifully, though only in quantity sufficient to satisfy the appetite.

In the diet, keep those things that heal within and without. A great deal of celery, lettuce and tomatoes, and especially use the garden blueberry. . .Also use plenty of watercress, beets and especially beet tops. These of course are to be used in sufficient quantity to satisfy the appetite but not to make any of them become as something disliked. So prepare them in many different forms. 3118-1

Beets are suggested as a good source of vitamins D and G. They may also have a beneficial effect on the optic nerves.

Do take D and G, but these more in the foods than supplementing in the combinations...that is, in the food value take... plenty of. . .beets. 1695-2

. . .add a great deal of vegetables that have a direct bearing upon the optic forces through the general system; such as carrots, green peas and green beans, onions, beets. All of these have a direct bearing upon the application of that assimilated for the optic forces. 3552-1

Because of the iodine and calcium in them, beets and beet tops can have a healing effect upon the lymph circulation and even destroy certain types of bacilli. The beet tops purify the *humor* in the lymph blood, absorbed by the lacteal ducts during digestion.

Do have oft for the body those properties that carry a great deal of iodine and calcium. . .especially. . .beets and beet tops. These are healing in their activity upon the lymph circulation. They are even capable of destroying certain characters of bacilli in the system. 3056-1

. . .beet tops. . .make for purifying of the *humor* in the lymph blood as this is absorbed by the lacteal ducts as it is digested. 840-1

Beets, celery and radishes are cleansing for the body.

Take as food values much that carries the iron, the silicon, the stabilizing condition for the system; such as we find in certain vegetables, as beets, celery, radishes; all of those natures that give the cleansing forces to the system. 257-11

[3316] was advised not to combine beets with vinegar. For [3405] fresh beets would be preferable to pickled ones.

. . .carrots, beets, watercress. . .should never be combined with any vinegar or acetic acid. 3316-1

. . .beets. . .preferably not those that have been pickled but fresh beets. 3405-1

Fresh young beets and beet tops are especially valuable.

Especially have beets, particularly those that are fresh and young. And do train the body to eat the beet tops as well as the young beets themselves. 2963-1

[482], who was suffering from stomach ulcers, was advised to abstain from eating the bulbs of beets although she could eat the tops.

In the evening meals. . .well-cooked vegetables, but only those of the leafy nature—or that grow in pods. . .no carrots, no beets, no turnips, nothing of that nature. The *tops* of these. . . may be eaten, but not the bulb. . . 482-3

Cabbage is nerve and blood building. For one person who needed blood building, only red cabbage was advised.

Let the diet be. . .nerve and blood building. If cabbage is taken let it be raw, rather than cooked.   3842-1

Evenings—cooked vegetables. . .those that are of the blood building. . .Those of cabbage, the red cabbage only. This. . . taken in small quantities.   5515-1

The readings explain that cabbage boiled with meat produces an acidity in the body when it is under the strain of fatigue or hyperactivity but that cabbage without the meat produces an alkaline reaction within the body under the same strain.

Study just a bit the vegetables and the general food values of *all* foods; as to how they react to the body. . .
When the body is under stress or strain by being tired, overactive, and then would eat heavy foods as cabbage boiled with meat—these would produce acidity; yet cabbage *without* the meats would produce an alkaline reaction *under* the same conditions!   1411-2

There are admonitions for particular persons against cooking cabbage with meats, with grease or with a quantity of grease.

Pot liquor and cabbage raw and cooked, but *not with meats*— cook them in their *own* juices, and with butter. . .   1560-1

The cabbage should be taken cooked and raw, but not cooked with grease.   415-8

Not the raw cabbage. Cabbage as prepared *without* too much grease is well, for it carries a great deal of iron and silicon, as well as traces of active forces in the system that are good so long as they digest well with the body.   1713-16

A 10-year-old girl with pinworms was advised to make raw cabbage the chief constituent of her three meals during one day and to chew this slowly and very thoroughly.

. . .have one whole day, morning, noon and evening meal, with practically nothing save raw cabbage; this eaten slowly, chewed very, *very* well. . .the worms. . .will be reacted upon by the day's use and activity of the cabbage upon the system.
1401-2

[719] who was suffering from duodenal ulcers and toxemia

was advised against eating sauerkraut.

Beware of stimuli. . .No kraut, or such.   **719-1**

However, a person suffering from constipation and poor assimilations was advised to take small amounts of kraut juice in the evening.

Small quantities of kraut juice would be well, but this taken of evening, not of morning.   **2595-1**

The hard tops of carrots contain vital energies which stimulate the reactions between kidneys and optics.

Q-1. What is the best diet for this body?
A-1. Now that which is a well-balanced diet. But often use the raw vegetables which are prepared with gelatin. Use these at least three times each week. Those which grow more above the ground than those that grow below the ground. Do include, when these are prepared, carrots with that portion especially close to the top. It may appear the harder and the less desirable, but it carries the vital energies, stimulating the optic reactions between kidneys and the optics.   **3051-6**

Carrots are a source of nicotinic acid. (See reference 1158-31 under salsify, this section.)
According to the readings a daily intake of carrots, celery and/or lettuce can keep a person immunized against infectious diseases.

Q-1. Are inoculations against contagious diseases necessary for me before sailing. . .?
A-1. So far as the body-physical condition is concerned, the adherence to the use of carrots, lettuce and celery *every* day at a meal. . .will insure against any contagious infectious forces with which the body may be in contact.
As indicated, if an alkalinity is maintained in the system—especially lettuce, carrots and celery, these in the blood supply will maintain such a condition as to immunize a person. 480-19

[3267] was to take plenty of carrots but no vinegar with them.

. . .take plenty of carrots, but not with vinegar.   **3267-1**

There is a warning against carrots that have had any preservative on them (doubtless against mold).

Use plenty of carrots, both raw and cooked. . .but these cooked in their *own* juices (as in Patapar paper) and never those that have had any kind of preservatives on same.

1970-2

Cauliflower may be eaten raw, doubtless in salads.

Q-12. Raw cauliflower?
A-12. This about twice a week would be sufficient [for this body].   1158-21

Cauliflower should not be creamed.

. . .cauliflower is very well when well prepared, but not creamed.   3642-1

We have just noted that a daily intake of carrots, celery and lettuce can immunize a person against contagious diseases, according to reading 480-19. Ingestion of celery and lettuce may obviate the need for smallpox vaccine, according to the following excerpt.

Q-10. Will the vaccination against smallpox be detrimental?
A-10. Depends upon when it is administered. When it [the child] is a little older give plenty of celery and lettuce, and you won't ever have to vaccinate, or if you will keep vaccine from milk or cow about the body, vaccine will not take.   3172-2

Celery is nerve and blood building. Most of its substance is assimilated.

Let the diet be. . .nerve and blood building. . .vegetables. . .as plenty of celery and the leafy vegetables.   3842-1

Q-3. Outline proper diet for body.
A-3. That as will give to the nerve system more of the *energy* . . .necessary. . .those. . .vegetables that are nerve building. Those that do not carry too much of the value of just weight, but that carry more *with* same that. . .is *assimilated* in system. As may be illustrated in this: In those. . .green vegetables. . .the celery; these do not carry so much dross, but are *mostly* all assimilated. . .   5475-2

Celery may be helpful to the eyes. It may improve blood coagulation. It may help to overcome constipation.

Q-3. What further treatment should be applied for her eye condition?

A-3. . . .give the body *plenty* of celery, lettuce and carrots. Have some. . .in the meal each day.   2004-4

Be sure there is plenty of. . .celery, as a part of the diet. This will enable the blood supply to be so improved as to make better coagulation when such would be necessary.   1787-3

Q-2. What should the body do to overcome constipation?
A-2. [Eat] a great deal of vegetables, especially those that give iron, as. . .celery. . .   1713-17

We are told that celery carries a high percentage of carbons and also B-complex.

. . .vegetables that carry a high percentage of carbons such as celery.   4439-1

We should have easily assimilated foods, but those very high in the adding of B-complex. . .as in celery. . .   3285-1

It is best not to combine celery and lettuce with radishes and onions.

Have plenty of vegetables and especially one meal each day should include some raw or uncooked vegetables. But here, too, combinations must be kept in line. Do not take onions and radishes at the same meal with celery and lettuce, though either of these may be taken at different times. . .   2732-1

We learned previously in "Ingestion of Food, Air and Water Containing Mineral Forces" under *Gold,* that gold, silicon and phosphorus may be found in eggplant if grown in certain (proper?) locations. (1000-2) This vegetable can contain iron, iodine and phosphorus in quantity.

Supply an overabundant amount of those foods that carry iron, iodine and phosphorus in the system. . .We will find much in. . .eggplant.   951-1

A person suffering from toxemia was advised to eat eggplant.

The eggplant. . .to be sure will assist.   569-25

For garlic, see text dealing with onions and garlic.
Cooked green beans were advised for cold and congestion.

Q-4. What vegetables are especially good for my body,

considering the condition of kidneys?

A-4. Cooked beans (and these should be green beans, or canned green beans—though not preserved with any preservative such as benzoate of soda). 404-10

The Jerusalem artichoke is insulin-reacting according to the readings and may, therefore, be used to curb diabetic tendencies or in the treatment of diabetes. Note, however, that in the excerpts below very particular directions are given as to the limited use of this rather potent vegetable. Different amounts are indicated for different stages of the affliction. It goes without saying that a person without diabetic tendencies who ingests a sizable amount of this tuber may find himself reacting in a fashion similar to that of the diabetic who has taken too much insulin for his circumstances. Such a reaction is not a pleasant one.

Q-4. [What about my] craving for sweets?

A-4. This is natural with the indigestion and the lack of proper activity of the pancreas. Eat a Jerusalem artichoke once each week, about the size of a hen egg. Cook this in Patapar paper, preserving all the juices to mix with the bulk of the artichoke. Season to taste. This will also aid in the disorder in the circulation between liver and kidneys, pancreas and kidneys, and will relieve these tensions from the desire for sweets. 3386-2

For *this* body, as indicated, the properties in the Jerusalem artichoke should be taken not more than once a week; and alternate the manner in which they are taken. One week cook same—this means one about the size of a hen egg. . .and this to be cooked in Patapar paper until it is done, but not overdone, but mashed in its own juices and eaten. The next week it may be taken raw—one about the same size. . .But do not take large quantities. And this is to be taken with *other* foods, as a part of the meal, and *not* alone. . . 2039-2

Occasionally—once a week or oftener—the Jerusalem artichoke should be a part of the diet. This will tend to correct those inclinations for the incoordination between the activities of the pancreas as related to the kidneys and bladder. These, as we find, even in this form, will make for better corrections. 1523-7

Q-1. Is the body diabetic?

A-1. A tendency. We find that these conditions exist: There is too much sugar in the activities of the kidneys. There is a torpidity in the activity of the liver. There is a slowing of the circulation to the head and to the heart *and* the general chest.

This. . .with the slowing activity, tends to leave a toxic condition; not that may be termed of a malarial-producing nature, but would eventually cause a strep formation in the blood, with the conditions which exist in the blood flow itself, and the excess tendency of activity of kidneys. . .[Directions follow for diet.]

And twice each week take the Jerusalem artichoke, about the size of a hen egg; first raw—say on Tuesdays—and the next time cooked, say on Thursdays, but cooked in its own juices (as in Patapar paper). Only eat one each time. . .When cooked, season it to make it palatable, but do not eat the skin—save the juices and mash with the pulp when it is to be eaten. Eat it with the meal, of course; whether it is taken raw or cooked. Do not take it between meals, but at the regular meal. . .*do not* take injections of insulin. If more insulin is necessary than is obtained from eating the amount of artichoke indicated, then increase the number of days during the week of taking the artichoke. . .   1963-2

Instead of using so much insulin; this can be gradually diminished and eventually eliminated entirely if there is used in the diet one Jerusalem artichoke every other day. This should be cooked only in Patapar paper, preserving the juices and mixing with the bulk of the artichoke, seasoning this to suit the taste. The taking of the insulin is habit forming. The artichoke is not habit forming, not sedative-producing in the body [so] as to cause accumulations of poisons as do sedatives; though it will be necessary to take a sedative when there are the attacks, but take a hypnotic rather than a narcotic—only under the direction, however, of a physician. . .   4023-1

And *especially* artichoke, preferably the Jerusalem artichoke; this not with vinegar, to be sure, but this should be taken—a little of it—for *every* evening meal! This carries those properties that are as of an insulin reaction, that will produce a cleansing for the kidneys as well as producing the tendency for the reduction of the excess sugar that is indicated in the inflammation noted in blood tests in the present.

Do not give the injections of insulin, but those properties as indicated that may act with same. [Other directions follow.]
                                                                        480-39

The Jerusalem artichoke should be a portion of the diet each day. This would be taken preferably cooked, but it may be

136

taken raw if preferable. The insulin from same—as it is easily assimilated for the activities. . .of the pancreas and spleen and liver activity. . .will aid in reducing the inclination for the inflammation and pus activity in the kidney itself. One artichoke the size of a duck egg or turkey egg, or thereabouts, should be taken each day, that is, the tuber of the Jerusalem artichoke. 1885-1

A very positive reaction may be had that will relieve a great deal of this tension, if there will be eaten each day—with the meal—a Jerusalem artichoke; one day cooked, the next day raw; one not larger than about the size of a hen egg. Preferably keep these fresh, not by being put in the refrigerator but by keeping them in the ground; by necessity protecting them from animals—dogs, hogs. . .or the like; for these will scratch 'em up—as would cats also!

There is needed that booster, or the effect of insulin as may be derived from the artichoke, for the system. . .As to the matter of diet (other than artichoke), refrain from those foods that tend towards creating sugar; as excess of starches or sweets.

A little honey may be taken occasionally.

Yellow corn meal is very good for the body, in whatever way it may be prepared; whether made into spoon bread, egg bread, cakes or the like.

The wheat germ oil would be beneficial, taken in moderation; that is, one to two drops a day; but *not* white flour or wheaten flour so much. Rather use the rye bread and the corn bread.

The meats should be rather fish and fowl—though no fried foods.

Use the leafy vegetables rather than those of the pod variety.
. . .If sweetening is desired. . .use either honey or saccharin.
2472-1

The juice of cooked kale is the most valuable portion.

Q-7. Are vegetables such as. . .kale, etc., good for me now?
A-7. Good if these are well cooked, but not in a lot of grease. These should be cooked in their own juices and the juice taken as well as the vegetable. For the effective or more healthful portion of kale is in the water that comes from same by cooking. 1688-8

Lentils are blood and nerve building. They serve as a counter-irritant to activity in the kidneys.

In the noon day those. . .vegetables that care for the blood and nerve building, and that will produce not an overactivity but. . .a counter*irritant*. . .activity in the kidneys, which will reduce the stimuli in the circulation in the hepatics. These we will find in. . .the vegetable forces that grow especially in pods, as. . .lentils.   5625-1

Lettuce may be eaten in its normal state or grated or juiced.

At least a portion of this meal should include lettuce. . . Arrange. . .[it] differently so it does not become abhorrent to the body; sometimes in. . .[the] regular state, other times grated, other times prepared in juice form.   2873-1

Lettuce can be helpful to the glandular system and also to the sensory system.

The condition to aid, then, is the *diet—and* that which *is* a stimulus to the glandular forces *and* the forces of body where assimilations are carried on.
Each day have. . .quantities of lettuce.   630-3

Have a great deal of. . .lettuce, mixed with gelatin. These are good for the body. They will aid in all portions of the sensory system, especially in the eyes, the ears, and the drainages through the antrum and the soft tissue of head for these supply elements that keep these portions of the body bettered.
                                                                   462-18

Lettuce carries a quantity of iron and salts.

. . .raw vegetables. . .carrying plenty of iron and of salts; such as. . .lettuce. . .   4605-1

Lettuce is a purifier which takes care of most undesirable influences attacking the bloodstream.

Q-7. Should plenty of lettuce be eaten?
A-7. Plenty of lettuce should always be eaten by most *every* body; for this supplies an effluvium in the bloodstream itself that is a destructive force to *most* of those influences that attack the bloodstream. It's a purifier.   404-6

Leaf lettuce is more sleep-inducing than the iceberg variety.

. . .lettuce. . .preferably that that does not head—for this body; more soporiferous than. . .the iceberg.   5557-1

The gluten in okra is body building.

...too often the inclinations have been for not sufficient of
the body building forces. Hence. . .all those foods carrying
quantities of gluten as okra. . .   694-4

Okra may also help with elimination and strengthen the
body.

Also it would help to keep better eliminations for the body
regularly. These may be controlled best. . .for this particular
body by the diet. So include often. . .okra. . .it will change the
general elimination and increase the strengthening of the
body. . .   3148-1

[2376] was advised against eating okra either fried or
prepared with vinegar.

...have plenty of okra whenever possible, even though it is
canned, but not that which has vinegar in same. These and
such characters, provided they are not fried, should be a
portion of the diet.   2376-1

Onions should be eaten both raw and cooked.

Plenty of onions, raw as well as cooked.   480-52

Cooking onions in Patapar paper will preserve the juices.

Q-5. . . .the best way for onions to be cooked. . .to get the
juice?
A-5. Steamed.
Q-6. Would cooking them in Patapar paper be a good way?
A-6. This is an excellent way. . .   572-2

Onions and garlic by stimulating thyroid activity can help
improve the skin on fingers and toes and also the condition of
the hair.

...there are conditions causing disturbances with this body.
These are because of improper coordination of the activities of
the inner and outer glandular force as related to the thyroid.
This allows for deficiencies in certain chemical forces,
especially as related to the epidermis, or the activities in the
toes and the fingers and the hair. . .
There is that which has caused much of the disturbance—a
long-standing subluxation existent in the 3rd and 4th lumbar

centers, which prevents the perfect circulation through the glands of the thyroid area. [Directions follow for osteopathic adjustments and other applications. Then]

Do eat more of seafoods, more carrots, and—while certain times will have to be chosen for such—do eat onions and garlic.

3904-1

In *Nature's Medicines* Richard Lucas devotes an entire chapter to garlic, "the bulb with miracle healing powers." He cites its use in cases of high blood pressure, tuberculosis, intestinal difficulties, colds, whooping cough and other disorders.[24] He also tells us of the discovery by a Russian electrobiologist, Professor Gurwitch, that onions emit a peculiar type of ultraviolet radiation, known as mitogenetic, which stimulates cell growth and activity. Cell proliferation is aroused when these rays from the growing center of one onion impinge on the growing center of another. Garlic and ginseng also emit this mitogenetic radiation. It appears to have a rejuvenating effect.[25]

Raw green peppers affect digestion, increasing pyloric action on the duodenum. They should be eaten in moderation, combined with other green salad foods.

Q-6. What is the food value of raw green peppers?
A-6. They are better in combinations than by themselves. Their tendency is for an activity to the pylorus; not the activity in the pylorus itself, but more in the activity from the flow of the pylorus to the churning effect upon the duodenum in its digestion. Hence it is an activity for *digestive* forces.

Peppers, then, taken with green cabbage, lettuce, are very good for this body; taken in moderation.   404-6

Although pokeweed is generally not considered a vegetable, in the springtime its burgeoning shoots are often eaten as a delicacy. With proper preparation they taste much like asparagus. The readings endorse this practice and explain that the young shoots act as a purifier for the body.

Eat very young poke—the tender shoots of the pokeweed—to act as a purifier for the body. Prepare it in this manner: When cutting sufficient to make a small dish or salad, put in cold water and let come to a boil. Strain or drain off, as in the

[24]Richard Lucas, *Nature's Medicines*, Award Books, New York City, copyright c 1966 by Parker Pub. Co., Inc., pp. 40-58.
[25]*Ibid.*, pp. 162-163.

colander—or put in a colander and let all the juice drain off. Then prepare or cook the remaining leaves with other greens, especially such as lamb's tongue and wild mustard—about an equal quantity. This eaten once a week will purify the whole body. 3515-1

. . .the foods that act as clarifiers or purifiers to the blood supply; such as poke salad. . .Cook the very tender leaves, allow to come almost to a boil and pour off the first water, then put in fresh, clear, cold water, and cook a few minutes. 2985-1

. . .carrots or beets or beet tops. . .These should be cooked, even the beet tops—very soon cook with the tender shoots of poke; not, however, without the poke having been first prepared, but these are especially blood purifiers, adding to. . . the body forces. Prepare the poke by first putting in cold water, letting it come almost to a boil; then drain, as through a colander—the water will be rather greenish. Then it may be cooked with the beet tops. 2948-1

Too many potatoes may cause excess liver activity in the production of fermentations. However, certain forms of potatoes (unspecified) may contribute to the better functioning of the thyroid and thymus glands.

As to the diet for the body—keep away from *fried foods!* or from those things that cause too much of the activity of the liver to be producing fermentations—as white bread or potatoes—though potatoes in some forms are well for the body, especially as they will make for a better activity for the thyroid and thymus gland, and thus cause better reaction as the corrections are made. 1935-1

The forms of potatoes recommended above would appear to be the peelings of Irish potatoes which are strengthening in their effect upon the glands. This may even result in bringing added luster to the hair. However, these peelings should be not boiled but cooked in Patapar paper to preserve the valuable properties.

. . .the peelings of. . .[potatoes] may be taken at all times— they are strengthening, carrying those influences and forces that are active with the glands of the system. 820-2

Q-4. What foods or treatments are especially good for bringing more of the luster—reds, coppers, and golds—back into the hair?

A-4. Nothing better than the peelings of Irish potatoes or the juices from same. Don't just put the peelings in water and cook them, because most of the necessary properties will go out, but put them in Patapar paper to cook them.   2072-14

This portion of Irish potatoes may be secured from their jackets if the potatoes are roasted, boiled or baked. It brings strength and vitality to structural parts of the body.

. . .the skins of Irish potatoes—whether roasted or boiled or baked—are well for the body; for the salts that are in same close to the peel will supply starch *and* carbohydrates in (such) a manner that the activities of the vitamins A and D are in such proportions as to build strength and vitality in the structural portions, and in the tendons and the muscular forces, such as to build resistance—and not build fat.   1073-1

The part of the potato directly under the jacket has in addition to the values cited, properties that are neither acid-producing nor too starchy.

In the diet, beware of too much starches of *any* kind; that is, do *not* include potatoes. . .However, *roast* potatoes with the jackets would be all right, if there would be eaten only the jackets and the small portion that adheres to the jacket—for this portion of the potato carries properties that are *not* acid-producing and not too great an amount of starch; but do not eat the bulk of the potato!   632-6

The bulk of Irish potatoes other than the peelings is of little value and might properly be discarded.

Add to the diet the Irish potato *peel,* but not the pulp a great deal. It would be better if the nice potatoes are cleansed, peeled and only the *peelings* cooked and eaten. Throw the other part away and give it to the chickens, or distribute it in some manner besides eating it.   1904-1

Pumpkins are a source of nicotinic acid. (See 1158-31 under salsify, this section.)
Radishes cut or grated or scraped provide more food values than those taken whole.

Radishes are also well, provided they are cut or grated or scraped. Taken in such a manner these release elements that are not released even in digestion, when taken whole. 3422-1

Rhubarb is mildly stimulating to the lymphatic and excretory systems of the body. It may, therefore, be useful as a slight laxative.

Eliminating foods, of course, are preferable. . .as in. . .any of the vegetables that are an active force for not too great a stimulation for the lymph and emunctory activity through the alimentary canal, but that are stimulating to same for better activity—as the pieplant [rhubarb], or similar foods that aid in such activity.   1885-1

Q-3. Would a mild laxative be advisable occasionally?
A-3. Those of any of the fruits (or vegetables) [that] tend to make for same. . .very good. . .Pieplant [rhubarb], figs, prunes, prune whip—these are, or would be laxatives for this system.
                                                                        348-13

When it is necessary to take any form of cathartic, that which is of the vegetable nature would be the better, but this will not be necessary if we will have at least one meal each day of wholly citrus fruit diet, or the pieplant—as is concentrated.
                                                                        5592-1

Noons. . .During those periods when there is little of the activity, so that there are not the normal eliminations, well that vegetables or fruits that are the more laxative in form be used as a portion of the meal; such as rhubarb. . .these should be either fresh or those canned without any superficial or artificial preservative.   3823-2

Salsify is an especially good source of niacin or nicotinic acid.

. . .nicotinic acid. . .the. . .source. . .in vegetables—carrots, squash, pumpkin and especially. . .what is called the oyster plant [salsify].   1158-31

Salsify tends to eliminate hardening centers in tendons. It supplies nature's sugars, nature's laxatives. It contributes to the strength, endurance and activity of mind and body. It is blood building.

. . .those foods such as salsify or oyster plant, especially— that carry. . .characters of salts that tend to eliminate these hardening centers in the tendons of the body.   2579-1

One meal each day we would supply principally. . .[of]

nature's sugars, nature's laxatives. . .A great deal of those forces may be found in. . .salsify.   951-1

Q-4. What special foods would give to the mind and body great strength, endurance and activity?
A-4. All of the vegetable, especially those of. . .salsify. . .
                                        3190-2

. . .cooked vegetables. . .those that are of the blood building in the vegetables—as. . .salsify. . .   5515-1

Salsify may be prepared with a little cream or used in soups and broths or cooked in its own juices. The author uses Patapar paper and a pressure cooker.

The oyster plant. . .prepared with not too much butter—but a little cream.   1302-1

Have soups, broths or the like, and these should include the oyster plant. . .   2873-1

. . .oyster plant. . .cooked in. . .[its] own juices, saving the salts or the water in which. . .cooked as a part of the diet. 1989-1

The green portion of spinach, lettuce and celery contains from twenty to forty percent more of the vitamins necessary for good health than does the white part.

When the spinach, lettuce or celery is selected, use the green portion rather than that which has been bleached. These portions have from twenty to forty percent more of the vitamins necessary for the sustaining of the better health, than those portions that are bleached by being covered or being forced into such a state.   920-13

Spinach may be eaten raw.

. . .the entirely green raw vegetables, such as. . .the raw spinach. These may be taken with whole wheat wafers with a mayonnaise or salad dressing.   631-6

Spinach. . .may be taken, either green, cooked, or in whatever way is most palatable for the body.   808-6

Squash contains nicotinic acid. (See 1158-31 under salsify.) In the discussion of the value of yellow vegetables (earlier in this section), we found that these vegetables carried vitamins

144

B and B-1. Squash, especially the yellow variety, was recommended for an intake of these. (1968-7)

Although tomatoes are normally classified as fruits, they are designated by the readings as vegetables. (See 584-5, following.) We will, therefore, so consider them. We are told that tomatoes, properly grown, contain more vitamins, well-balanced and easily assimilated, than any other vegetable does. However, if they are not vine-ripened, they may have a harmful effect on the body. In most cases canned tomatoes are more uniform in content than raw and, therefore, preferable. Tomatoes are generally non-acid-forming; but at times the body may react to them by forming an acid of its own. This may explain why they should not be eaten with meats, sugar, a great deal of starch, vinegars or acetic acids. (For further discussion of this subject see *Ill Effects of Improperly Ripened Fruits* under the section "Fruits, Grains, Beans and Nuts.") Tomatoes, if properly ripened, may be used with lettuce as a salad. Eating them alone with just a little salt is especially beneficial. In general, tomatoes should be eaten three or four times a week; but taking too great a quantity may affect the pancreas, the prostate and other glands.

Q-2. *What has been the effect on my system of eating so many tomatoes?*
A-2. Quite a dissertation might be given as to the effect of tomatoes upon the human system. Of all the vegetables, tomatoes carry most of the vitamins in a well-balanced assimilative manner for the activities in the system. Yet if these are not cared for properly, they may become very destructive to a physical organism; that is, if they ripen after being pulled, or if there is the contamination with other influences.

In *this* particular body...the reactions from these have been not *always* the *best*. Neither has there been the normal reaction from the eating of same. For it tends to make for an irritation or humor. Nominally [normally?], though, these [tomatoes] should form at least a portion of a meal three or four days out of every week; and they will be found to be *most* helpful.

The tomato is one vegetable that in most instances (because of greater uniform activity) is preferable to be eaten after being canned, for it is then much more uniform.

The reaction in this body, then, has been to form an acid of its own; though the tomato is among those foods that may usually be taken as the *non*-acid-forming. But these [tomatoes] should be of the best in *every* instance where they are used! 584-5

Q-10. Are tomatoes harmful?
A-10. Tomatoes that are pulled green and ripened off of the vine are harmful. Ripened on the vine, no.
Q-11. Are there any special foods with which tomatoes should not be eaten?
A-11. These should not be eaten with meats, sugars or vinegars. 379-10

Q-3. Are tomatoes good?
A-3. This depends, too, upon what combinations. If they are taken with a great deal of starch, no. If taken with vinegar or acetic acids, or such combinations, no. If they are taken with lettuce as a salad, as a part of the meal, very good. If taken alone with a little salt, *very* good. 257-210

Tomatoes good, but not in excess, for they would rather influence the juices of the pancreas—some portions, especially along the prostate and other glands of this nature. 228-1

A woman suffering from eczema and athlete's foot was advised to avoid the mixture of acids resulting from ingestion of tomatoes and peaches at the same meal. Each could be taken separately.

. . .*never* combine peaches with tomatoes at the same meal— but either of these in moderation may be taken occasionally.
2332-1

Yellow yams contain vitamins B-1, A and G.

. . .keep. . .plenty of the vitamins, especially B-1, A and G. These will be found. . .in. . .yellow yams. . . 2015-8

The need to use only very fresh vegetables, whether in raw or cooked form, is brought out in the following.

As it is so well advertised that coffee loses its value in fifteen to twenty to twenty-five days after being roasted, so do foods or vegetables lose their food value after being gathered—in the same proportion in hours as coffee would in days.
340-31

Vegetables are important for an active brain.

Vegetables will build gray matter faster than will meat or sweets! 900-386

They also stimulate the blood supply, which brings nerve energy.

Q-4. *Any particular diet for this body?*
A-4. . . .if we take these properties into the system we are giving here for blood force as the gold and soda, the natural tendency and call for the system will be for those things that are increasing the life-giving fluids in the body. Blood makes nerve energy, nerve force, nerve-supplying energies to the arterial and venous active principles so that what the system calls for let it have. You will find it will be much [more]. . . vegetable matter that will be taken rather than meats. Only occasionally, if ever, any meat taken or used in the system.
3975-1

. . .especially nerve building forces in blood. . .vegetable matter that grows above the ground. . .   **4120-1**

Fruits, Grains, Beans and Nuts

The food values to be obtained from fruits, grains, beans and nuts—all the end products of plants—have been touched on previously in the section "Ingestion of Food, Air and Water Containing Mineral Forces." It seems timely to review this material briefly before adding to it.

Calcium, we learned, is found in watermelon, limes, grapefruit, oranges, almonds and filberts; gold in fruits and nuts; iodine in oranges and especially pears; iron in apples and pears particularly, in whole grains, buckwheat, all berries, yellow fruits, including yellow peaches, yellow apples, lemons, oranges, grapefruits, all citrus fruit juices and pineapples; iron and phosphorus in combination in fruits, including citrus fruits, and nuts, especially almonds; iron, silicon and lithium to build the blood supply in fruits; phosphorus in citrus fruit juices; phosphorus and gold in fruits and nuts; and silicon in fruits and nuts.

Fruits

Apples
We have previously noted that apples, especially yellow apples, were recommended in the readings for their iron content (1968-7) and that they affect the blood. (4841-1) However the variety of apples used is very important. Jonathan or jenneting apples are preferable, whether raw or

cooked. These include the Black Arkansas, the Oregon Red, the Sheepnose, the Delicious, the Arkansas Russet. (The jenneting variety resembles an early pear.)

In the following references both the kind of raw apple and details of the three-day raw apple diet are brought out.

We would use first the apple diet to purify the system; that is, for three days eat nothing but apples of the Jonathan variety if possible. This includes the Delicious, which is a variety of the Jonathan. The Jonathan is usually grown farther north than the Delicious, but these are of the same variety, but eat some. You may drink coffee if you desire, but do not put milk or cream in it, especially while you are taking the apples.

At the end of the third day, the next morning take about two tablespoonsful of olive oil. 780-12

If a three-day purge is to be taken, *we* would advise rather the three-day diet of *only* raw apples; though a little coffee or tea may be taken if desired, but eat all the apples you can! Then on the evening of the third day, upon retiring, take two tablespoonsful of *pure* olive oil.

Q-6. *May I take something to insure daily bowel movements. . .*

A-6. If the purge is taken of the apple diet, and then the proper osteopathic manipulations given—especially in the areas indicated. . .it shouldn't be necessary for some time.

1158-30

Q-2. *Would it be well for the body to go on the three-day apple diet for cleansing of the system?*

A-2. Would be well.

Q-3. *Are the apples we have in the house. . .all right for this?*

A-3. All right for this. Those that pertain to. . .the Jonathan variety. . .or the jenneting; the Black Arkansas, the Oregon Red. . .the Sheepnose, the Delicious, the Arkansas Russet; any of those that are of the jenneting variety. 294-182

At the end of the third day of the apple diet, take half a cup (teacup) of olive oil. 361-7

Don't try to work like a horse when you are on the apple diet! or else. . .it will be more detrimental than helpful! But these cleansings will prevent the accumulations of gas, the pressures that make for the neuritis through the portions of the body. 307-14

Q-16. *Why did the apple diet fail and was it harmful?*

A-16. . . .this would not have failed if there had not been the needs for undue changes during those periods. It is often necessary for this to be repeated more than once, to become really effective.   1158-31

Raw apples are not well unless they are of the jenneting variety.   820-2

From the above references we find that the olive oil follow-up to the apple diet may be either two tablespoonsful or a half a cup and that the first may be taken on the third evening or the following morning while the latter should be taken at the end of the third day. The person on this three-day diet should not work unduly. Sometimes it is necessary to take this treatment more than once if the body needs a great deal of purification.

The next reference underlines the desirability of cooked apples also being of the Jonathan or jenneting variety.

Cooked apples if they are of the jenneting variety may be given. None of those of the more woody variety, as those of Ben Davis or of Winesap, or of the fall or woody variety. These should *not* be given this body in *any* manner.   142-5

For some persons raw apples were not acceptable except when used in the three-day diet. However roasted (or baked) apples were.

No raw apples; or if raw apples are taken, take them and nothing else—three days of raw apples only, and then olive oil, and we will cleanse *all* toxic forces from any system!. . .Apples cooked, apples roasted, are good.   820-2

The fruits that may be taken: plums, pears, and apples. Do not take raw apples, but roast apples a-plenty.   5097-1

Stewed apples, likewise, were advised.

. . .stewed fruits (as figs, apples, peaches, or the like). . .623-1

Raw apples are not good for such conditions as gastritis (5622-3) and ulcerative colitis. (5178-1)

Q-1. Is raw fruit harmful [for 5622]?
A-1. *Apples* but not other fruits. Pears and all citrus fruits are *good*. Grapes without the seeds, well. Figs are very beneficial, whether the ripe or those as packed.   5622-3

> Fruits: beware of raw apples or of very sour peaches, but pears in season and plums will be well. The small fruits, as the berries, not too many of these.   5178-1

It would seem, however, that the eating of raw apples was allowable for some persons. [1968] was told that cooked apples were preferable, but the raw ones were not ruled out. [255] was advised to eat "some character of apples," obviously of the jenneting kind. [538] was told to alternate an apple with other raw fruits as an adjunct to a small dose of olive oil. (See reference under *Olives and Olive Oil.*) [913] was advised to eat an apple at every meal except breakfast, either raw or cooked. It was to be well ripened.

> . . .yellow apples (preferably the apples cooked, however). . .   1968-7

> In the fruits. . .some character of apples. . .   255-3

> At each meal, save the morning meal, have an apple (this may be raw or it may be cooked for this body). . .just so. . .[it is] *well* ripened; not the green nor those that have been stored too long.   913-1

For some years the author has personally enjoyed eating raw Golden Delicious apples, organically raised.

In a formula given for application to the skin, apple vinegar was recommended in place of synthetic vinegar or acetic acid. The inference is that the apple vinegar is more acceptable to the body.

> Not vinegar made from acetic acid or synthetic vinegar, but the use of that made from apples.   276-7

Bananas

The readings approve of the eating of bananas in moderation, but only those ripened on the plant. There is a warning against ingesting those that have been stored too long, also against eating bananas when under stress.

> Do not overtax the system with bananas, unless these are ripened in their natural state; for the activity of these in the beginnings of their deterioration—before they are palatable—makes for a hardship upon the system. But those that are overripe, or that have been gathered or prepared when they

were fully matured, may be taken in moderation at certain meals or times. 658-15

Q-6. Should she eat bananas now, raw or cooked?
A-6. Occasionally these may be taken, *raw.* Let them be well ripened though. 4281-17

Q-5. Are bananas all right? Do they have a bad effect on body?
A-5. Bananas if they are ripe are very well, but rarely is there a ripe banana in this vicinity [Virginia Beach].
257-210

No bananas unless you are in the territory where they are grown and ripened there. 820-2

. . .at each meal, save the morning meal, have. . .a banana. . . just so [it is] *well* ripened; not the green nor those that have been stored too long. 913-1

. . .whenever there is a great anxiety or stress, do not eat. . . bananas nor fruits of that nature which are acid-producing. . .
1724-1

Berries

Berries carry a large amount of dissolving fluids, which are needed in the body.

We would keep at all times sufficient quantities of a vegetable nature carrying a great amount of the dissolving fluids in the system, such as we find in those of the citrus fruits, berries and some of the vegetables that grow above the ground. . . 228-1

Some berries are more acid than others due to their place of growth. A person eating them needs food with silicon and iodine to balance.

Some [berries]. . .carry a great deal more acid than others; dependent a great deal upon where they are grown; that is, they carry too great a quantity of potash and thus require that an equal balance be created by taking sufficient quantities of such natures as carry silicon or iodine. 3823-4

Berries carry iron, silicon and phosphorus. Those growing close to the ground have extra iron. However berries should not grow on the ground.

...using fruits, berries...that carry iron, silicon, phosphorus and the like... 480-19

Diet for this body will be the greater force, these that carry as much of iron as possible, principally, of fruits in this character and nature such as. . .in berries, especially, those that grow on the ground, close. 4889-1

Let the diet be...nerve and blood building. Fruits...berries—provided they grow off of [the] ground, not *on* the ground... 3842-1

Berries help to build nerve forces and keep the eliminating properties in the blood. They are high in vitamin B and the vitamin B complex.

The diet...all those that lend energy to nerve building forces and those that give to the blood force the eliminating properties—berries and fruits... 4730-1

We should have. . .foods. . .very high in the adding of B complex, or the vitamin B—as in...berries whatever may be obtained... 3285-1

Berries may be eaten canned if fresh are not available.

Canned berries may be used if the fresh are not practical. 849-50

Berries are nature's sugars.

One meal each day we would supply principally of...nature's sugars...berries of most natures—any of the active principles in such...provided they are without any of the preservatives; currants and their derivatives... 951-1

Garden blueberries have properties that are healing to the body within and without. They should be stewed and eaten with their own juices and only a small amount of sugar.

In the diet, keep to those things that heal within and without. A great deal of celery, lettuce, tomatoes, and especially use the garden blueberry. (This is a property which someone, some day, will use in its proper place!) These should be stewed, but in their own juices, little sugar but in their own juices. 3118-1

Gooseberries carry iron and are blood building. Do not use them with preservatives.

Those [foods] that. . .[are] blood building, and especially carrying iron. . .berries—especially gooseberries—may be taken. 2597-6

...gooseberries in any of their preparations—whether those that are preserved or otherwise, provided they are without any of the preservatives. 951-1

Dark raspberries are preferable to the bright red variety. For incoordination of the glands:

Apples raw should be abstained from; also bananas; also some characters of berries, as strawberries or gooseberries or the like. Other berries may be taken in moderation, especially those that will soon be in season, as the raspberry—preferably the dark variety rather than the red would be more helpful. These may be taken in the morning meal with the cereals or they may be used in a salad made of fruits occasionally. . . 906-1

Strawberries should be avoided by those who need to keep more alkaline or who need more iodine in the system.

Let the diet be not of meats or too much sweets, but of vegetables and fruits—no tomatoes or strawberries [or] any other fruits of the acid state. 3751-6

Q-4. Are strawberries all right for me to eat?
A-4. Strawberries are rather excess acid-producing, and especially carry too much of potash when iodines are needed for the system. 307-9

When strawberries are eaten, only saccharin or honey should be used to sweeten them.

...berries of any nature, even strawberries if so desired. (No, they won't cause any rash if they are taken *properly!*) [to be eaten with whole wheat cereals]...The sugar used should only be saccharin or honey. 3823-3

Cherries
Cherries are nerve and blood building.

Let the diet be. . .nerve and blood building. . .Fruits. . .[such as] cherries. 3842-1

Citrus Fruits

We have just noted above, in 228-1, that dissolving fluids come from citrus fruits. These fruits were also mentioned frequently in the section "Ingestion of Food, Air and Water Containing Mineral Forces." Under *Vegetables* it was brought out that vitamins B and B-1 are to be found in yellow fruits as well as yellow vegetables. However, just how citrus fruits and juices should be added to the human system is not a simple matter.

Orange and lemon juices may be mixed in a certain proportion; also, orange and lime; grapefruit and lemon; grapefruit and lime; and lemon and lime. Lemon juice should have a little water added.

Take plenty of citrus fruit juices; even if this is a part of the meal each day, it is well. With the orange juice put a little lemon—that is, for a glass of orange juice put about two squeezes from a good lemon, not a dry one, so that there will be at least a quarter to half a teaspoonful [of lemon juice added]. With the grapefruit juice put a little lime; about eight to ten drops. Stir these well, of course, before taking.　　2072-3

It will be much better if you will add a little lime with the orange juice, and a little lemon with the grapefruit—not too much but a little. It will be much better and act much better with the body. For many of these are hybrids, you see.

3525-1

Combine a little lemon with the orange juice, or grapefruit juice.　　1208-14

Q-5. Is lemon juice, as being taken now, helpful?
A-5. It is a good alkalizer. Squeeze a little lime in with it also, just two or three drops in a full glass of the lemon juice taken. Best to mix the lemon juice with water, of course. Use half a lemon, or a full lemon to a glass of water, depending upon how soon the lemon is used after it is fully ripened or prepared for the body.　　1709-10

We note from the foregoing that it is because many of the citrus fruit varieties are hybrid that the juices should be mixed before being added to the human system.

It is best to have the juices fresh, not canned.

...we would have citrus fruit juices, fresh; not those that are canned. . .For this body those. . .preservatives that are in most are *not* so good. 1187-9

The frozen citrus fruit juices obtainable today *may be* preferable to the canned, since fruits, the readings tell us, do not lose much of the vitamin content from freezing; and it would seem that freezing would make preservatives unnecessary.

Q-13. Considering the frozen foods, especially vegetables and fruits that are on the market today [in Edgar Cayce's time]—has the freezing in any way killed certain vitamins and how do they compare with the fresh?
A-13. So far as fruits are concerned, these do not lose much of the vitamin content. Yet some of these are affected by freezing. 462-14

Citrus fruits taken alone will act as eliminants. However, taking citrus fruits or juices or even apples or tomato juice with starches other than whole wheat bread has a disturbing effect on most bodies. There is an additional reason for the admonition against eating citrus fruits and cereals at the same meal. The milk taken with the cereal forms into a curd which requires a different digestive element from that required for the citrus.

Mornings—citrus fruit juices or dry cereals with milk, but do not eat the cereals and the citrus fruit juices at the same meals; else we will find we change the activity of citrus fruit juices with the gastric juices of the stomach, by combining those that are acid and those that are alkaline reacting but of an acid nature. . . 549-1

Q-3. What foods should I avoid?
A-3. Rather is it the combination of foods that makes. . .for disturbance with most physical bodies, as it would with this... do not combine. . .the reacting acid fruits with starches, other than *whole wheat bread!* that is, citrus fruits, oranges, apples, grapefruit, limes or lemons or even tomato juices. And do not have cereals (which contain. . .[a] greater quantity of starch than most) at the same meal with the citrus fruits. 416-9

If cereals are taken, do not mix them with the citrus fruits—for this *changes* the acidity in the stomach to a detrimental condition; for citrus fruits will act *as* an eliminant when taken alone, but when taken with cereals it becomes as *weight*—rather than as an active force in the gastric forces of the stomach itself. It requires a different element for the digesting of citrus fruits with cereals of any nature that are taken with milk; for curds with acids of fruits are as pouring milk in tea that has lemon in it. It produces a curd.   481-1

The pineapple is classed among citrus fruits according to the readings, so it also should not be taken with cereal.

When other citrus fruits are taken, as pineapple or grapefruit, they may be taken as they are from the fresh fruit.
3823-3

Do not eat cereals at the. . .meal when citrus fruits are taken, but alternate these, taking cereals one morning and citrus fruit the next; such as oranges, grapefruit, pineapple, lemon. .
3185-1

For a person with toxemia neither lemon nor lime was to be added to pineapple.

Do not add lemon or lime to. . .pineapple. . .   1593-1

Another reference explains that if the cereal (acid) is taken with the citrus (acid but normally alkaline-reacting), the combination in the system becomes acid-producing.

Oranges. . .may be taken. These are *not* acid-*producing*. They are alkaline-reacting!
But when cereals or starches are taken, do not have citrus fruit at the same meal—or even the same day; for such a combination in the system at the same time becomes *acid-*producing!
Hence those taken on different days are well for the body.
1484-1

[2448] was to eat the pulp of citrus as well as the juice to insure the bulk needed for lacteal activity.

. . .do not have the citrus fruit *and* cereals at the same meal. In most of the fruit take the pulp *with* the juices themselves, for the reaction of this *bulk* is needed in the activity of the lacteals.
2448-1

Citrus fruit should not be taken at the same time with food that contains gluten.

Oranges, grapefruit, lemons and limes. . .provided they are

not taken close with any food that carries *gluten*—which would tend to change these in their activity with the gastric flows of the digestive areas. 710-1

In the section under "Vegetables" we found that okra contains quantities of gluten. Obviously gluten bread contains a sizable amount, too.

Citrus fruit has a cleansing effect on the blood.

Adding. . .a great deal of the citrus fruit, especially for the breakfast meal, we will find the blood *cleansed,* and much of that disorder as gives rise to the soft tissue in the head, nasal cavities and the stomach, or that as is of a catarrhal nature, will be relieved. 849-7

Citrus juices should not be served with stewed fruits such as figs, apples and peaches.

Mornings—citrus fruit or stewed fruits (as figs, apples, peaches or the like), but do not serve the stewed fruits with the citrus fruit juices; neither serve the citrus fruits with a dry cereal. 623-1

Citrus fruits and juices can help build enamel on the teeth through their effect on the glandular secretions of the body. At the same time they can help thyroid activity.

Q-3. What can I do to prevent the teeth from wearing down?
A-3. Use more of an alkaline-reacting diet; as quantities of orange juice with a little lemon in same, as four parts orange juice to one part lemon; grapefruit, raw vegetables, potato peels. . .these will materially aid in adding those elements necessary for the correcting of the glands with the system that make for the proper secretions to the body for the building of enamel, and for the activity—of course—of the thyroid.
365-4

Dates and Figs

Dates and figs prepared in a special manner may be used as a food for spiritually developed individuals. This concoction is also advised for better eliminations from the body. (Good elimination would naturally be helpful for a body seeking purity and spiritual development.) In the following references one suggests crushed wheat as an alternative to corn meal, a constituent of the mixture. The others include *only* corn meal.

At. . .meals [other than breakfast] there may be taken, or included with the others at times, dried fruits or figs, combined with dates and raisins—these chopped very well together. And for this especial body, dates, figs (that are dried) cooked with a little corn meal (a very little sprinkled in), then this taken with milk, should be almost a spiritual food for the body; whether it's taken one, two, three or four meals a day. But this is left to the body itself. . .

But for this particular body, equal portions of black figs or Assyrian figs and Assyrian dates—these ground together or cut very fine, and to a pint of such a combination put half a handful of corn meal, or crushed wheat. These cooked together—well, it's food for such a spiritually developed body as this!   275-45

Q-6. Any further suggestions for maintaining maximum health this winter?
A-6. Do these, as we find the better conditions for the body.

It is well for this body, or growing bodies, or elderly individuals also, for strength building and for correcting the eliminations, to use this as a cereal, or a small quantity of this with the cereal, or it may be served with milk or cream:

Secure the unpitted Syrian or black figs and the Syrian dates. Cut or grind very fine a cup of each. Put them on in a double boiler with just a little goat's milk in same—a tablespoonful. Let come almost to a boil. Stir in a tablespoonful of yellow corn meal.   1188-10

Q-3. What bulk does she require that can be disguised in food or drink?
A-3. We would prepare a mixture to be taken as food, in this manner: Chop together a cupful each of black figs and dates. Put this on the stove in a cupful of milk (from which the cream has not been separated). Just before it comes to a boil, stir in same two tablespoonsful of corn meal. This will not only make bulk but will be the character of bulk as a food that will act with those properties for better eliminations, and give food values of a nature most helpful for the body in the present. This quantity might be used three or four meals, and this means it might be taken once or twice a day, dependent upon the ability to get the body to take same.   1553-15

To be sure, keep the eliminations in good order. An aid to this would be found in the use of a food prepared in this manner: 1 cup black figs, chopped or ground very fine; 1 cup dates (not seeded);* ½ cup yellow corn meal (not too finely ground).

Cook this for twenty minutes in sufficient water (2 or 3 cups) for it to be [of] the consistency of mush, or cook until the meal is thoroughly cooked in same. Eat a tablespoonful of this mixture of an evening, not all at once but let it be taken slowly so as to be well assimilated as it is taken. This will be most helpful for the body.

*[I think the reference to dates "not seeded" means that you should use the big dates that have not been pitted, and take the seeds out yourself just before preparing them. Gladys Davis]

1779-4

Another strengthening food for this body would be a combination prepared in this manner, that will work with the eliminations, to assist in absorbing those inclinations for the formations of gas owing to the inability of perfect mastication of most foods:

Take a cup of black Syrian figs and a cup of dates. Seed them. Cut or grind these together. Then add half a cup of water. Let it *almost* come to a boil. Then add a tablespoonful of yellow corn meal.

This will be almost as a gruel when fully prepared, and would be kept upon ice or in a place for the preservation of its abilities to be active without fermentation. This quantity may last for at least two days. It may be taken at each meal if so desired, and may be taken with milk or cream or without, just as is preferable to the body.

1907-2

Then follow the regular diets that aid in eliminations. Use such as figs; or a combination of figs and dates would be an excellent diet to be taken often. Prepare same in this manner: 1 cup black or Assyrian figs, chopped, cut or ground very fine; 1 cup dates, chopped very fine; ½ cup yellow corn meal (*not* too finely ground).

Cook this combination in 2 or 3 cups of water until the consistency of mush. Such a dish as a part of the diet often will be as an aid to better eliminations, as well as carrying those properties that will aid in building better conditions throughout the alimentary canal.

2050-1

For alcoholism and for toxemia:

An excellent food for the body of an afternoon and evening would be this combination: 1 cup black figs, or packed figs, chopped or ground very fine; 1 cup dates, chopped or ground very fine; ½ cup yellow corn meal (not too finely ground).

Cook this in sufficient water (2 or 3 cups), for 15 to 20 minutes, to make it [of] the consistency of mush.

A little of this taken each evening or night will be found to supply energies for the system that will be most helpful—especially combined with the osteopathic corrections, and the effect produced upon the nervous system as well as the glandular system from the quantities of the gold taken in the manner indicated. 2055-1

Q-4. Since babyhood, the mother has been perplexed as to what food is best for this entity. What caused this condition?
A-4. We haven't the physical condition but feed the entity oft the foods which were the basis of the foods of the Atlanteans and the Egyptians—corn meals with figs and dates prepared together with goat's milk. 5257-1

Figs by themselves may also be an eliminant.

...we would make more of an *eliminant*...or give more fig in the diet, in the various preparations of same. 275-4

Pieplant, figs, prunes, prune whip—these would be laxatives for this system. 348-13

Under *Citrus Fruits* we noted that figs might be served stewed. They may also be eaten pressed or raw.

...have plenty of such as figs—stewed, pressed, raw or the like. 2479-1

The desirability of using natural eliminants such as figs is pointed out in the following references.

If there is the constant dosing or constant application of synthetic influences, these become at times hindrances to the body. But if there are those activities from nature's storehouse, then...these work with the creative energies and impulses of an organism to create and to bring about coordinating influences in the system. 1173-8

Little of minerals should ever be the properties within the system, save as may be taken through the vegetable forces, save where individuals have so laxed themselves as to require or need that which will make for an even balance of same. 364-11

When it is necessary to take any form of cathartic, that...of the vegetable nature would be the better, but this will not be necessary if we will have at least one meal each day of wholly ...the fig, or the syrup of same, or those as carry properties that make for the activity of the muco-membranes from the salivary glands to the jejunum...or to the action of the glands that make for separations in the system—or lacteals. 5592-1

Grapefruit Juice and Grapes

A cleansing diet of grapefruit juice and grapes combined was advised for [133], suffering from colitis. A poultice of grapes would accompany it.

For at least three to five days, let the diet be only grapefruit juices and grapes. Grapefruit juices. Not oranges, but grapefruit juices and grapes only.

We would make a poultice of grapes with the hull on and put it over the abdominal and kidney area, or encircling the body at the 9th to the 12th dorsal area. [Directions follow for taking certain medicinal substances, colonics and adjustments.]

Q-1. Should the grapefruit juice and grapes be taken at the same time?

A-1. No! One at one time, one at the other. Or the grapefruit juices, of course, may be taken between the regular periods. But eat quantities of grapes—whether two, three, four, five or ten *pounds,* even! 133-3

In a later reading for the same person:

At those periods (which should be from one to two days at a time) the only diet would be grapes; not grapefruit, but at other times grapefruit juices are to be taken. . .at one meal or a period of the day. . .

The grape poultices across the intestines and bowels have been most helpful. These should be worn each day, for periods of three days, and the grape diet should be the whole diet during the three days. . .letting about three days elapse between each period of such treatments at first, and gradually increase the time elapsing between the use of these until there would be ten days between each period of grape treatment. But the grape poultices should be made a little bit thicker. Let them be an inch and a half thick rather than the half an inch ...You see, the heat from the body will cook the grapes. Don't [you] cook them. Apply them raw. Only mash them and put in those containers. . .with the hulls, yes, but mashed.

Between the periods of the grape and grapefruit [juice] diet, in the beginning use a liquid diet consisting of the citrus fruit juices of mornings. . .and the vegetable juices at other meals; gradually—that is, in eight to ten days—beginning to add the semi-solid foods. . . 133-4

Grapes

Grapes and grape juice, without the grapefruit juice addition, were frequently recommended in the readings.

We have noted the advice to [780] to go on the three-day apple diet. This person was given an additional suggestion: At the end of the apple diet, drink grape juice and water a half hour before meals and before retiring in the proportion of three ounces of juice to one of water. Carbonated drinks were to be eliminated and the intake of sweets trimmed down. Even honey and honeycomb were to be taken in small amounts. This formula would in time eliminate stiffness in the feet, hands and limbs.

Then begin with taking (that day if you desire), about one half hour before each meal and before retiring at night, three ounces of grape juice in one ounce of plain water.

Do not take any carbonated drinks. Cut down on sweets, but if you wish, honey may be taken or honeycomb at times, but not too much of this either.

These. . .will remove the tendencies for cricks in portions of the body; stiffness in the feet, hands and limbs at times.

780-12

Grape juice was also recommended for weight control.

Q-15. Why should the body take grape juice?
A-15. To supply the [necessary] sugars without gaining or making for greater weight.   **457-8**

Also for weight reduction we would follow the grape juice way; that is:

Half an hour before each meal and at bedtime, drink two ounces of grape juice (preferably Welch's) in one ounce of plain water (not carbonated water).

Keep away from sugars, pastries and the like.

These will keep better conditions in the assimilation and elimination also.   **1567-3**

Grape sugars were recommended for [487].

Keep the body from too much sweets—though *sufficient* of sweets to form sufficient alcohol for the system; that is, the kind of sweets, rather than sweets. Grape sugars—hence jellies or of that nature are well.   **487-11**

The grape diet was suggested for purification in various

instances. There were slight variations in the recommendations for different individuals. Note these in the following references, also that at times the grape poultice was to be applied.

Some days, for at least three or four days, eat only *grapes*— morning, noon and night—*grapes!* Not with the seed, to be sure. . .preferably those of the purple variety; not the larger but those that are good and *not* those that have been shipped or kept too long.   1703-1

. . .have as much as the body can possibly assimilate of *grapes!* every character, or all that may be taken of the grapes, and grape *juice.* This will act as an aid in reducing those tendencies for gas. When using the juice, extract it from the fresh grapes or else use Welch's grape juice—but eat as much of the fresh grapes as possible to assimilate.   2140-1

Note: Welch's grape juice was obviously recommended because of its excellent quality. Since Edgar Cayce's time a number of other brands have come into being which presumably utilize the juice of grapes raised organically. One or more of these can generally be found in a quality health store.

For at least three days (and rest during the period) we would eat only grapes, or fresh grape juice. Do not eat the seeds in the grapes, of course.   352-2

For a person with tendencies toward colitis:

Also we would have a diet. . .mostly of grapes—or grape juice; the same character of grapes as those used for the poultice—but not the same, of course, that are used over the abdomen! But do not eat the seeds. Of course, the seed may be left or should be left in those used for the poultice, but they should never be eaten—nor in the juice taken. The Concord grapes are the best, if it is possible to obtain them. If not, use the purple grapes that may be obtained—as the California grapes, but *not* the white grapes!   324-7

. . .*entire* grape diet, for at least three-day periods; then to the regular normal diet that has been indicated. Quantities of grapes! And should there appear any disturbance in the stomach and duodenum through these periods, make a poultice of the grape hull and pulp—between cloths—and apply over those areas; or over the abdomen and liver area, you see. Make this about an inch and a half thick—that large a quantity, you see, all over. Plenty of water but just grapes for three days—*quantities*—all that the body may eat.   757-6

For skin cancer—along with animated ash, ultraviolet, violet ray and infrared treatments:

We would let at least a week to ten days be between the three-day grape diet. . .and we would have at least three series of the grape diet before a re-check. This will give the opportunity for the proper balance.

Q-5. In making the grape poultice, should the grapes be heated or anything mixed with them?

A-5. Nothing mixed with them, and *not* heated. Let them make the heat from the body by drawing onto the system in a normal manner. Well that they be rolled, you see, retaining the hull *with* the pulp. Any type of the grape is well, at the present season.   757-6

For tumor:

. . .it would be helpful to have three or four days each month when *only* grapes would be used as the diet. And during those three to four days we would apply the grape poultices across all the abdomen itself.

Q-3. The kind of grapes—does that matter?

A-3. Concord grapes are preferable.   683-3

The effect of the grape poultices in helping to eliminate poisons through perspiration, as well as the desirability of stopping their use when the desired result has been achieved, is brought out below.

Not the grape poultices now, in these particular conditions. For the absorptions from the acids of same have had their effect upon the superficial circulation, or through the perspiratory glands of the system—or the sweat glands through which much of the poisons may be eliminated.

988-7

Grapes and raisins (dried grapes) are advised as a help with eliminations.

Q-1. Please advise as to diet.

A-1. We would add those foods that tend to make the eliminations improved; that is, fruits—fresh or raw, as well as cooked; and we would include those that produce better eliminations—figs, raisins, grapes, pears, and the like. 69-4

Melons
There is a warning against eating cantaloupes not grown locally.

Have raw vegetables also, but not a great deal of melons of any kind, though cantaloupes may be taken if grown in the neighborhood where the body resides; if [a cantaloupe is] shipped, don't eat it. 5097-1

Watermelons contain properties cleansing to the kidneys.

In the diet—do live mostly, for a while, on watermelon. . . having these almost daily. The watermelon is for the activity of the liver and kidney. 3121-1

Keep those conditions. . .as indicated through the watermelon taken occasionally, or rather often—three to four times a week; for this keeps sufficient of the properties that will act with the kidneys, keeping them cleansed. 540-6

Olives and Olive Oil
For [257] olives of every character were to be part of the diet, as well as olive oil. The latter would act as a lubricant and also a food for the digestive system, especially that below the duodenum. The value of olive oil as a food was brought out in other readings also.

Olives of every character. . . 257-11

Well, then, that those properties as of small quantities of olive oil (which the body likes very well) be taken as food values. . .Not sufficient that this become rancid in the system . . .but that acts as a lubricant and as a food for the digestive system, especially that *below* the duodenum.
Q-10. What laxative or purgatives should the body take and when?
A-10. Olive oil would be sufficient, used in the proper way and manner, with the food as has been outlined. . . 257-13

Then, we would take about a quarter teaspoonful of olive oil four times a day; just so it does not come at a time when it interferes with the meals—owing to the necessity of the body, in its temperament, to have some food of one character or another following such a dose. Do not use just crackers always. Sometimes take a piece of toast, some grapes, a pear or an apple, or a tomato, or especially celery. This will take away the taste of the oil, as well as act with the gastric flow. This will not be at all palatable at first, but will be found to be most beneficial. Keep this up, for it is a food to all of the intestinal system; but *do* keep the oil fresh. Do not take this much when there is the belching from that already taken; just take a smaller dose but take it just as often. 538-66

Then, we would begin first by taking small quantities internally each day of pure olive oil; not so much as to cause regurgitation or the body to belch same, but a quarter to half a teaspoonful two, three to four times a day, for periods of ten days at a time. Then leave off a few days, and begin again. This will act as a food for the whole of the alimentary canal.

2454-1

Quantities that will be assimilated of olive oil will always be well for the system. 313-4

A small amount of olive oil daily is good for almost everyone.

Q-8. Would it be well to take a small quantity of olive oil daily?
A-8. Well for most everyone. . . 2072-16

Olive oil or vegetable oils should be used with raw salads instead of vinegar.

Noons—such as vegetable juices, or combined with. . .meat juices and a combination of raw vegetables; but not *ever* any acetic acid or vinegar or the like with same—but oils, if olive oil or vegetable oils, may be used with same. 275-45

We have noted previously the use of olive oil as a follow-up to the three-day apple diet.

Peaches
The value of yellow fruits, including yellow peaches, has been discussed previously. There is a warning against overly ripe peaches.

. . .peaches. . .these are all well for the body. . .Be sure that all [fruits] taken are fresh, firm, and not that that is *overly* ripe; that is, fermentation not already begun. 2261-1

Pears

In the section "Ingestion of Food, Air and Water Containing Mineral Forces" we have found that pears affect glandular activity (1049-1) because of iodine content and also have an effect on the blood (4841-1) because of iron content and are, therefore, helpful in treating anemia. Under *Grapes,* this section, we have found that pears, as well as grapes, help eliminations. (69-4) A question concerning avocado pears elicited an answer implying that they contain a great deal of iron. Generically pears were declared to be helpful to anyone, especially when there was a need to build up the blood. They should be eaten in the morning and evening rather than the middle of the day when the body is generally most active.

Q-6. Do avocado pears contain much iron and copper, and are they good for anemia?
A-6. They are good for anemia. They contain most iron. Pears are helpful to *anyone,* especially where body and blood building influences are needed; for they will be absorbed. These are best to be taken morning and evening; not through the active portions of the day. 501-4

Persimmons

A 25-year-old man was advised to eat persimmons to restore the hair on his head.

Q-4. What treatment should be followed to restore hair on head?
A-4. Eat the peelings of Irish potatoes. Eat persimmons as soon as they are in order—even the large persimmons are very well. 1710-5

Plums

Plums contain iron and are blood building.

[Foods] that have blood building, and especially carrying iron. . .plums. . .may be taken. 2597-6

Prunes

Prunes were recommended as helpful for eliminations and preferable to laxatives.

In the foods, we would have more of the relaxing or bulky nature, that tend to make for laxatives through the system. These if possible to be had are preferable to taking cathartics

or laxatives that are of an irritating nature to the flow of the peristaltic activity of the ailmentary canal. Then, use such as bran with figs and such foods combined with same; as prunes, pieplant [rhubarb] and this character of foods. These will aid in relieving the distresses [which included digestive disturbances and the equilibrium being upset in the lacteals].

2811-1

Pieplant, figs, prunes, prune whip—these. . .would be. . . laxatives for this system.   348-13

. . .prunes, prune juice. All forms of this character of fruit tend to aid eliminations. . .   1188-10

Preparation of Fruits

The readings also advised ingestion of fruits other than those mentioned previously and ingestion of fruits in a stewed as well as raw state.

In the reference from 5097-1 under *Apples,* this section, we noted that plums and pears might be taken, presumably either raw or cooked as there was no prohibition given against taking them raw as there was in connection with apples for the same person.

Stewed and canned peaches and canned pears were suggested. In the case of the canned fruit it was not to be preserved with benzoate of soda.

Mornings—citrus fruit or stewed fruits (as figs, apples, peaches or the like), but do not serve the stewed fruits with the citrus fruit juices; neither serve the citrus fruits with a dry cereal.   623-1

. . .as sliced peaches, pears, or the like. Those that are canned may be taken, provided they are not canned—or preserved— with the benzoate of soda.   5672-1

Stewed raisins and apricots were advocated.

Occasionally stewed fruits, as baked apples with cream, stewed figs, stewed raisins, stewed prunes or stewed apricots— these may be taken. . .   840-1

We will find that those food values are best that make for the eliminating forces of the body through the alimentary canal; that is, leafy vegetables will make for the better eliminations—also, as a part of the diet (in the mornings or evenings), use either stewed figs, raisins, apricots, or pears occasionally. All of these will be found to be most helpful to the body in these directions.   480-24

Small quantities of preserved quinces were especially recommended for [1005], who suffered from inactivity of the liver and of the eliminating and excreting systems. This brought about inflammation of the type coming from an acid condition while at the same time in parts of the body great quantities of alkalinity were shown. Prunes, figs and nuts were also suggested.

We would find then that prunes (they are acid-producing, to be sure) would be well; also figs, nuts, especially quince or such fruits—these canned or preserved are very well in small quantities as a portion of the diet.   1005-16

Desserts for [275] could consist of fruits combined with jelly (gelatin). Note that fresh pineapple is included here as well as are apricots and peaches.

Evenings. . .using as the. . .dessert. . .blanc mange or Jello, or jellies, with fruits—as peaches, apricots, fresh pineapple, or the like.   275-24

Apparently it is best to use either raw fruits *or* raw vegetables in a salad but not both together. In the following reference note that [935] was one of the persons advised against raw apples and that papaya and guava were fruits suggested for use in salads.

Principally (very seldom altering from these) raw vege- tables or raw fruits made into a salad; not the fruits and vegetables combined. . .these may be altered. . . Use in the fruit salad such as bananas, papaya, guava, grapes; *all* characters of fruits *except* apples. Apples should only be eaten when cooked; preferably roasted and with butter or hard sauce on same, with cinnamon and spice.   935-1

Ill Effects of Improperly Ripened Fruit
[633] suffered from toxic poisons, which affected the lymph circulation in the jejunum to the extent that the walls had become thinned and seepage had occurred. It was being thrown off through the perspiratory system in the form of body rashes. This young man of twenty-three was advised against eating

fruit which had been harvested in an unripened state since it would bring accumulations harmful to the circulatory system. Certainly the same advice against ingesting such fruit is useful for us all.

Beware of bananas; of apples (unless they be cooked—roasted, especially, would be well). Beware of berries, especially those that are out of season in the *surrounding* territory in which the body resides; that is, don't use shipped-in strawberries, blackberries, or any of those fruits of that nature. Peaches, melons, when grown in the *surrounding* country, would be very well; but not shipped fruit—for all fruits containing acid, that are gathered in a state that is not of ...[their] own *ripening,* maintain for such a condition as with this body very *harmful* reactions; for the benzoates or the picric or tetric or citric acids, that are accumulations from such, are harmful to the circulatory system. 633-1

Wine

Wine made from fruits will now be considered. In the section "Ingestion of Food, Air and Water Containing Mineral Forces" under *Calcium* we found that wine might be taken as a food. The stipulations were that the wine should be red and the amount taken one and a half to two ounces; that it should be drunk at two, three or four o'clock in the afternoon and brown bread eaten at the same time. (578-5) The next reading also advises the use of brown or black bread, sour bread, as the accompaniment.

Q-7. Would a small quantity of wine be. . .[of] benefit, when retiring?
A-7. Not when retiring; but about two ounces of red wine in the late afternoon—with black or brown bread—would be very, *very* well. It is strengthening, blood and body building. Let the bread, though, be sour bread; preferably what is ordinarily known as "Jew bread." 340-31

This wine should be taken at least a half hour to an hour before a meal.

Ordinarily—wine may be taken as a food in the late afternoon, or before dinner. This should be at least half an hour to an hour, though, before the meal; and as a food, not as a drink. 357-10

Red wine taken in this way aids circulation through the

hepatics and stimulates gastric flow, thereby helping the activity of the pancreas, spleen and kidneys.

Red wine—taken of late afternoon as *food* and not as a drink—would be helpful; not only in aiding the activity of an already disturbed circulation through the hepatics, but in stimulating the gastric flow [so] as to aid a better activity through pancreas, spleen *and* the activity of the kidneys.

1889-1

The nature of red wine becomes apparent in the following selection.

Q-11. What is meant by red wine?
A-11. Means *red* wine! Not white wine, not sour wine; not that that is too sweet but any of those that are in the nature of adding to the body the effect of grape sugar.
There is a variation, to be sure, in the character of sugars and the necessary forces and influences of that carried on in the system in producing assimilation.
Foods must ferment, naturally, from acid, the action of acid and alkaline. These passing into the duodenum, especially, become then certain characters of sugars; as produced by the activity of the pancreas juices upon the effect of juices from the liver and the spleen, in digestive forces.
Then the addition of red wine, which is carrying more of a tartaric effect upon the active forces of the body, is correct; while those that are sour or draw out from the system a reaction upon the hydrochlorics become detrimental.   437-7

Wine, properly taken, is good for everyone.

Q-4. Any kind of intoxicating drinks?
A-4. *Wine* is good for all, if taken alone or with black or brown bread. Not with meats so much as with just bread. This may be taken between meals, or as a meal; but not too much— and just once a day. Red wine only.   462-6

As indicated, wines—for the stomach sick [stomach's sake?— I Timothy 5:23] are helpful.   440-3

. . .red wines. . .Take as. . .food, or as a booster action for the digestive system.   257-210

Wine homemade from blue grapes, properly fermented, was suitable for [404] to use as a "food." Blackberry wine was not as desirable as it has a tendency to produce constipation.

Q-4. Is the homemade wine made from the blue grapes good for this body?

A-4. If fermented a sufficient period, very good for the body; if taken as a food, *not* as a drink! Take with sour bread or *brown* bread at those periods when there is needed the stimulation from the general activity of the system; that is, at three, four to five o'clock in the afternoon is the period when an ounce to an ounce and a half may be taken with the bread and be beneficial.

Q-5. Is blackberry wine better?

A-5. Blackberry wine is *not* as good! Its tendency is to produce constipation.   404-6

While red wines strengthen the body, light wines or champagnes stimulate it. At times the latter are indicated as being helpful.

The light wines or the champagnes or the like are for stimulation, while the red wines are strengthening. . .325-68

And in the early mornings it would be well for the body to be stimulated with very light wine, which would be helpful to the whole assimilating system; such as Tokay, claret or the like—a small quantity; but this in the mornings, *not* in the evenings.
                                                                        583-8

. . .at no time take any of those things that carry reproduction of intoxicating forces for the body, save light wines at the evening meal, and these preferably taken when the meat course is served.   257-129

Wines and mild stimulants well for the body, champagne, sauterne, or any of those stimulants that aid the kidneys in functioning without irritation to the intestinal system.
                                                                        325-13

For a person whose severe lung condition seemed to indicate cancer:

White wine as. . .stimuli will be most helpful for the body. These should be very light; that is, the alcoholic content not more than six percent.   5374-1

The role of light wine as a digestive force is pointed up in the following selection, but it is emphasized that we produce a similar fermentation within our own bodies, which should not be augmented to the extent that overbalance occurs.

Q-3. Are light wines good or bad for me?

A-3. In moderation they are *well* for the body. Just so the activities are not such as to become detrimental to digestion, but *light* wines with the digestive forces are beneficial. An overamount of same, or activity produced by taking with improper foods—with foods that they do not *coordinate* with—is harmful for the system. Whether the bodies would have it or not, *foods* produce that *within* the system that is the same fermentation that is called wines, or beer, or liquor, or ales, or such, *for* the digestion to be proper in a body! That man overbalances same, by engorging, or taking too much into the system and making a dog, or a hog of himself, is to be pitied for the man!   275-21

For a person who had been ill with poliomyelitis, light wines or malt extracts might accompany an evening meal of designated foods.

In the evenings—flesh may be taken in moderation, but none that does not have the hoof divided and that does not chew the cud...these should not be rendered in other than their *own* fat, and should *not* be in any grease other than their own—whether boiled, fried or roasted. This will, of course, include breads also. Rye, whole wheat, or it may be mixed. At this meal light wines or malt extracts may be also taken as drinks.

135-1

For a person recovering from an appendectomy, which reading 256-3 termed "a beautiful job," wine was to accompany a suitable quantity of olive oil one day a week.

Also the alimentary canal should be kept rather clear. Not by the use of purgatives, but rather those that will produce proper assimilations through the system. We would keep those eliminants that make for elasticity and activity of the intestinal tract itself, as related to the membranous activities of the lymph circulation. Added to those being used, at least for two days each week take all the olive oil that may be assimilated; for this is well with the activities of the intestinal system, and will be found most beneficial. One of these days that this is taken, it would be well that it be mixed with wine when taken—but do not take other stimuli into the system to excess while those forces are producing the proper coordinating in the assimilating forces of the body, for these would tend to weaken the activities of the gastric juices of the assimilating system and make for a tendency of scar tissue to become more in the nature of tautness, so that these would make for

adhesions that would finally become lesions and very
detrimental to the body.   256-3

Grains

Wheat

The role of grains in human nutrition, particularly that of
wheat, is emphasized in the readings.

. . .as is generally known and seen, in each land there is that
prepared. . .by nature or the creative forces—to make for the
body-development of those within that particular environ.
And in how many lands is *wheat?* It is the greater portion and
should be the greater portion of that which is to supply not
only body-heat but body-development for an equal balance in
the mental influences upon the physical forces of man in his
activity.   826-5

*Q-7. Would I be successful as a writer of books on health,
finance, economics, or other subjects?*
A-7. On any or all of these subjects. But. . .that which is the
motivative influence from the spiritual *angle* would be the
first. Take in thine own self, take the farmer in thine own
environ, thine own surroundings. Build him as to a power in
the earth from his application of the spirit of truth and life that
is in the light of that which is prepared and builded for the
building of the more perfect bodies, the more perfect activities
of thought; and [show] that these are not as shams that may be
builded from drugs that are even made from the synthetic and
not the pure and true! Build these into those things about thine
men or thine characters in same. *Wheat!* call the book. 826-2

Q-6. Should Wheat *be a book of fiction?*
A-6. Of fiction. . .with the basis of. . .[the] activity [of wheat]
in all the varied lands—and as the staff of life in the material
world.   826-4

For. . .that work pertaining to what has been well said to be
the "staff of life" in the sojourns of individuals as individuals
in the earth plane—or a book *Wheat*—should be the *crowning*
effort of the entity; in its giving to the general public or to its
peoples in many lands that which will show how that as there
are added to the body-physical the elements of the soil in their
proper ratio, these bring to the balanced mental and physical
reactions the necessary forces for keeping the moral, the
mental, the soul, the spiritual balance in the individual. And
thus this is given out to the groups, to the masses in *their*
reaction.   826-5

The need of man's body for natural foods as opposed to synthetically fashioned ones is strongly brought out above. In fact, the mental and spiritual are shown to be dependent on a pure physical basis.

Whole Grain Products

The importance of using foods made from whole grains rather than refined ones is also brought out in the readings. This is clear in respect to both cereals and breads.

A well balanced diet—whole grain cereals. . .   257-252

In the diet we would give whole wheat grains as cereals, whether dry or cooked. . .   1788-12

Mornings—whole wheat toast, browned. . .   935-1

For persons having digestive problems of the stomach or intestinal area cereal grains were to be cooked slowly for a long time in a covered container, not aluminum.

When cooked cereal is used, preferably use only the whole wheat. This may be merely rolled, crushed or ground—but the *whole* of the grain is to be taken; because of the influence and vitamins, as well as the iron, as well as the very natures of the life of the wheat itself that are needed. . .and cook for at least three hours—but do not cook same in an *open* kettle nor in an aluminum kettle. Use either glass *or* enamelware with the top on at all times.   1703-1

Also we would take cereals, as the cracked or crushed wheat cooked a long time, and cracked or crushed oats, but *not* rolled oats.   2140-1

In the matter of diet. . .those of the wheat or oaten, preferably in the whole grain rolled—not soured before rolled, but rolled—and made in a gruel. *These*. . .should be *well* cooked . . .at least three to four hours—in double boilers *preferably not* aluminum.   505-1

However, the use of a steam cooker also results in well-cooked cereals, the nutriments of which are released in the most desirable fashion.

Mornings. . .Whole wheat bread, preferably toasted. . . [cereal] only crushed wheat, whole wheat; not cooked so as to destroy any of the vitamins that carry the iron, the silicon and those influences that build with body and nerve and blood building forces, but in such measures that these are retained—which would be as cooked in preferably [a] steam cooker of such nature that will [not] only break up the elements but release for the body the proper nutriments from same. These may be combined at times with the cereal known as Maltex, which is a combination of barley with wheat, which breaks up the activities of some influences. Do not ever, though, have the citrus fruits *and* the cereal at the same meal.   831-1

At least three mornings each week we would have the rolled or crushed or cracked whole wheat, that is not cooked too long so as to destroy the whole vitamin force in same, but this will add to the body the proper proportions of iron, silicon and the vitamins necessary to build up the blood supply that makes for resistance in the system.   840-1

The products of various grains were recommended for different individuals. We have just noted that [2140] could use oats and [831] barley. There is mention of buckwheat, rye, corn, corn meal and various prepared cereals in addition.

Yellow corn, yellow corn meal, buckwheat—all of these are especially good.   1968-7

Q-5. What is raw cereal?
A-5. Rolled wheat, rye, or oats, are usually termed the *raw* cereal.   275-21

Of mornings: Cereals—these changed from dry to the cooked. Cream of Wheat or Wheatena, or oatmeal, or Grape Nuts, or Corn Flakes, or Rice Flakes—with the cream *mixed*—not full raw.   142-5

Under Jerusalem artichoke we noted that yellow corn meal, made into spoon bread, egg bread, cakes or the like, would be good for [2472]. A question elicited the answer that the yellow corn meal products would in time have a laxative effect.

Q-2. What would be a good laxative for this body?
A-2. Gradually the yellow corn meal mush, cakes or bread, will become as a laxative.   2472-1

In the preceding section under *Dates and Figs* it was brought out that corn meal was part of the diet of the Atlanteans and Egyptians (5257-1) and various recipes were given combining this meal with dates and figs to make a dish which was a fit food for spiritually developed individuals and which also was a good eliminant.

For those who wish to reduce, rye products were suggested.

In the matter of the diet, keep to those foods that tend to make for a reducing of the body as to avoirdupois. Let most of the bread ever consist only of Ry-Krisp or rye bread, but principally the Ry-Krisp.   603-3

Wheat Germ

Wheat germ oil may be used in conjunction with gold for regeneration of the system.

Every other day we would also give internally two drops of wheat germ oil. After six to ten drops have been taken it will be found that this will be helpful with the activity of the gold in regenerating the activities through the system.

Q-1. Should gold given by mouth be increased now?

A-1. We would keep the same amount; only adding the wheat germ oil which will make it more efficient—since conditions have arrived at that point where such improvements are indicated.   1553-25

Wheat germ itself was also recommended.

Do for the body-forces use wheat germ in the morning meal with the cereal, which may be taken a teaspoonful over a good bowl of cereal, then add the cream and a little sugar if desired.
                                   5347-1

Also, at least once each day take wheat germ. This may be taken with foods or cereals, but preferably with cereals.
                                   5073-1

Values in Whole Grains

In a preceding section "Ingestion of Food, Air and Water Containing Mineral Forces," certain food values in whole grains have been brought out—those of iron and vitamins B and B-1 (480-55) under *Iron* and those of iron, calcium and phosphorus (1131-2) under *Iron and Phosphorus*.

Beans

Beans have been mentioned previously. In the section "Ingestion of Food, Air and Water Containing Mineral Forces" under *Calcium* the reference from 1785-1 recommends beans and lentils for calcium intake; that from 540-6 points out that butterbeans supply calcium and lime; the selection from 243-19 informs us that calcium is found in early peas. Under *Iodine,* lentils, beans and peas are called to our attention as sources of this mineral. (313-4) Under *Iron and Silicon* beans and lentils are recommended. (275-27 and 275-28) In the section on "Vegetables" there is mention of the dissolving fluids to be obtained in English peas and butterbeans. (228-1) Also, it is brought out that wax beans are rich in vitamin B-1 (5319-1); that lentils are blood and nerve building and act as a counter-irritant to too much activity in the kidneys (5625-1); and that green beans can help the optic forces and may be used to help eliminate cold and congestion. (3552-1)

Fresh beans, peas, lentils or other beans should be cooked in Patapar paper.

It would be especially well at the evening meal to have *red* cabbage, provided it is prepared in its *own* source—as cooked in Patapar paper, so that all the juices and vitamins may be retained in same. It should be the same with fresh beans, peas, lentils, or beans [that] may be a part of the diet.   3823-2

Soybean milk is not advisable for everyone nor in all situations.

Though the soybean milk product is not well for *every* body, in these particular conditions here it is very good. . . 1206-8

Q-1. Is it advisable for the body to drink soybean milk?
A-1. This will depend much upon the activities of the body. If there is sufficient of the energies used for physical activities to make same more easily assimilated, it is well. If these energies are used for activities which are more mental than physical, it would not be so well.   1158-18

Pod vegetables such as beans stimulate the nervous system.

. . .stimuli for the nervous system. . .especially. . .the vegetable forces that are of the pod nature. Beans. . . 758-2

Beans should not be combined with a great deal of bread.

Do not combine quantities of starches with proteins; as beans (white beans), lima beans, or roughage—do not combine these with quantities of bread. . .When these are taken, do not eat bread.   926-1

There are two bean products whose values are freely discussed in the readings—namely chocolate and coffee.

Chocolate
A limited amount of good chocolate can add energy to the body and supply it with carbohydrates in a proper way.

Not too much sugars, to be sure, but at certain periods—say once or twice a month—eat some good chocolate. This adds energies and carbohydrates in a manner that is well. 2737-1

Plain chocolate, without corn starch or much cane sugar, is the desirable kind. This was available in 1927. However, chocolate prepared just prior to and during World War II was another matter, and warnings were given against this variety.

Keep the body from too much sweets—though *sufficient* of sweets to form sufficient alcohol for the system; that is, the kind of sweets, rather than sweets. Grape sugars—hence jellies or of that nature are well. Chocolates that are *plain*—not those of any brand that carry corn starches should be taken, or those that carry too much of the cane sugar. Grape sugar, or beet sugars, or of that nature, may be taken. [Reading given 9/8/27]   487-11

Q-4. Are daily heavy chocolate malted milks detrimental?
A-4. Chocolate that is prepared in the present is not best for *any* diet. This, too, the chocolate is not produced in the vicinity of -----. Those foods that may be taken from the vicinity or food values of that nature are the better. Take plenty of milk—you will find some of that around. [Reading given 4/1/44] 4047-1

Q-2. Is bitter chocolate, or bittersweet chocolate hard for me to digest?
A-2. Any of the chocolates are hard to digest at the present. These may be taken in moderation as conditions progress but should never be taken in any quantity. [Reading given 1/13/41]   2426-1

A chocolate drink is preferable to chocolate candies.

In the diet keep away from chocolate candies. . .   3607-1

Q-4. What about chocolate?

A-4. This should be very, very seldom given. But after these conditions are improved, or removed, this will be helpful in the form of a chocolate drink, rather than in candy. [Reading given 10/27/39]   2004-2

It would appear that the readings envisioned a return to plain chocolate after World War II. For the consumer today it would be well to examine the labeling on chocolate and chocolate products to see whether they conform to the standard suggested in the reference from reading 487-11.

In the section "Ingestion of Food, Air and Water Containing Mineral Forces" under *Calcium* we found the beverage cocoa, which is derived from chocolate, recommended for calcium content. (1785-1, given 1/10/39)

Coffee

For some persons the caffeine in coffee is hard on the digestion. It should therefore be taken along with bread, meat or sweets. In the case of [404] it was even desirable that the tannin (caffetannin?) be mostly removed. The resulting product could then be drunk two or three times a day if taken without milk or cream. Other persons eliminate the caffeine satisfactorily.

It is less harmful to take cream with coffee than to take milk with it. However, coffee in excess *with* cream can become a poison, as can excess coffee with a quantity of sugar in it. Coffee taken properly is a food.

Q-8. Is coffee good? If so, how often?

A-8. Coffee taken properly is a food value.

To many conditions, as with this body, the caffeine in same is hard upon the digestion; especially where there is a tendency for a plethora condition in the lower end of the stomach.

Hence the use of coffee or the chicory in the food values that arise from the *combinations* of coffee with breads or meats or sweets is helpful.

But for this body it is preferable that the tannin be mostly removed. Then it can be taken two to three times a day, but *without* milk or cream.   404-6

Coffee is. . .[one] of those. . .stimulants to the nerve system. The dross from same is caffeine. . .[which] is not digestible in the system, and must necessarily be eliminated. When. . . allowed to remain in the colon, there is thrown off from same poisons. Eliminated as it is in this system, coffee is a food value and is preferable to many stimulants that might be taken. . .

294-86

Q-9. Is the chemical reaction of raw milk in coffee the same as cream in coffee in relation to the digestion in the stomach?
A-9. Well, this depends—to be sure—upon the activity of the system at the time. Cream. . .is less hard, or more easily digested—and produces *less* of that hard to be assimilated by portions of the system. But in coffee it is *preferable* for the body to use neither cream nor milk. Of course, cream is less harmful—and of course carries more food value, of a different nature. But there is a portion in same that becomes gradually hard upon the activity of the juices from the pancreas and spleen to the activities upon the system through the lacteals in their absorbing from digestion.

275-45

Coffee, fresh—without cream, is a food. In excess, *with* cream—or with quantity of sugar, it becomes as a poison, or hard for a digestive system—if taken in excess. This may be taken in moderation.

684-1

Q-1. Does it hurt me to use sugar in my coffee?
A-1. Sugar is not near so harmful as cream. [You] may use sugar in moderation.

243-22

We previously learned under *Vegetables* that coffee loses food value as time elapses after its being roasted. (340-31)

Nuts

In the section "Ingestion of Food, Air and Water Containing Mineral Forces" the very first reference cited, 480-46, recommended nuts such as filberts and almonds for calcium value. Under *Gold* nuts were suggested where there were deficiencies of gold, silicon and phosphorus. (1000-2) Under *Iron* a lack of iron and silicon was to be eased by eating nuts. (480-19) Under *Iron and Phosphorus* we learned that for a person whose body was deficient in iron, calcium and phosphorus, the ingestion of almonds, English walnuts and pecans was advisable.

Noons. . .nuts; especially those that are of the fruit of trees—almonds, English walnuts, pecans. . .The walnuts known as black walnuts are not good for this particular body; neither are the Brazil nuts particularly good.

1131-2

For a person suffering with arthritis and incoordination of the glands, one meal almost entirely of nuts and nut oils was advised.

Supply an overabundant amount of those foods that carry iron, iodine and phosphorus in the system. . .
Then there should be one meal almost entirely of nuts, and the oils of nuts. . . 951-1

For a person suffering from adhesions and lesions, nuts would be helpful.

In the diets be mindful that we keep those things that add iron, silicon and gold in the system. . .let the diet [include]. . .
Nuts, in salads. 1055-1

Nuts produce an alcohol reaction in the system. They are natural sweets.

. . .those things that produce an alcohol reaction in the system; such as nuts. 1985-1

Keep the natural sweets—as with. . .nuts. . . 773-16

Nuts may take the place of meats.

Have plenty of. . .nuts, as a portion of the meal; rather than so much meats. . . 1303-1

Nuts are good but do not combine same with meats. Let them take the place of same. 1151-2

. . .use the fruit and vegetable diet. The fats should be more from nuts than meats [for 1000]. . . 1000-11

The advice to secure products grown locally applies to nuts as well as vegetables and fruits.

Use. . .nuts. . .of all natures or characters that are grown in the environ of the body, especially. 1771-3

For [710] black walnuts, pecans and coconut meat were to be taken sparingly because of richness. Nuts advised were almonds, peanuts, English walnuts, Brazil nuts and filberts.

Beware of. . .very rich foods where too much of the nuts of

certain natures are used. *Not* black walnuts, nor pecans nor [those] of such natures. Not coconuts. . .Nuts such as almonds, peanuts, English walnuts, Brazilian nuts and filberts are very good. 710-1

An intake of nut butter, nut oil or nut milk was recommended for some persons.

Not too much. . .grease of any nature, though butter— preferably those of the nut variety may be used. 91-1

Peanuts are very good. . .and peanut butter is especially very good for the body. 984-3

Do refrain from eating too many peanuts with candy. Peanut butter will be found to be better. . . 1747-6

. . .the *oils* of *nuts*. These are good for this body, *rather* than meats. 5557-1

Morning—[as] much of the oils of nuts may be taken as will be well assimilated—not overtaxing same. . . 5641-2

Q-5. *Is peanut oil taken internally good for my body?*
A-5. Not good if taken by itself. If this is taken in combination with olive oil, or alternated, it would be very well.
1688-8

Also take internally once a day about a teaspoonful of peanut oil. Let this be taken. . .[in] very small sips, assimilated. Do this just before retiring at night. 5334-1

Use not the vegetable oils in the cooking, but either the peanut oil or the. . .margarine—for this especially carries D in a manner that conforms with those properties in preparation for assimilation by the body. 826-14

Q-6. *With lacteal area disturbed, shall I continue to drink so much sweet milk?*
A-6. This is not so well, for the casein as well as the quantity of calcium in same makes for a hardening of those activities through the lymph flow in the intestinal system.
If this is altered to the milk that is a natural creation from nuts it would be much better. . .particularly almonds and filberts will be helpful and carry with same elements that are much preferable to so much milk. 1140-2

The Almond

The almond is a nut especially recommended in the readings. It is presumed that the sweet almond is indicated rather than the bitter since the former was the more common one at the time the readings were given.

The following beautiful extract combines symbolism and fact concerning the potency of this nut.

An almond a day is much more in accord with keeping the doctor away, especially certain types of doctors, than apples. For the apple was the fall, not [the] almond—for the almond blossomed when everything else died. Remember this is life!
3180-3

A scholarly discussion of this symbolism, as well as a great deal of information about the almond, is presented in an article "An Almond a Day" by W.H. Church, found in *An Edgar Cayce Health Anthology.*[26]

On a material level the almond, according to the readings, carries more phosphorus and iron in a combination easily assimilated than any other nut.

The almond carries more phosphorus *and* iron in a combination easily assimilated than any other nut. **1131-2**

Eating two or three almonds a day is suggested in the readings as a preventative for cancer.

...those who would eat two or three almonds each day need never fear cancer. **1158-31**

A reading given for a woman with cancer advised that after surgery she should eat one almond a day to avoid recurrence of the condition.

Eat an almond each day—one almond—the body will have no more trouble or recurrence of this nature through the system.
3515-1

Two almonds a day can eliminate skin blemishes and result in elimination of blemishes in body forces.

And know, if ye would take each day, through thy ex-

[26]W.H. Church, "An Almond a Day," *An Edgar Cayce Health Anthology,* A.R.E. Press, 1979, pp. 62-75.

perience, two almonds, ye will never have skin blemishes, ye will never be tempted even in body toward cancer nor towards those things that make blemishes in the body forces themselves. 1206-13

Retention of Food Values from Plant Products

The retention of food values from plant products depends on a number of factors, of which the first two are the age (past maturity?) and length of time kept. The need to use fresh vegetables has been brought out before but is reemphasized in the second excerpt below.

[Retention of food values] depends upon preparation of same, the age and how long gathered. All of these have their factors in the food values. 340-31

...this doesn't mean green in color only but those [vegetables] that are raw and fresh, not stale vegetables. 906-1

We see that the preparation is another factor. For various methods of cooking, refer to the section *Avoidance of Minerals Proceeding from Kitchen Utensils,* in which the use of Patapar paper and a steam or pressure cooker is highly recommended and in which other utensils are discussed. The following excerpt tells us that steam pressure cooking preserves rather than destroys vitamins.

Q-14. Consider also the steam pressure for cooking foods quickly. Would it be recommended and does it destroy any of the precious vitamins of the vegetables and fruits?
A-14. Rather preserves than destroys. 462-14

Preservatives in commercially canned products are another matter to consider. We have previously learned under *Preparation of Fruits* to avoid canned peaches, pears or the like which are preserved with benzoate of soda. (5672-1) There are other warnings in the readings against this preservative.

. . .never use for the body. . .*canned* [products], unless they are those that are free of the benzoate character of a preservative. Do not use those! 1001-1

Tomatoes, if they are *ripened on the vine;* otherwise those that are canned *without* preservative—or especially benzoate of soda. (Do not use such [tomatoes] as use that as preservative.) 135-1

The readings tell us that the freezing process does not cut down much on certain vitamins in fruits but that it does affect vegetables markedly. We must remember that in Edgar Cayce's day the freezing of fruits and vegetables was just being perfected and that it is possible that these evaluations do not hold entirely true for our day.

Q-13. Considering the frozen foods, especially vegetables and fruits that are on the market today—has the freezing in any way killed certain vitamins and how do they compare with the fresh?
A-13. . . .Some are affected more than others. So far as fruits are concerned, these do not lose much of the vitamin content. Yet some of these are affected by the freezing. Vegetables— much of the vitamin content of these is taken unless there is the reinforcement in same when these are either prepared for food or when frozen. 462-14

Note: For diet and eating habits in regard to plant products consult the later section "Considerations Concerning the Eating of Meat and Vegetables."

Plant Products for Healing

In the Edgar Cayce readings it is made abundantly clear that although we primarily need to work with the spiritual and mental aspects of our problems, we also are provided with natural means to correct the physical imperfections which have resulted from our malfunctioning. For every ill there is a natural remedy.

The entity was in the earth during those periods when the first of the settlers crossed the mountains of the native land, when there were the turmoils and strife over the salt lands. . . the entity gained through the experience; for, through the applications of self in attaining the relationship with the natives of the western, the southern, and the northern lands. . . the *entity* became associated with—not the ordinary medicine man, but—that one that oft would speak with the entity even in the present—Red Feather.
In that experience the entity learned much of those things that would bring to those peoples the allaying of the fevers and the healings, the strengthening of the weary in body and mind; and thus gained from nature—or the storehouses of the influences themselves that make for material manifestations in an earthly kingdom—the powers of creative energies.
688-2

For the entity had caught that vision in the experience [as a faith doctor or healer] that there *is* that principle in every herb, yes in every element, that is creative within itself that gives that inclination for *healing* to a physical body...1458-1

Then the motivative element [to rid the body of physical disturbances] may be within the attributes of nature itself, whether it be through mechanical applications or medicinal properties of herbs. *Whose* herbs are they? Whose force or power is used? They are *one!*   1620-1

Yet the entity from that sojourn is a lover of nature, one that appreciates nature, the *natural* sources; and that there is within the grasp of man all that [is] in nature that is the counterpart of that in the mental and spiritual realms, and an antidote for *every* poison, for every ill in the individual experience, if there will but be applied nature, natural sources.
                                                          2396-2

In light of the above information we shall now take up suggestions in the readings for plant products to be used for healing. Of course, the selections on vegetables, fruits, grains, beans and nuts given previously have pointed out how these foods supply varied bodily needs, thus inducing *healing*. The references to follow now, however, deal not with food as ordinarily obtained but with special items, some taken orally, others inhaled or applied to the skin.

Oral Applications

Clarification of the Nature of Teas
Before we deal with teas, it is well to bring out the fact that what is generally regarded by Americans as tea is merely a special mixture of dried leaves and that it is of no great value to the system.

Q-20. Is [the use of] tea and coffee harmful to the body?
A-20. Tea is more harmful than coffee. Any nerve reaction is more susceptible to the character of tea that is usually found in this country, though in some manners in which it is produced, it would be well.   303-2

Q-4. Are tea and coffee harmful?
A-4. For this particular body tea is preferable to coffee, but in excess is hard upon the digestion. To be sure, it should never be taken with milk.   1622-1

Q-3. Is coffee or tea good for this body?
A-3. Coffee is better than tea, though the body may prefer the tea. . .There is very little food value in tea, though it is a stimulant.   462-6

For the same person later:

Q-3. What about tea?
A-3. Tea might be taken when the body is resting—but this is rather a pick-up for the body and does not last as long with the body even as coffee, and coffee is more of a food than tea.
462-14

. . .nor of any [food] that will produce improper fermentation, as. . .tea. . .   5558-1

Q-8. Is ice tea harmful to the body?
A-8. Tea is rather hard on most bodies. If it is taken with lemon it is preferable.   850-2

Q-1. Does honey or tea cause high blood pressure?
A-1. Honey does not cause high blood pressure. Tea, with other combinations, does. These. . .may be moderately taken, not too strong a tea, nor too much of the honey; but these. . .in combinations. . .do cause high blood pressure. Be mindful as to the other combinations made with same.   1010-20

However, there are other blends of tea besides that one generally used in this country. Some of them are mentioned in the readings as specifics for various conditions. They will be included in this section. Remember that, in every instance, tea leaves should be finely chopped before steeping.

Agar
Agar may be used in conjunction with colonic irrigations to alleviate chronic constipation.

Q-11. What causes chronic constipation?
A-11. Natural from the too full a capillary and too little an internal circulation. Hence the colonic irrigations, and the use of agar in those forms that will assist peristaltic movements, are well for the body.   4091-2

One person, however, was advised that agar was not very good for him, moreover, that his use of it along with Castoria was improper as the two substances should not be combined.

Both are suitable in their proper places and for individual conditions.

It [agar agar] is not very good for the body!...While both [agar agar and Castoria] are laxatives, [they] do not work the same with the system. These should never be combined as laxatives. Each in...[its] proper place and with individual conditions...well.   257-186

Aloe

Aloe may be used to help elimination through the alimentary canal. A combination of it and several other substances will act along with the gastric juices of the stomach so that the spleen, pancreas and liver may coordinate their activities.

For a person needing a tonsillectomy, whose state of acidity needed to be considered:

We would keep an increased elimination through alimentary canal, with an intestinal antiseptic following same occasionally. This should be preferably of an alkaline reaction, such as ...Glyco-Thymoline or Lavoris, or...magnesia and...aloe, or phenolphthalein—these, in quantities under the supervision of ones handling the operative forces.   5660-1

For incoordination of eliminations with tonsils in a poor state:

We would...*increase* the *eliminations* in the system, both by colonic irrigations—[so] as to cleanse near nominally [normally] the colon itself—and by taking into the system properties...[which] will aid or *stimulate* the liver in its activity; not merely by exciting the gastric juices of the system, [so] as to cause an overacid forming, especially through the bile ducts—but...[also by acting] in conjunction with the gastric juices of the stomach itself, causing spleen, pancreas *and* liver to *all* be active *together* in a *coordinating* way and manner. These...*with* the eliminations increased through colonic irrigations, would be best found in those properties of colocynth, calomel, aloes, and hyoscine. These may be found in the properties combined in that proportion as prepared by Sharp and Dohme [as of that date] or they may be compounded together in a prescription in such a manner as to be active upon the system in *small* doses—which will be found to be a great deal better than large quantities at a time. Take small doses, extending over a greater period of time, so that the system— the functioning organs themselves, are able to absorb sufficient so that the *functioning* of the organ is stimulated *to* exercise *its* own functioning, not *increasing* the functioning of the gastric juices or exciting any of the functioning organs to a state. . .[so as] to produce an excess or a *drain* on the organ in its functioning. [Directions for removing part of tonsils follow.]   5499-2

Alum Root

An individual with a serious complaint, manifesting in diarrhea, was advised that diarrhea due to overactivity of the lymph circulation through the alimentary canal may be lessened by alum root, *heuchera americana,* which has an astringent effect.

Then begin with small doses of *this* as a compound: to 6 ounces of distilled water, add: alum root, 1 ounce; Indian turnip, 20 grains; ginseng (wild), 1 dram. Reduce by slow simmering to ½ the quantity. Strain while warm and add 2 ounces of grain alcohol with 1 ounce of simple syrup. The dose would be a few drops in the beginning, every hour, until there is relief through the alimentary canal, and a tendency for the stopping of the diarrhea.   5631-1

[348], originally given directions by the readings for alum root therapy, instead had surgery for a stomach ulcer. On later occasions, he sought further advice. Alum root was still recommended, this time to be chewed, if desired, rather than taken in a liquid compound.

Those properties as have been given, as to change the vibratory forces of the body—or just to have small quantity of the alum root and to occasionally nibble or chew a small quantity—will be found to be most helpful.   348-12

These (physical difficulties). . .may be aided the best by using those properties that were once given. . .alum root, Indian turnip, wild ginseng, compounded with simple syrup and alcohol—or just the alum root may be carried in pocket and eaten or chewed on just occasionally. This will act as an astringent, but not as a deteriorator, of the muscular activities of the general system as related to digestion.   348-13

First, for a long period there have been those inclinations for a diathetic [diathesis, catarrhal?] condition—or a diarrhea, or an overactivity of the lymph circulation through the alimentary canal.

This tends to weaken the system, naturally prevents a gaining of vitality as a stored energy.

Then, with the poisons that accumulate, and that are added [to] by the condition of the teeth. . .there is produced an indigestion, and an overflow of the gastric juices in this particular condition.

All of these conditions, then, must be taken into consideration.

First, then, we would have the teeth—the mouth conditions—corrected.

Begin with a small piece of alum root (dried) to be put in the mouth and chewed—a little piece of this the size of an English pea—put in the mouth about half to three-quarters of an hour after each meal, and gradually chewed—and the juice swallowed. This will gradually correct the condition through the digestive system. . .

Q-1. What causes the tightness of muscles, and how may this be corrected?

A-1. This is a combination of reactions from the overflow of the gastric juices or the lymph through the intestinal system; and is a part of the general debilitation, which will be aided and assisted by the properties from the alum root.   348-23

The readings indicate that ulcerative chronic colitis may also be helped by a preparation made from alum root and that even sores in the mouth may be helped by alum water.

Prepare this also in a fusion: Put ¼ ounce of alum root in 4 ounces of distilled water and let come to a boil, then strain. Be sure the alum root is crushed. Add to this, ½ ounce of simple syrup and take 1 ounce of grain alcohol or rye whiskey and add. This is only to be taken, one teaspoon when there is cramping through the alimentary canal or colon.

Two or three days after this has been taken, though, take an irrigation to remove the inflamed [inflaming?] fecal forces in the colon.   5057-1

Q-2. What can be done for the sores in the mouth?
A-2. A little alum water will be helpful. . .   757-3

Balm of Gilead
[2790] was told that balm of Gilead may help to stimulate the functioning of the organs of the pelvis with the action of the kidneys. (2790-1, *Tonics*, this section)

Balsam of Tolu
[5664] was told that balsam of tolu can be of help to the

digestive system. (5664-1, *Tonics,* this section) It also appears to accentuate the special effect of a compound while improving its taste. (643-1, *Ginseng,* this section)

Black Snake Root

[636] was told that essence of black snake root affects the lacteal ducts, the secretions from which stimulate capillary circulation. (636-1, *Ginseng,* this section)

Buchu Leaves

According to the readings buchu leaves (or *diosma,* meaning "divine order"[27]) cleanse the kidneys of poisons; buchu leaves and mandrake root together specifically affect the hepatic circulation (643-1, *Ginseng,* this section); and buchu leaves and elder flowers affect the kidneys and pelvic organs. (1278-1, *Ginseng,* this section)

Camomile

The author's introduction to herbal remedies came from that childhood classic *The Tale of Peter Rabbit* by Beatrix Potter. The reader will recall that after Peter had sampled Mr. McGregor's vegetables and been frightened off by Mr. McGregor (which, also, doubtless had an effect on his digestive system), his mother restored him with camomile tea. This choice appears to have been an excellent one, as the readings tell us that camomile is useful in settling the stomach and reducing disturbance in the intestinal tract.

At least three times each day give a mild camomile tea, to reduce the disturbance in the intestinal tract and especially to settle the stomach. Pour a pint of boiling water over a teaspoonful of the camomile and allow to steep as tea. These would be the proportions. The dosage would be a teaspoonful three times a day—of the tea. . .made in the manner indicated.
1788-8

References to this tea in the readings chiefly suggest that it be alternated with saffron.

We would, then, have an altering of the yellow saffron water with the camomile. . .   18-2

. . .those combinations of the active forces in same [an

27Robert O. Clapp, "Blessed Ragweed—The Most Hated of Weeds," *An Edgar Cayce Health Anthology,* A.R.E. Press, 1979, p. 46.

eliminant] that keep for the non-acidity in system. . .those that come from the combination of the forces as in teas of saffron and of camomile. [Other suggestions added.]   19-3

. . .a mild form of camomile tea, or saffron tea, that is palliative to the digestive system, and that will make for the proper eliminations, preventing the accumulations of drosses that would affect the system in any way by not being eliminated.   4798-1

. . .we would change or alternate this [saffron tea] at times with camomile tea. For these tend to form, in the regular activities of the body, the best in the gastric flows for the intestinal disorder.   641-7

We also will find that occasionally camomile tea, made in the same way and manner [see reference for this reading number under *Saffron*]—this used instead of the saffron, will enable the system—with these being kept in the line as has been outlined—to create more of a mucous membrane in the stomach and intestinal system. . .   2884-3

Camomile tea was reported to be useful in keeping the capillary circulation in order.

For a 2½-year-old child, who apparently had the measles:

Precautions and care should be taken with the body at this time to prevent such activities indicated in the system from affecting the glands in the body.

Hence. . .the body should be kept quiet. Keep it out of drafts. Then, give sips of such tea as the camomile, to keep towards the capillary circulation. Put about a pinch of camomile to a whole cupful of hot water, and give it in sips when water is desired. In this manner give a teaspoonful or two to three teaspoonsful about three to four times each day. [Other directions follow.]   324-4

Cinchona Bark

[1278] was told that cinchona bark (quinine) clarifies the blood supply in the liver and that this bark in combination with wild cherry bark clarifies the lungs of carbon. (1278-1, *Ginseng,* this section)

Elder Flowers

Elder flowers affect the functioning of the pelvic organs with the action of the kidneys according to 2790-1 under *Tonics,* and

1278-1 under *Ginseng,* both in this section. They can help to change the vibratory forces in all of the mesenteric system according to 5664-1, *Tonics,* this section. The mesenteric membranes hold in position the organs in the pelvic area as well as associated blood vessels, nerves and lymphatics.

Elm Bark
A pinch of powdered elm or elm bark put into water a few minutes before drinking may be helpful in coating the walls of the intestines, thus preventing strains there.

Then when this [drinking water with lithia tablet dissolved in it] is to be taken, once or twice a day we would have just a pinch of the elm bark (between the thumb and forefinger) in a glass of water—the ground elm bark. If it is. . .preferable, it may be used with a small piece of ice in same; this would be all the better, but stir same and let it stand for a minute or two before it is taken.   840-1

The water that is taken [by this individual in his condition]— *most* of same should carry. . .elm, and this should be prepared just before taking, but should *always* be cool, or cold. . .
Q-1. What quantity of elm. . .should be used?
A-1. For each glass of water a pinch between the finger and thumb of the ground elm, stirred well, with a small lump of ice in same; prepared about two to three minutes before it is drunk.   5545-1

For a person with colitis:

Drink plenty of water at *all* times. In the water taken, outside of that used with the medicinal properties mentioned, put a pinch of powdered elm in same; stirring and letting. . .[sit] for a few minutes before drinking. Do not keep this made up. Should this become foul, it is *very* detrimental. If quantities of it produce belching, then take a small quantity of baking soda or Upjohn's citrocarbonates—which will reduce the acidity.
                                                                                                    133-3

Q-4. How long take elm bark, and what does it do for body?
A-4. As indicated, this would be taken when it desires water—or if it sours in the stomach—or because of foods, or those conditions that arise from a condition in the system— leave off.
This again is to supply that coating along the walls of the intestines themselves, [so] as to prevent the strains from which blood has appeared.   257-215

Ginger

Ginger stimulates the ducts and glands in the liver, thereby working directly with the gastric flow. (1019-1, *Tonics,* this section) A combination of ginger and ginseng acts directly on the organs affected by gland production. (1278-1, *Ginseng,* this section)

Ginseng

The reader's attention is called to an excellent article "An Introduction to Herbs in the Edgar Cayce Readings" by Cecil Nichols.[28] There is a special reference to ginseng in it.

We have already noted under "Onions and Garlic" that ginseng emits mitogenetic radiation, which appears to have a rejuvenating effect.

Many of the Edgar Cayce readings recommend the use of wild ginseng.[29] That this is the wild American ginseng, *panax quinquefolium* or five fingers root,[30] rather than the oriental variety, seems to be substantiated by the fact that the American herb was used at the time by those receiving the readings without any later correction yet uncovered from the readings themselves.[31] Such use of an American plant by Americans ties in with the statement we noted under the section on vegetables:

> **For, in the consideration of the whole, it will be found that products grown in individual localities are best suited to the needs of individuals living or dwelling within those same localities.** **1797-3**

For an Oriental, the *panax schinseng* would doubtless be better.

Ginseng grows wild in the eastern part of the United States as far north as Michigan and Wisconsin and as far south as northern Florida, Alabama, Louisiana and Oklahoma. A heavy concentration occurs in Appalachia. There the "sang" hunters for many years have added to their families' scanty supplies of cash by harvesting this foot-tall, five-foliolate-leaved perennial, which in the autumn exhibits bright red

---

[28] Cecil Nichols, "An Introduction to Herbs in the Edgar Cayce Readings," *An Edgar Cayce Health Anthology,* A.R.E. Press, 1979, pp. 39-44.
[29] William A. McGarey, M.D., "Notes from the Medical Research Bulletin," *The A.R.E. Journal,* May, 1973, pg. 134.
[30] Lucas, pg. 155.
[31] Nichols, pg. 42

berries. Since it grows in isolated patches and one or two plants must always be left to insure future harvests, this ginseng collection by the mountain men involves long walks through their native forests. The wild ginseng brings a better price than the cultivated herb (approximately 67% more). The roots of the cultivated kind are lighter in weight and without the growth rings of the wild variety.[32]

Wild ginseng is characterized in the readings as the life principle.

> . . .the life principle as we have in the wild ginseng. . .839-1

Its effect is a glandular one as will be noted in the following four references. The readings suggest its use only in conjunction with other herbs.[33] These other herbs were to affect specific parts of the body while the ginseng would activate the whole. The function of a number of these other herbs is, likewise, clarified in these same four excerpts.

> **There are some disturbances that need attention in the physical forces of this body. These have to do with the eliminations as related to the general change in the system [female, 45 years old], and a condition of a general catarrhal nature through the intestinal system itself—or the effects or strains upon the flow of the lymph through the digestive area.**
>
> **. . .we would prepare a compound that would tend to overcome this colitis condition, or the drawing of the cords along the intestinal system—and that feeling which occurs in the pit of the stomach and through the intestines at times, as of something** *moving*. . .**These are the reactions of the nerve and muscular forces, and the lack of proper balance in the circulation through the system in these areas.**
>
> **So, we would prepare a compound in this manner for this body:**
>
> **To 4 ounces of distilled water, add 2 ounces of strained honey. Let this come to a boil; of course, skimming off the fumes until it is perfectly clear, but just let it come to a boil—or sufficiently so that the skim may be cleared. Then, before it cools—or while still tepid (though not boiling, or hot) add (to the 6 ounces, or then it will be a little better than 5¼ ounces)—in the order named: elixir or extract of wild ginseng, ¼ ounce; essence or elixir of Indian turnip, 10 minims (this is rather**

---

[32]Arnold and Connie Krochmal, "Ginseng, Panacea of Five Leaves," *Garden,* September/October 1978, © 1978 by The New York Botanical Garden, pp. 25-28.
[33]McGarey, *op. cit.*

hot!); tincture of stillingia, ¼ ounce; syrup of sarsaparilla, ½ ounce; alcohol, ½ ounce.

Shake this solution together before the dose is taken, which would be ½ teaspoonful 3 times each day, taken just before the meal; that the activities of the properties may be with the gastric flow as digestion takes place.

And this will be found to remove those strains upon the system, those tendencies for the lack of proper eliminations, and the activities with the digestive forces and through the intestinal system. . .

The carrier of water with honey is combined to make for that which may assimilate with the system.

In the compound we have first the wild ginseng, which is an essence of the flow of the vitality *within* the system itself. It is an *electrifying* of the vital forces themselves.

The Indian turnip is an emit and a stimulation to the gastric flow, which would cut off the flow of the secretions in the glands of the stomach that supply to the glands of the thyroid.

Other properties, as in the stillingia, make for the activity with the pulsations between the liver, the heart, the kidneys, in such a manner as to *still* the circulatory forces there.

The compound syrup of sarsaparilla makes for an emit that carries to the gastric flow of the stomach and to the intestinal digestive force an equalizing in the body, or in the flow of the lymph to these portions of the system. . .

Then, the preservative, or the alcohol—which preserves the elements in their state of being made into an essence, which makes for an activative force in all elements combining with the gastric flow in the system. Hence it is only a stimulation, sufficient to add *to* that lacking in the body; as the body has often refrained from sweets when they would have been helpful!   404-4

For a man afflicted with non-malignant cysts, who was given particular directions for using animated ash and ultraviolet ray:

We would also prepare a compound to be taken internally to work with the blood supply and to create an activity with the glands and the assimilating system [so] as to alleviate the conditions; so that not only may there be the overcoming by the releasing of oxygen for the blood supply through the ash and the electrical forces in same—that gives a surcharge, as it were, to the red blood cells themselves. . .[but also] the eliminations and assimilations and activity of glands— through this compound of properties—may aid in creating the *correct* balance for the body. It would be prepared, then, as follows:

To 32 ounces of *distilled* water, we would add (each ingredient to be *crushed* before adding, but added in the order named): wild cherry bark, 2 ounces; sarsaparilla root, 1 ounce; wild ginseng, 1 ounce; Indian turnip, ½ ounce; yellow dock root, 1 ounce; buchu leaves, 1 dram; mandrake root, 15 grains.

Reduce this by slow boiling to 16 ounces. Strain while warm and add (while still warm) 3 ounces of grain alcohol with 1 dram balsam of tolu cut in same. Shake the solution well together before the dose is taken, which would be a teaspoonful 4 times each day—before the meals and before retiring. . .

For each of these ingredients in the compound has a special function to perform.

The wild cherry bark is an expectorant and a purifier, as combined especially with the other ingredients for the blood supply.

The sarsaparilla root is an emit, or a *strengthener* to the activities of the secretions in the stomach and *intestinal* tract.

The wild ginseng will act directly with these combinations to stimulate the activities of the glands of the system; the genitive glands, the lacteal ducts, the lachrymal ducts, the adrenals, the thyroid, all will—with these combinations—make for an activity that is purifying and body building.

The yellow dock root is an emit and blood purifier, an active principle with the secretions of the liver.

As is also the mandrake root, and it—with the buchu—is specifically active with the hepatic circulation. Mandrake, of course, is of the podophyllum activity. . .and is productive towards the increased secretions through the alimentary canal; while the buchu cleanses the kidneys from any of these poisons in such a manner as to make for bettered conditions.

The alcohol with the tolu; the one is a preservative, the other an active principle to make the whole compound more palatable—and yet specific in its activity.   643-1

For a beauty shop operator:

Q-4. Please give me a formula for a medicine to be taken internally to restore natural color to hair.

A-4. This would necessarily be put up under the direction of a pharmacist, unless. . .an organization was formed for the manufacture of same; which would be a combination in these proportions, whether making two ounces or four hundred gallons: To 4 ounces of simple syrup, add: lactated pepsin, 1 ounce; black snake root extract, ¼ ounce; essence of wild ginseng, ¼ ounce; Atomidine, 40 minims; extract of liver (preserved in alcohol, of course, or Armour's liver extract), ½ ounce; grain alcohol, ¼ ounce.

The dosage of this would be half a teaspoon three times each day, just after meals, for periods of ten days with five-day rest periods. This taken in such a manner over a period of several months will be effective to glands, to those secretions that will not only make a digestion that will be much improved in health but—with any good scalp treatment, especially such as we have indicated—it'll turn graying hair. . .back to normal; or where it has been streaked even by various forms of dyes, its *growth* will come normal.

Q-5. Please give me a formula to improve and recondition the nails.

A-5. There is not much better than that already prepared by Cutex for the care of the nails, provided the glands (. . .from the thyroids, of course) are producing the proper amount of secretions in the system. So, then, what you use to care for the hair will care for the nails also. . .for they are the *outgrowth* of the same secretions in the system. While there may be occasions when. . .[persons] with very thin or brittle nails may have very excellent hair, it's because such persons eat their own nails!

To turn again to why such a formula as given would affect the body-functioning, [so] as to change the outward activity of the functioning of glands in a body:

The syrup, surely, is the carrier.

The pepsin is active [in] such [a way] that the ingredients given may be effective upon the basic influences within the body that would produce in the varied offices of the body those proper functionings to stimulate in the proper proportions the activities of the cuticle and the epidermis.

So the basis of. . .the complexions of body would be changed. . . to be more in a healthful and thus in an activative force to beautifying of that which is to man his crown of strength and to woman her head of beauty; for to man hair in the head is as strength—to woman is as beauty.

Then, the essence of the black snake root is an active principle with the lacteal ducts that make for secretions in the system that stimulate a capillary circulation; aided in same and purified through the wild ginseng essence, that is—according to the ancients—the basis of the stimulation of life in its very essence in the body of man.

The Atomidine—that is activative in the glands, especially the thyroid, the adrenal and all the ductless activities through the atomic forces in iodine, the one basic force [along] with potash—makes for a balance throughout the functionings of the body itself.

While the extract of liver. . .[and] the preservatives, in the activities with the other portions of the body, become beautifiers. Hence, proportioned as indicated, are activative with a body—healthy; the nails, the cuticle, the epidermis, and the adorning of the beauty of the body—*beautiful!*   636-1

For general debilitation:

We would prepare, then, this: To ½ gallon of rain water, or distilled water, we would add: wild cherry bark, 2 ounces; sarsaparilla root, 1 ounce; wild ginger, 1 dram; ginseng, 1 dram; cinchona bark, ½ ounce (that's quinine bark—cinchona. . .); buchu leaves, 1 dram; elder flower, 1 ounce.

Reduce this by simmering, or slow boiling, to one-half the quantity. Strain while still warm. Best were this strained through the filter paper. Then add, 2 ounces of grain alcohol, with 2 drams balsam of tolu cut in same.

Shake solution together before the dose is taken. The dose should be [a] teaspoonful 3 times each day, taken preferably half an hour *after* the meals—and eat the meals; but be mindful of the *character* of the meals. There should *not* be any white bread. There may be whole wheat or rye, or even the mixtures of same. There should be the *juices,* or soups of the vegetables, in which all of the protein from the meats should be put; but not much of the meats, if any. These, though, may be taken at *times,* when the body feels it absolutely necessary. . .

Q-4. What causes backaches, and what can be done to help?

A-4. With the application of the properties as given, we will find the changes—for these are the effects of the various properties, and—as will be seen—these have been given due consideration. The effect of this combination in the system is: In that, first, of the barks, to *clarify* the blood as related to the respiratory system, or that through the activity of the lungs, in the carbon condition created in system. In those of the ginger and ginseng, act directly with the organs as are affected by the gland production in system. Those of the quinine bark, are those that are to *clarify* the blood supply, as is related to the liver. [Those] of the buchu leaves and elder flower, are for those effects in the kidneys and the pelvic organs. Those others are the *carriers* and *assimilating* forces in the system, see?   1278-1

The functions of the various herbs mentioned in the preceding four extracts are summarized below:

Wild ginseng is an essence of the flow of vitality within the system, electrifying the vital forces. When combined with wild cherry bark, sarsaparilla root, Indian turnip, yellow dock root, buchu leaves and mandrake root, the wild ginseng will act directly on the glands of the system—genitive glands, lacteal ducts, lachrymal ducts, adrenals, thyroid—as a purifier and body builder.

It appears that the Indian turnip can cut off the secretions from those stomach glands which normally supply the thyroid, in this way stimulating gastric flow.

The stillingia soothes those circulatory forces which set up pulsations between the liver, heart and kidneys.

Compound syrup of sarsaparilla equalizes the lymph flow related to the gastric stomach flow and the intestinal digestive force.

Wild cherry bark is an expectorant and purifier for the blood supply.

Cinchona bark (quinine) clarifies the blood supply in the liver.

Wild cherry bark and cinchona bark together clarify the lungs of carbon.

Sarsaparilla root strengthens the secretions in the stomach and intestinal tract.

Yellow dock root and mandrake root are both blood purifiers, actively affecting the secretions of the liver.

Mandrake root, which belongs to the podophyllum family, also increases secretions through the alimentary canal.

Buchu leaves cleanse the kidneys of poisons.

Mandrake root and buchu leaves together specifically affect the hepatic circulation.

Buchu leaves and elder flowers affect the kidneys and pelvic organs.

Balsam of tolu, while improving the taste of a compound, appears to accentuate its special effect.

Essence of black snake root affects the lacteal ducts, the secretions from which stimulate capillary circulation.

Ginger and ginseng together act directly on the organs affected by gland production.

It is well to note here that the Atomidine (atomic iodine) included in the 636-1 compound is extremely potent and for many persons completely inadvisable to use. We must remember that individuals have varied needs, weaknesses and strengths. Information that becomes apparent from the references is for study. Direct application of any of these compounds is not advised.

For the smoking of ginseng seeds, consult a later section on mullein.

Golden Seal

Golden seal in mild form was suggested to correct conditions in the lining of the stomach, to produce a better reaction between the intestines and the blood supply and to activate a depleted condition through nerve and muscle forces.

Note that prescriptions given here were—as usual in the readings—for specific individuals.

Well, too, that occasionally. . .golden seal be given in a mild form. The active principle of this is as an astringent and as an effective issue for conditions. . .[which] exist in the lining of the stomach itself proper; is to *prevent* temperature, or to intestinally produce better reaction with the blood supply. . .

1866-5

. . .depleted condition, or the incentives of the muscle or nerve forces to carry out their whole function, and functioning . . .below normal.

To give a better incentive to all of the nervous centers and to give correct incentives to the functioning of the organs themselves, without disturbing their equilibrium and to overcome the conditions. . .through the system causing this condition, it would be better if the body would travel. Ocean would be best. Rest and water. Or, for the present surroundings and conditions, [that] which would be slower and not as certain to the amending of the conditions would be to take into the system those elements that would give the incentive, with as little resistive force produced in the body as possible. We would take this: To one gallon of rain water, add: four ounces of wild cherry bark; two ounces of sweet gum; two ounces of yellow dock root; one half ounce of blackberry root; one half ounce of golden seal.

This would be reduced by simmering to one quart; strain and while warm, add four ounces of grain alcohol, and twenty grains of ambergris.

The dose would be two teaspoonfuls three times each day.
Let the diet be of vegetables rather than meats.   3888-1

For a person with a "complication of disturbances" for which various measures were suggested, including this for digestion:

First, we would have a compound prepared to be taken internally.

To a gallon and a half (1½) of distilled water, add—in the order named and in these proportions: wild cherry bark, 2 ounces; sarsaparilla root, 1 ounce; golden seal, 1 ounce; snake root, ¼ ounce; yellow dock root, ½ ounce; cinchona bark, ½ ounce.

Reduce by slow simmering until the quantity when strained off is 1 quart. Then, while warm, add 1½ ounces of pure grain alcohol with 2 drams of balsam of tolu cut in same.

This would be as a tonic, as an emit, and as a corrective for the digestive forces. The dose would be half a teaspoonful three times each day, *after* the meals.   1109-1

For an 8-year-old girl in whom cold and congestion had brought on a serious condition, causing high fever and affecting assimilations:

Give as a mild tea those properties either of golden seal or of yellow saffron, the proportion being one to forty...This may be given whenever water is desired by the body...Given warm, however. Let the body drink as much as it cares for. 4611-1

Indian Turnip or Jack-in-the-Pulpit

It appears that the Indian turnip, *arisaema triphyllum*,[34] can cut off the secretions from those stomach glands which normally supply the thyroid, in this way stimulating gastric flow. (404-4, *Ginseng*, this section) It may also act as a stimulus to assimilation in the duodenum. (5664-1, *Tonics*, this section) It can increase the activity of the ducts and glands within the liver area itself. (1019-1, *Tonics*, this section)

Life Everlasting

Life everlasting may help to create a high vibration in the blood supply used by both the respiratory system and the heart. (5664-1, *Tonics*, this section)

A tea made from mullein and life everlasting can add to the vitality of the circulation.

...also make a tea in this manner: To 16 ounces of distilled water add ½ ounce of the mullein leaves or the dried mullein and ¼ ounce of life everlasting. Steep this as a tea and take sips of this three or four times a day, about an ounce during the day, preferably warm...While insipid in taste, if sipped when it is warm it will add that vitality in the circulation.   360-5

---

[34]Euell Gibbons, *Stalking the Healthful Herbs*, David McKay Company, Inc., N.Y., 1966, pg. 249.

Mandrake Root

Mandrake root, which belongs to the podophyllum family, increases secretions through the alimentary canal. It is a blood purifier, actively affecting the secretions of the liver. Mandrake root and buchu leaves together affect the hepatic circulation. (643-1, *Ginseng,* this section)

Mullein

[243] was advised that a tea made from mullein leaves, preferably green, may be of great help to the circulation through the veins, particularly in the legs, and that it can help eliminate acid in the system as well.

. . .the acute conditions that are the more disturbing in the present are those of the varicose veins—that are the more aggravating and tiring to the body. Thus the great distress that is caused when the body is on the feet for any great length of time; causing not only the disorders through the lower limbs and thighs but in the feet also.

And this general pressure, with the body attempting to go, causes the nerve pressures that become reflexly aggravating throughout the body.

Parts of this, of course, have a reflex in the general condition which has existed—where superacidity has caused distress. And this has caused undue activity to the kidneys as well.

As we find in the present, those pressures that exist in the lumbar and sacral axis, as well as in the lower portion—or coccyx end of the spine—are the areas that need the more adjustment to alleviate those tendencies for the circulation that carries blood away from the heart, and yet is so slow in the return of same; thus causing the enlarging of the veins in the lower limbs.

We would also take mullein tea. This should be made of the fresh, green, tender leaves [finely chopped]. Pour a pint of boiling water over an ounce of the mullein leaves and let steep for about twenty to thirty minutes. Then strain and keep in the ice box, so that it may be kept fresh. Take about an ounce to an ounce and a half of this each day. Make this fresh at least every two or three days. Keep this up, and it will aid in the circulation, in the elimination of the character of acid in the system, and aid in the circulation through the veins—that are disturbing.

When there is the ability to rest, apply the mullein stupes to the areas in knee and along the thigh, and just below the knee where the veins are more severe. But the tea taken internally will be more effective.

Do keep up eliminations.

Massage the feet and lower limbs daily in a tannic acid solution or that preferably obtained from using old coffee grounds—which carries a mild tannic acid as well as other properties that would be beneficial—that is the coffee made from same. . .Boil these and use these, as well as the liquid, to bathe feet in—of evenings.

Do have the corrections osteopathically made in lumbar—sacral axis, *and* the coccyx area; and coordinate the rest of the body, for the tiredness and for the relaxing of the nerves, when these are done. 243-38

Since the reading references on mullein deal with the use of both the tea and the stupes, we will consider both at this time.

The preceding excerpt advised mullein stupes on thigh, knee and leg below the knee to relieve swelling. The following ones refer to stupes on liver and gall duct area, kidney area, side, neck, ankle, foot and abdomen as well. In summation, 988-7 points out the effect of mullein on the body—i.e., it absorbs poisons and throws them off through the respiratory tract. Since this tract consists of both the lungs and the pores of the skin, it is easy to see how the poisons can be removed by mullein tea through the action of the lungs and to some extent that of the pores and how accumulations of poisons can be particularly relieved by the action of the stupes since the warmth opens the pores, making it easier for the poisons captured by the mullein forces to be thrown off in excessive perspiration.

Also each evening—and *early* morning, that is, in the evening before retiring, and at the early morning period when the body becomes restless by the sediments that tend to gather in the kidney and bladder, and the irritation that comes from same—we would apply the green (if possible to obtain) mullein stupes. These should be applied over. . .the liver and gall duct area, and over the kidney area from the back. These should remain upon the body for at least twenty to thirty minutes to an hour, depending upon the ease that same brings, to be sure. In making the stupes—let these be prepared with the *green* mullein if possible—this bruised and then the hot water poured on same (in a crock or enamel container). Have them at least two thicknesses over the body, with a gauze and then heavy padding afterward—and even an electric pad over both areas would be beneficial. 1885-1

Q-7. What is the remedy for swollen side, caused by pleurisy and swollen veins? in abdomen, neck and side?

A-7. Application here. . .would be the mullein stupes. These [swellings] are produced more from the condition in the *respiratory* system, as has been outlined, and when. . .[it is] brought to a normalcy much of these will disappear.   130-1

(If the feet and limbs give a great deal of trouble). . .we would apply mullein stupes over those areas of the ankle and foot. Put these on hot and then bind about with padding or wadding to keep the heat. Apply these stupes at least twice each day. Preferably use the green or fresh mullein. This would be bruised, put in very hot water and allowed to stand a few minutes, then dipped out and applied between gauze over the affected area.   2227-3

We would apply the mullein stupes now more to those areas that are the *sources* from which the limbs receive their circulatory activity, and those positions about the limb to reduce the swelling. Apply these about once a day, and for about an hour. The mullein made into a tea would also be well, but not of the same leaves used on the leg, of course! About two ounces of this would be taken each day.   1541-6

But to overcome the dropsical or fluid forming portions in the limb and in the abdomen, use the mullein stupes. . .These are to be used at least twice a day. The activities of same upon the body itself will tend to make for the accumulations to be thrown off through the perspiratory system, excessively. Hence it is necessary after each of these stupes that there be used an alkaline or an acid (preferably an acid) antiseptic solution, for the cleansing of the limb and the abdomen. These stupes may be given for a period of half an hour to an hour, so long as they are kept in a manner that they will be active to remove the accumulations.

These are the properties in same, then, and how they affect the body. The heat from the very activity or application of the stupes, to be sure, *opens*. . .the pores. And the very nature of the mullein is to absorb poisons from the body itself; relieving pain and causing the accumulations to be thrown off through the respiratory system.   988-7

Mullein stupes may be used for ulcerated as well as swollen areas.

Q-2. Should the mullein stupes be applied directly to the body or between gauze?
A-2. They may be applied directly *or* between gauze, depending on the severity of the ulcered area from time to

time. Only the green mullein would be applied in the stupes, though the dried mullein may be used in the tea. Of course, the green may also be used for the tea, though it doesn't require so much [as dried leaves]—about half the quantity—but do not let it boil; just steep as tea, by pouring hot water over same. Let it stand for fifteen or twenty minutes. . .   2714-1

The effectiveness of mullein is emphasized by its application in cases of osteochondritis (involving both bone and cartilage). [275] was threatened with cancer. One of the directions given was for the use of mullein stupes to "strike in" to the affected area and help with the healing of the structural tissue.

Well were the stupes used *too,* that there may be created in exterior portions that as will *strike* in, for the healing of the tissue that becomes involved in the structural portion, building up.   275-5

One reading points out that where there is acute discomfort from swelling, mullein stupes may be supplanted by the smoking of mullein seed. The latter would not be a curative measure but a hypnotic one (inducing sleep).

For a painful case of gonorrheal synovitis (?), involving the urethra and a swollen knee:

About those portions of system—in the testes, and in those portions where the pain or the acute attacks occur, or reoccur—well were these kept with mullein lotion or stupes of mullein or mullein with the leaves bruised and in hot applications applied to the body, and these would bring relief. As would the smoking of seeds from those of the mullein or of ginseng—these would bring relief for this *particular* condition; though are not curative forces, but only as a hypnotic for the condition.

. . .following these as has been outlined would bring the better general physical forces for this part of the body. . .

Q-1. Can they obtain the mullein there?

A-1. In the vicinity, in the country around. Grows in most fence corners. Ginseng grows most about the lots, outbuildings, etc. Only the seeds, not the green portion—but the seeds and the pods, which are now ripening.

Q-3. In what manner should the smoke be used?

A-3. Smoked as any other smoke! Use as stupes, as applications for the portion of the body.   849-5

Although mullein stupes may be a specific in certain cases,

acquisition of a number of the green leaves is not always possible. Mullein tea may often be more easily obtained. In addition, in the excerpt which opened this section, [243] was advised that mullein tea taken internally would be more effective than the stupes.

Although the directions for making the tea given previously in the excerpt from reading 243-38 seem to the author to be the best from a general viewpoint, others will now be added. One points out that some of the flowers may be included with the leaves. Another mentions only flowers when the tea is to be used to help the kidneys and urinary channels to expel a kidney stone. A third gives slightly different directions for brewing the tea, apparently primarily concerned with the use of dried mullein when fresh cannot be obtained.

Also we find that a weak mullein tea would aid in reducing the tendencies for the accumulation of lymph through the abdomen and limbs. Prepare same in this manner.
To 1 pint of water add 1 ounce of the mullein well bruised (with some of the flower included would be well). Let it come *almost* to a boil. Then set it aside to cool. Keep it on ice, of course, and make fresh every day or two. Take a tablespoonful of this about twice or three times a day.   409-36

Also we find that a tea made from the mullein flower would be well. The proportions would be about a level teaspoonful to a pint of water, and let this steep as tea. Taking about an ounce of this twice a day will aid in. . .the activity of the kidneys to expel—and the channels through the system for expelling [the] stone.   843-6

Also prepare mullein tea, which we would begin [taking] after the elm water has been taken for about ten days. Use the green mullein if it can be obtained; otherwise use the dried mullein. Crumble it, put a teaspoonful in a glass or crock container and pour a pint of boiling water over it. Allow this to stand for thirty minutes, strain, then cool and drink; not necessarily all of it at one time, but in the course of three to four hours after it has been prepared.   3373-1

Reading 457-14 advises that taking mullein tea occasionally may be helpful to anyone.

Q-13. Would the mullein tea be good for body now also? If so how much?
A-13. Not unless there is trouble with varicose veins or the

tendency for a dropsical condition through the pelvic areas. This taken occasionally is not bad for any body and it will be good for you. 457-14

Since the value of tea made from *fresh, green* mullein is so thoroughly brought out in the readings, a discussion of methods of obtaining it, even in winter, would seem to be in order.

Reading 849-5 above advised that mullein could be found in the country in fence corners. Reading 3287-2 located it in cow pastures and stated that it was a moss which came from a cattle grazing operation, of cows especially. In this connection it is interesting to note Euell Gibbons' comment that mullein thrives in pastures because grazing animals will not eat it but that it is often given cattle as a veterinary medicine, particularly in the form of an infusion of the leaves to relieve coughs.[35] Gibbons' comment, however, has been qualified to the author by the report of a farmer that goats, browsing rather than grazing animals, do eat mullein leaves, though very sparingly.

Q-1. Where can I get mullein in Florida?
A-1. Wherever cows graze in Florida or anywhere else, mullein grows. It is one of the mosses that comes from feeding cattle—cows especially. 3287-2

Keep in mind that these directions for locating mullein come from Edgar Cayce's time. Today fence lines are often sprayed with herbicides to discourage weeds. Pesticides are used in connection with farming. Mullein growing by the roadside may be polluted by fumes from the traffic going by. So using mullein obtained from an expedition into an unknown countryside may be very questionable and conceivably could result in adverse effects. It is better that it be raised in good garden soil enriched by organic methods. (See later section on the best cultivation of plants.)

The following suggestions are offered. The mullein seeds should be planted in the spring. They are extremely small (like pepper) and should be covered with soil only as required to hold them in place. They should be watered sufficiently to bring about germination. If transplanting is undertaken, spacing between adjacent plants should be approximately two feet. Mullein plants thrive with plenty of sunshine, but can also be

[35]Gibbons, pp. 224-225.

assisted by watering during dry periods.

By the end of the first summer abundant leaves should be in evidence. Some of the bottom ones can be harvested, but not to the extent which would endanger the plants, which can be assisted through the winter by covering with straw, pine needles or other light mulch at times when the temperature drops to approximately 20° F or below.

When the covering is removed in the second spring, the plants should grow rapidly and be ready for harvesting by early summer. A few plants, however, should be permitted to go to seed. They will probably reseed themselves in the surrounding area, but it is prudent to collect a few seeds "just in case"— or perhaps to start some new beds. In any event they will be ready and eager to start up in the following spring, thus completing the biennial cycle.

For the well-being and continued life of the plants, leaves can be picked to only a limited extent in the autumn; they are harvested chiefly at the onset of the flowering period during the second summer.

Providing tea made from green leaves at any time during the two-year cycle is not difficult. It can be made in bulk according to the directions in reading 243-38, then chilled and later frozen, preferably in small containers. When needed, a quantity sufficient for three portions (4½ oz.) can be melted. Of this the first 1½ oz. should be consumed promptly and the other two portions at 24-hour intervals during the ensuing 2 days. (The readings specify that the tea is to be kept for use no longer than 2 or 3 days.)

Since we are told in various readings to allow an interval between successive applications of a therapy, it seems advisable to take the dosages in groups of 3 at 24-hour intervals, then skip 48 hours before starting the following group. This sequence has been followed with excellent results.

Passion Flower or Maypop

Passion flower or maypop is an important part of the passion flower fusion used in the treatment of epilepsy. According to Dr. William A. McGarey this non-habit-forming herbal compound, although not a sedative, does have a calming effect on the nervous system. It aids in activating eliminations, helps retard muscular contractions and through its effect on the sympathetic nervous system lessens congestion accumulating at the base of the brain after seizures. The readings indicate that these effects may stem from the action of the pyloric end of the stomach on the lacteals and through them on the glandular system. The readings advise that passion flower fusion should be given along with Dilantin, Phenobarb or Mysoline until the latter can be gradually stopped.[36]

The readings explain:

> . . .the maypop is for the nerve system and the blood supply, as is hindered by the improper incentives through the connection between the glands at the base of the brain and the hypogastric nerve center, which governs the digestion and the assimilation in portions of the system. . .   4678-1

Plantain
The use of fresh or green plantain rather than dried is advisable.

> Use. . .the plantain in its original state rather than the dried.
> 3751-6

Plantain tea is healing. [3515] was advised to have breast surgery for cancer; later when healing commenced, a cup of plantain tea, prepared according to directions, was to be taken every other day.

> Afterward, when there is healing, begin taking internally a mild plantain tea, prepared in this manner: Cut fine tender plantain leaves, sufficient to fill a tablespoon. . .not heaping too high. Put this in a cup and fill with boiling water. Let stand for thirty minutes. Strain and when sufficiently cool, drink. Take this amount every other day.   3515-1

Prickly Ash Bark
Prickly ash bark affects the blood supply as it is acted upon by the emunctory forces of the liver itself. (2790-1, *Tonics*, this section)

Psyllium Seed
Psyllium seed may be helpful in establishing proper intestinal elimination.

> . . .we would begin with the psyllium seed, as will make for. . .

---

[36]William A. McGarey, M.D., "What Is Adequate Therapy for the Epileptic?" *An Edgar Cayce Health Anthology*, A.R.E. Press, 1979, pg. 166.

a *cleansing* of the body—this taken two doses, not over a teaspoonful—with at least 4 times as much water. The blond is the better. . .especially for this body, and this taken of mornings with the fruit or the cereal diet, or evenings with those of the vegetable diet. Eat as a cereal. 404-2

Q-6. Is it all right to take the alophen pill at night as he has been doing?
A-6. . . .it is necessary that there be the proper eliminations ...without the activities and with that little that can be taken it would be preferable to take the psyllium; though the alophen is well to take at times. And the psyllium is not too rough for the system; about a tablespoonful twice a day. This, of course, is put in hot milk or hot water and allowed to jell; and the jelly may be taken with the meal or taken alone; preferably with the cereal of a morning and with the curds or with the supper—or in the evening meal. 1424-2

Ragweed or Ambrosia Weed
A scholarly discussion by Robert O. Clapp is here recommended to the reader. Titled "Blessed Ragweed—The Most Hated of Weeds,"[37] it deals with this subject in depth. Outstanding features of the article will be included in the following treatment.

There are more than 125 references to ragweed in the readings indexed under "Prescriptions: Ragweed."

Its alternate name, "ambrosia weed," would seem to indicate its great value. Ambrosia was the food of the Greek gods, of which according to legend they partook on Mt. Olympus and which doubtless was supposed to contribute to their immortality. Ambrosia weed can be of help in both assimilation and elimination. In this way it could lengthen the life span of many persons with problems in these connections.

. . .[Take] small quantities of [ragweed], occasionally, to assist in the proper assimilation. 953-18

...[ragweed] is a good eliminant with a vegetable base. But it must be chosen very young, and the leaves alone chewed—don't spit it out because it's bitter! It's not poisonous, and it's a good eliminant. . . 903-35

To be exact, the vibrations of ragweed help to clarify assimilation and to normalize the equilibrium which must be

---

[37]Clapp, pp. 45-51.

maintained between the activities of the pancreas, spleen, liver and hepatic circulation—all this without being habit-forming or causing the intestinal tract to develop a need for cathartics.

For a person with a tendency to diabetes:

[If there will be taken] in the system, at regular intervals, those properties that are not habit-forming, neither are they effective towards creating the condition where cathartics are necessary for the activities through the alimentary canal— whether related to the colon or the jejunum, or ileum—yet these will change the vibrations in such a manner as to keep clarified the assimilations, and aid the pancreas, the spleen, the liver and the hepatic circulation, in keeping a normal equilibrium. These properties would be found in those of the ambrosia weed, made in this manner.

To 6 ounces of distilled water, add 3 ounces of the [finely chopped] *green* ragweed, or ambrosia weed. Steep for sufficient period to reduce this to half the quantity. Then strain, adding to this 2 ounces of simple syrup, with 1 ounce of grain alcohol. Shake the solution before the dose is taken. The dose would be half a teaspoonful twice each day, when the period for taking has arisen—or take it about once each month, for three or four days. This will aid the digestive system, will aid the whole of the *eliminating* system.   454-1

Note that *green* ragweed leaves are to be used in this preparation. The addition of syrup is probably to mitigate their bitter taste.

At times the readings suggest ragweed combined with other substances, depending on the needs of specific bodies. One of these blends is with senna. For [1010] the addition of horehound and sweet gum was indicated. For [666] stillingia, wild ginseng and sarsaparilla were added.

To meet the needs of the conditions at the present, we would first cleanse the system with a mild cathartic; preferably that as would be found in combining the ragweed with senna. This combination: To 3 ounces of ragweed add 8 ounces distilled or rain water. Reduce to half the quantity. Strain, adding sufficient alcohol to preserve same. Adding, *then* to same 2 grains of senna. Shaking well together, the dose would be a teaspoonful every evening until at least half to two-thirds of the quantity is taken.   3826-1

For sedimentary forces in both liver and kidneys, especially the bladder and urinary canal:

Take this in the system only when the body feels it is needed to give the balance, so should be kept on hand and only taken occasionally: Take 2 ounces of the ragweed in its green state gathered as we would find at the present [Nov. 24, 1922]; this we would put into 6 ounces of water and steep until reduced to 4 ounces; to this we would add the same quantity made from the green plant known as horehound; add to this 4 ounces of grain alcohol with 2 drams of sweet gum dissolved in it. Take [one] tablespoonful when necessary for the correction of the condition through the intestinal tract.

Let the diet be only vegetable forces. Do not lower the plane of development by animal vibrations.   1010-1

In 4 ounces of simple syrup we would add: tincture of ambrosia weed, 2 ounces; tincture of stillingia, ¼ ounce; tincture of wild ginseng, ¼ ounce; syrup of sarsaparilla compound, ½ ounce.

Shake the solution together before the dosage is taken. The dose would be half a teaspoonful three times each day. The addition of these properties...will change the digestive forces as to assimilation, causing or producing less of an acid in the digestive system, clarifying a coordinating force (that is, with the correction and the vibration added with same) between the liver and the kidneys, and making for a nearer normal balance.   666-1

In Edgar Cayce's day Simmons' Liver Regulator was still on the market, which it is not today. It contained ragweed, licorice and a little senna according to reading 304-18. For some persons the regulator was adequate to correct their conditions. Others needed the green ragweed derivative.

The Calcidin is well, as is also the alophen, but *better still* would it be were those properties for the eliminant to be *oils— with* those of either the ragweed or the Simmons' Liver Regulator, which is ragweed and licorice and a little senna. These would be *more* effective, and the *oil necessary* to take the inflammation out, or through the intestinal tract. . .

Q-2. How much oil should be given?

A-2. Two teaspoonsful of the Russian white oil and *half* a teaspoonful—in about half an hour afterwards—of the Simmons' Liver Regulator, or it may be compounded in that of the ragweed, or ragweed tea, made in *this* manner: This would be preferable to make it from the original.

To 6 ounces of distilled water, add ambrosia weed 2½ ounces. Steep, or slow boil, for 20 minutes. Strain off. Then add: licorice in solution, ½ ounce; syrup of sarsaparilla compound,

214

¼ ounce. Cut in ½ dram balsam of tolu in 2 ounces of alcohol and add to same. The dose then would be, after the oil...about half to three-quarters of an hour—half a teaspoonful. Take until there is a thorough evacuation from the bowel. 304-18

Q-3. Have the sweats and massages been given correctly?
A-3. They have been given very well, but not in just the manner indicated.
We would keep up the eliminations. The liver needs stirring more...These we would carry through to stir the liver to better activity; not with the minerals as much as with vegetables. As we find, the Simmons' Liver Regulator now would be the better, whether it is in the powder or in the liquid form. But these we would keep up, so that there are at least two or three eliminations daily.

Q-4. Did the colonic do any good [apparently it only irritated]?
A-4. It did good. Thus the needs for the colon to be drained so as to allow the better assimilations for the body.
Q-5. Is the mineral oil I am taking good for me?
A-5. Not unless the rest of the pockets of the colon are cleansed.
Q-6. Should I take olive oil, say a teaspoonful with each meal?
A-6. This is very well, but what is needed is to cleanse the colon and the secretions of the liver and the gall duct increased. Thus the form of vegetable forces indicated. For this is ambrosia weed, with sufficient of the licorice and cascara to aid in stimulating and in fitting it for the body— though the better way would be to eat the ragweed itself!
404-13

Then after the [castor oil] packs have been given for five days, begin with taking small doses of the essence of ambrosia weed. *Preferably* this would be taken green, or *new;* prepared in this manner:
Put about half an ounce of the green ambrosia weed in a pint of water. Let this come thoroughly to a boil (after the weed has been bruised and put in the water...). Then take off and strain; and to the quantity that is left—which would be about two-thirds of a pint...add one ounce of pure grain alcohol, that it may be preserved.
The dose of this would be half a teaspoonful three times each day (after meals), until there are *thorough* eliminations through the alimentary canal from the taking of same; that it may act upon the liver.

This is better for the body than taking even the Simmons' Liver Regulator; which is of the same, but is combined with licorice and other compounds that, for *this* body, would *not* be so well.   1880-1

For persons wishing to make up a ragweed preparation for use in winter, the following formula should be helpful as the ragweed base is to be dried.

Q-1. Is the Simmons' laxative which I took, the same as Simmons' Liver Regulator recommended in reading 369-11?
A-1. Not exactly the same; this was made to take the place of the liver regulator and to meet some requirements that were necessary. Where this is given for anyone, the better preparation would be to make it out of the ragweed, which is the basis of same—either the green (but dry same) or the dry, which may be preserved or bought in bulk, and made in the form of a tea—in this manner (This isn't for this body in the present—may be necessary later; but we have given those things necessary for this particular body in the present), and in this proportion:
To 8 ounces distilled water add 3 drams dried ragweed. Reduce to 6 ounces, or reduce to the quantity. . .[where] it is necessary to add even more water to *make* 6 ounces. Then add a preservative, which would be 1 ounce of grain alcohol.
And you have better than Simmons' Liver Regulator for activity on the liver. This for anyone! This is the *best* of the vegetable compounds for activities of the liver. Of course, if made commercially we would add some few other things to it.
                                                                369-12

The introduction of ragweed vibrations into the system was also suggested to ward off hay fever and asthma occurring at the time of ragweed bloom. Regular amounts of a ragweed brew were to be taken prior to the season.

Now, as we find, there are conditions which tend to disturb the body at specific periods. Hence. . .there are certain seasons or periods when the vibrations of the body, or the relationships which are established in the nerve centers, are such as to cause the body to become allergic to conditions which exist in or under certain environs, or certain pressure experienced by climatic reactions in the body.
These reactions come from what may be called or set up as vibrations in certain centers between sympathetic and cerebrospinal system, and thus the body in such periods is subject to conditions which manifest in irritation to mucous

membranes of the nasal passage and throat, bronchi and larynx, or, as sometimes called, rose fever or such natures. These, for this body, are particularly from the ragweed.

Thus, we would find in this particular season, before there is the blossoming of same, the body should take quantities of this weed. Brew same, prepare, take internally and thus war or ward against the activity of this upon the body itself.

Then, through the period, also take that as an antiseptic reaction upon the nerves of the nasal passages, or the olfactory nerves of the body.

These will prevent, then, the recurrent conditions which have been and are a part of the experience of the body. This will enable the body to become immune because of the very action of this weed upon the digestive system, and the manner it will act with the assimilating body, too. Well, just don't get too heavy, for it will make for an increase in the amount of assimilation and distribution of food values for the body.

Thus we would prepare the compound in this manner; Take a pint cup, gather the tender leaves of the weed, don't cram in but just fill level. Put this in an enamel or a glass container and then the same amount (after cleansing of course, don't put dirt and all in but put in same amount by measure) of distilled water . . .Reduce this to half the quantity by very slow boiling, not hard but slow boiling, strain and add sufficient grain alcohol as a preservative.

Begin and take it through the [last] fifteen days of July and the whole of August, daily, half a teaspoonful each day.

Thus, we will find better eliminations, we will find better assimilation, we will find better distribution of the activities of foods in the body.

Then, use through the latter portion of August and September, this as a combination: Prepare in the manner indicated, putting together the ingredients only in the order named. First we would prepare a bottle with a large mouth, two vents through the cork and these vents capable of being corked themselves with a small cork. Neither of the vents is to enter the solution, so use a six-ounce container. In this container put four ounces of grain alcohol (at least 90% proof), then add in the order named: oil of eucalyptus, 20 minims; rectified oil of turp, 5 minims; compound tincture of benzoin, 15 minims; oil of pine needles, 10 minims; tolu in solution, 10 minims.

When this is to be used, shake the solution together, remove the corks from the vent, inhale deep[ly] through the nostril so . . .[that the fumes will] enter the nasal passages, also to the upper and back portions of throat, both passages. Shake between each deep inhalation.

Do these and we'll have better conditions for the body. Do

for the body-forces use wheat germ in the morning meal with the cereal, which may be taken a teaspoonful over a good bowl of cereal, then add the cream and a little sugar if desired.

Do these and we'll have bettered conditions for this body...

Q-1. To the amount of the ragweed we would use how much alcohol?

A-1. That should be done by the prescriptionist or the chemist, just to preserve same. 5347-1

Red Root

Red root stimulates pancreatic secretion and also the functioning of the spleen as it destroys blood corpuscles. (2790-1, *Tonics,* this section)

Saffron

A most excellent and detailed article, "The Healing Powers of Saffron Tea," by Robert O. Clapp is recommended in its entirety to those interested in the subject.[38] Salient features of this will be included in the following discussion.

The herb saffron was suggested for use at least two hundred and fifty times in the readings. Approximately two hundred of these times it was to be administered in the form of tea.

There are two saffron herbs. The one pointed out by the readings is *carthamus tinctorius,* more commonly known as saffron, bastard saffron, safflower and American saffron.

The American saffron will be found to be most helpful. This is really preferable to the Spanish saffron which is much more expensive. 428-12

The effect of saffron tea on the body is described in the following excerpts.

For psoriasis:

The activity of this [saffron tea] upon the gastric flow of the stomach and duodenum and through the alimentary canal will tend to allay, and to work with the activities that supply the mucous membrane flow along the canal itself, thus aiding the body. 3112-1

For poor eliminations:

Also during the period when the colonic irrigations and the

[38]Robert O. Clapp, "The Healing Powers of Saffron Tea," *An Edgar Cayce Health Anthology,* A.R.E. Press, 1979, pp. 52-61.

osteopathic treatments are being given, we would take a great deal of the saffron tea (made from American saffron), that it may aid in creating better activity through the peristaltic movement of the eliminating system.   1930-1

For intestinal gas:

And about twice a day (this between the meals) have half an ounce of yellow saffron tea; not too strong. This as we find will prevent the accumulations of gas and the inflammation to be absorbed by the activities of these properties through the system.   428-11

Q-2. How may he prevent food causing gas?
A-2. The specific activity. . .of the saffron. . .will work with the gastric activity, especially of the duodenum from which source most of the gas emanates.   556-16

For measles:

The saffron tea is very well as an intestinal antiseptic. . .
                                                               487-26

The readings make it clear that this tea has a beneficial effect on the gastric flow through the stomach, duodenum and alimentary canal; that peristalsis is improved; and that gases and mucous no longer tend to accumulate.

Such an effect is particularly helpful with psoriasis, a condition dealt with in the following selections.

Q-4. Please give me the cause and cure for the so-called psoriasis with which I am troubled.
A-4. The cause is the thinning of the walls of the intestinal system, which allows the escaping of poisons—or the absorption of same by the mucous membranes which surround same, and becomes effective in the irritation through the lymph and emunctory reactions in the body.

An effective cure for same is first being mindful of the diet, during the periods when these necessary elements would be given for creating those activities within the system to close such conditions:

In the system we would use elm water and saffron water. These would be taken in the ordinary drinking water, during periods of one, two to three weeks at a time. All the drinking water carrying, then, either a small quantity of elm or the saffron.

For this adds to the assimilating system those properties

that become effective to the aiding of building within the system itself those conditions that will overcome such activities in the system.   289-1

There has for so long a time remained that condition wherein the mucous membranes of the digestive system, and of the intestinal tract even proper—or the walls, are thinned by this impoverishment. Hence a tendency for the lymph and the mucous membranes to pick up, through these small orifices—and through the improper eliminations of the poisons, and create in the lymph and emunctory circulation those as of the rash, or abrasions, as occur on portions of the system; the body attempting to eliminate poisons, yet when the body is impoverished, so that these would not occur, the whole general system suffers under same, and—as the condition is seen—the system has just been a little too much overloaded, so that the digestive and assimilating juices, or assimilating system, are not able to take care of the conditions in a *normal* way and manner. . .

We would also prepare to be taken of mornings, that of yellow saffron tea. This should be steeped, not too strong, but about a teaspoonful [of the finely chopped leaves] to the pint of water and allowed to brew or steep as tea. . .This may be. . . strained and set aside in a cool place, and should last for 2 to 3 days, taking a tablespoonful of same in a glass, or half a glass, of water—of mornings. . .after the cereal or fruit has been taken.

We also will find that occasionally camomile tea, made in the same way and manner—this used instead of the saffron, will enable the system—with these being kept in the line as has been outlined—to create more of a mucous membrane in the stomach and intestinal system. . .and keep up those rubs as given for the limbs, and we will find changes coming about, betterments for the body.   2884-3

We would keep to the taking, more often, the saffron tea. . . and we would change or alternate this at times with camomile tea. For these tend to form, in the regular activities of the body, the best in the gastric flows for the intestinal disorder.

                                                                641-7

To the normal water that may be had in the surroundings, we would add to each gallon (to be kept for drinking water. . .) a five-grain lithia tablet. Dissolve this and it would make about the proper proportion, and it would be added and dissolved in same preferably after the ordinary water had been boiled—or had come to a boil and strained or filtered off before used. Then when this is to be taken, once or twice a day we would have just a pinch of the elm bark (between the thumb and forefinger) in a glass of water—the ground elm bark. If it is. . .preferable, it may be used with a small piece of ice in same; this would be all the better, but stir same and let it stand for a minute or two before it is taken. We would also. . .[with] the same type of water, have the yellow saffron—the American saffron is correct, or may be used if so desired. This would be [in] the proportions of about a heaping teaspoonful to a gallon of water. This preferably we would make in an enamel container or in a glass container, preferable to the aluminum. This would be allowed to steep as would tea. Then it may be drawn off and kept as a portion of the drinking water to be taken at the regular intervals when the body desires water. Not that there would never be any of the regular routine or drinking of water outside, but let the most—and as much as possible all—that is taken either carry one or the other of those properties as indicated. This would be the first precaution, for—while it is, of course, slow acting—it will make for a cleansing of the kidneys, a better activity through the alimentary canal, clear those tendencies for the poisons to accumulate through the lymph and emunctory circulation, and overcome these tendencies for toxic forces to arise in the body that affect. . .the body throughout. 840-1

Saffron tea may also be used for lacerations such as stomach ulcers.

These. . .have been lacerations and the better the condition will be if there is the following of those suggestions that have been made, making more milk in the diet where it is practical. Keep away from fats and oils, and it will be better. Do use occasionally the charcoal tablets prepared by Kellogg's. These are the better absorbents and will protect the area. Use the saffron tea also. . .once a day, preferably in the evening when ready to retire. This will be well for the condition. 270-49

Take mornings and evenings *small* quantities—half to a teaspoonful—of pure olive oil.
In the mid-morning and before the afternoon drink (of the red wine), take a teaspoonful of yellow saffron tea. Use the American saffron and brew it just as tea. These properties act upon the gastric flow of the digestive forces, not only with the salivary glands (in the mouth) but the upper portion or cardiac portion of the stomach itself. This mixing with the gastric flow (that is started by the activity of the olive oil—not at the same period, but taken as has been indicated) will reduce the acidity,

will prevent or allay the plethora or swelling as produced in the pylorus and through the duodenum; and thus aid the body in better assimilations. 1481-1

Because of the tea's effect it is most understandable that it should be used for problems of elimination.

. . .there are some acute conditions arising from a cold and congestion in the liver and in the digestive system itself; with acute conditions through the lower portion of duodenum and the gall duct area; with pains—by lack of digestion—through the alimentary canal.

First, we would apply the castor oil packs. Before these are begun, however—about three hours before—take a good dose of yellow saffron tea, about two and one-half ounces. Put about two pinches of the yellow saffron in a crock and pour the boiling water over same, allowing it to stand for about ten minutes. Strain and drink. This may be cooled, of course, to make it more palatable.

Then in about three hours after taking the saffron tea, apply the castor oil pack for about an hour. The next day apply again, and then the next.

Then take at least half a teacup of olive oil. 852-18

To meet the needs of these would be to set up proper eliminations. Well that the body rest for two to three days, and well that sweats be taken to start capillary elimination. Taking internally sage and saffron tea, hot—hot as can be taken—and sweat this *through* the body. . .These may be made in the ordinary way and manner as any tea—saffron and sage—and may be taken separate or together, but at least half a pint of each would be taken each day, and a sweat taken. . . *These* will set up elimination, and these will start *proper* eliminations through the alimentary canal. 2597-1

Then begin taking. . .the saffron tea, a cupful each day—or at least two ounces. Put a pinch of the American saffron in a teacup and pour boiling water over it—allow to stand for twenty to thirty minutes—strain and drink. A pinch between the thumb and forefinger, in the cup of boiling water. Drink two ounces of this, once each day.

Also at the same time begin taking mullein tea, prepared in the same manner—one dram to a cup of boiling water, allowed to steep—drinking only an ounce of this, once each day.

3287-1

Condition of person described in the preceding reading:

Poisons in the system as has been indicated that must be eliminated by increasing the eliminations. 3287-2

These we would keep active with a mild form of stimuli to the respiratory system, especially from the digestive and lymph area, as a mild form of camomile tea, or saffron tea, that is palliative to the digestive system, and that will make for the proper eliminations, preventing the accumulations of drosses that would affect the system in any way by not being eliminated; keeping the intestinal tract rather active, keeping the body quiet, and the diet rather that of the liquid diet. Plenty of the juices of fruits; little or no nuts. Soups or mild broths, with little vegetable—no meats. 4798-1

A question as to how long saffron tea therapy should continue elicited this answer:

This should be kept up not in a haphazard manner, but until there is a better condition physically created throughout the alimentary canal. Take it for two, three, four, five days, a week, ten days—leave it off a few days, and then have it prepared again and take again. This is the best manner.
It stimulates better strength through the activities of the lymph and emunctory circulation in the alimentary canal. 257-215

The following references supply simple directions for preparation of saffron tea.

As for the properties to be taken, not a great deal of what would be called "medicinal" properties; but [have such] as these:
To 3 drams of yellow saffron add about 16 ounces of water. Let this steep as tea for half to three-quarters of an hour; not boiling but just steeping...Use this as a drink 3 times each day. Take a *glassful* of it in the mornings before any meal is eaten, and before the evening meal (for we would have the raw vegetables in the middle of the day) and at night before retiring. 633-1

Hence, we would begin taking internally once each day, preferably just before retiring, a cup of saffron tea. Put a pinch of the American saffron in a cup of boiling water, or put it in the cup and pour boiling water over it and allow to stand for thirty minutes (covered during that period, of course). Then strain, cool, and drink. Use a good pinch of saffron...between the thumb and the forefinger, to the cup of boiling water. Make this fresh each time. 3112-1

Sage

The reference to sage and saffron teas (2597-1 under *Saffron*) will be included here in greater detail to make clear the exact difficulties arising from too few eliminations from other parts of the body and overstimulation of the kidneys.

...for some time back there has been the tendency towards the non-eliminations in the proper channel, and with the constant effect of an overstimulation of the kidneys has brought that of the uremic force to be active in an improper manner. Not that this is as uremia, or uremic poisoning, but that of an overactive kidney gives to the whole system that of the improper distribution of eliminating forces in body to the excess of the liver and to the excess of capillary or the lymphatic circulation, and eliminations. Hence we have the character of hindrance through congestion in the intestinal tract, and a form of lesion as produces stitch in side. Pressure produced on nerves of the limbs brings tautness and inactivity through the nerves *of* the limbs. Then the condition becoming acute, these are brought about in an acute form.

To meet the needs of these would be to set up proper eliminations. Well that the body rest for two to three days, and well that sweats be taken to start capillary elimination. Taking internally sage and saffron tea, hot—hot as can be taken—and sweat this *through* the body...These may be made in the ordinary way and manner as any tea [leaves finely chopped and steeped in boiling water]—saffron and sage—and may be taken separately or together, but at least half a pint of each would be taken each day, and a sweat taken...These will set up elimination, and these will start proper eliminations through the alimentary canal...Then we would have, after rest (for these will weaken some)—after resting for two or three days, proper stimulation osteopathically to set up the proper coordinating in the nervous system.   2597-1

Sarsaparilla

Sarsaparilla can help in alleviating cold, congestion and superacidity in the system.

For a catarrhal condition caused by bacilli in the blood supply:

...to bring the greater assistance to the physical balancing of conditions in the body...To 1 gallon of rain water...add sarsaparilla root, 4 ounces; wild cherry bark, 2 ounces; yellow dock root, 2 ounces; burdock root, 2 ounces; black root, 2 ounces; prickly ash bark, 1 ounce; mandrake root, 20 grains;

buchu leaves, 30 grains.

Reduce this by simmering (not boiling) to 1 quart. Strain, and while warm add 4 ounces pure grain alcohol, with 3 drams of balsam of tolu cut in same.

The dose. . .would be [one] teaspoonful 4 times each day, before meals and before retiring.

Reduce the diet to practically. . .the vegetable diet, save as beef juices, or fish or fowl in small quantities may be taken. Never any meats save [of] this character, though the juices of meats may be taken—not in soups but juices. . .   4649-1

The arising of the trouble, then, is from a low vitality with superacidity, and the conditions that arise of specific and contributory natures from same.

. . .then, in meeting the needs of the conditions for this body, necessarily one portion must not be builded to the detriment of the other—but all portions must be considered and the applications made that will make for the better and proper coordination throughout the whole system. . .

First we would begin with that which will meet or combat the cold, the congestion, and the acidity in the system. So, we would have a compound prepared in this way and manner: To 2 ounces of strained honey add 2 ounces of distilled water. Let this come to a boil, for a carrier. Then sct aside, and add the following ingredients (in the order named): syrup of sarsaparilla compound, ½ ounce; syrup of horehound, ¼ ounce; essence of wild ginseng, ½ ounce; syrup of rhubarb, ½ ounce.

Shake this solution well before the dose is taken, which would be three, four, five times each day; at least *four* times, and at other periods if necessary. The dose would be a teaspoonful, which may be taken before the meals or between the hours for meals.

This compound. . .will act upon the mucous membranes, stimulating the digestive forces of the system, stimulating the activity of the excretory forces of the kidneys and the secretive forces of the liver and those activities of the pancreas. These activities will create, then, a better balance throughout.

                                        1014-1

The effects of sarsaparilla are given clearly in two excerpts. Sarsaparilla root strengthens the secretions in the stomach and intestinal tract. (643-1 under *Ginseng,* this section) Compound syrup of sarsaparilla equalizes the lymph flow related to the gastric stomach flow and the intestinal digestive force. (404-4, *Ginseng,* this section)

Sassafras

Sassafras clarifies the blood stream and helps to allay nerve pressure. (5664-1, *Tonics,* this section)

Stillingia

Stillingia affects the gastric flow.

. . .the stillingia as an emit and an active force with the gastric flow.   839-1

Specifically it soothes the circulatory forces which set up pulsations between the liver, heart and kidneys. (404-4, *Ginseng,* this section) It clarifies the blood stream and helps to allay nerve pressure. (5664-1, *Tonics,* this section) Combined with other herbs, it can help to cleanse the kidneys and thus build up the blood supply and add to the gastric flow. (1019-1, *Tonics,* this section)

Watermelon Seed

A mild watermelon seed tea may be used to clear the kidneys of poisons. The nitre in it affects the entire circulatory system involved in the upper and lower hepatic (liver) area. Directions follow for application.

We would clarify the activity through the *kidneys* with a weak watermelon seed tea. . .Crush the seed. . .add a dram to six ounces of water, and steep as you would tea. This would be the correct proportion. It may be kept cool or warm, and little sips given two, three, four times each day—preferably warm.
632-17

Prepare and take internally a mild watermelon seed tea, prepared in. . .these proportions: Take a tablespoonful of watermelon seeds (before they are crushed or cut). Then crush or cut same, and put in a pint of boiling water—or put them in a tea container (crock) and pour a pint of boiling water over same. Let steep for at least thirty minutes. Take this quantity during a day; taking a tablespoonful to two tablespoonsful two, three, four times a day. . .this should be repeated at least two or three times each week, so that there may be [not only] the activity. . .of the nitre that is an active principle in same— upon the whole of the circulatory system as related to the upper and lower hepatic circulation, but. . .[also] a purifying of the system in the activity of same with the combinations. . .of that stimulation from the mullein stupes on the areas indicated.
1885-1

Watermelon seed tea acts as a diuretic and can remove quantities of fluid from the abdominal area.

Take internally the tea. . .made from watermelon seed, prepared as a tea; to reduce this activity through the kidneys' affectations, and to alleviate the quantities of water that accumulate through the abdominal area. The proportions would be half an ounce of the crushed seed to a quart of water, allowed to steep for twenty to thirty minutes. This may be kept and should be taken about a glassful each day.   1148-1

This tea should be used intermittently. The schedule for its use depends upon individual needs.

We would also make a tea of watermelon seed. Put a tablespoonful of cracked or crushed seed in a pint of water and let steep as tea. Strain and make palatable. This will act upon the kidneys with sufficient nitre to cause an activity most effective in this *particular* condition. Take a tablespoonful of the tea twice a day for two or three days; then leave off a day or two days, then take again.   647-3

Take internally small quantities of watermelon seed tea. Take this about once or twice a week. Crack the kernel, about half an ounce to a pint of water, allowed to steep as tea. Drain off. Take two to three ounces once or twice during a week; dependent upon activities of eliminations through kidneys, especially.   1151-2

For a pregnant woman:

Because of conditions that will be left by the activities of the kidneys, these should be purified by the very small doses of watermelon seed tea after the birth. Grind, crack or crush a teaspoonful of watermelon seed and pour a pint of boiling water over same, using only an enamel or crock container, covered. Let this stand for twenty minutes, strain, and then put in the refrigerator. Take this amount during two days. Then don't take any more for at least three to four days afterwards. Then repeat this.   951-7

Occasionally, about once a week, take watermelon seed tea prepared in this manner. Crush or cut a teaspoonful of the seed and put in a cup, and fill with boiling water. Let stand for thirty minutes, strain off. When cool, drink. This should be done once a week for five to six weeks. . .   3614-1

When there was acute need for passage of a kidney stone, watermelon seed tea was recommended to relax the (urinary?) system so that the stone could be expelled more easily. Other directions were also given.

It would be well for there to be taken a mild tea made from crushed or ground watermelon seed. The proportions would be about a teaspoonful of the ground seed to a pint of water, allowed to steep as ordinary tea. About two ounces of this would be taken every four hours...until there is the relaxation to the system.   **1839-1**

A person with diabetic tendencies, affecting the kidneys, was told to use the (Jerusalem) artichoke but if it was difficult to do this to substitute watermelon juice and pulp or watermelon seed because of the nitre-like content.

...there is still...an irritation or tendency for the activity of glandular forces as related to pancreas to become more active. Hence we find an increase in the activity of the kidneys, or those tendencies for too oft but sparse activity in most instances—as to the discharges from same, or from the bladder. But the [Jerusalem] artichoke should correct this. Don't take the properties by the hypodermic, but take the artichoke. Or now if there would be taken two to three drops of sweet spirits of nitre it would be well, or else eat a good big watermelon provided more of the juice is taken than the pulp. Or if this is not convenient, take watermelon seed tea—until there is the ability to get more of the artichoke.   **470-36**

However, it was made clear in the readings that watermelon seed tea possesses not only nitre-like properties but also others, actively affecting the rest of the (bodily?) system.

For a man 83 years old, who had been told to take watermelon seed tea:

...while carrying properties as in the nitre, it has an active force with the rest of the system that is not obtained in nitre.
304-43

We would not take more of the nitrate—the sweet spirits of nitre (it is a nitrate). We *would* take now the watermelon seed tea, which forms a different combination.   **540-10**

Wild Cherry Bark

Wild cherry bark is an expectorant and purifier for the blood supply, according to 643-1, *Ginseng,* this section. Wild cherry bark and cinchona bark together clarify the lungs of carbon. (1278-1, *Ginseng,* this section) Wild cherry bark together with other ingredients stimulates the lungs, throat and bronchials and the organs above the diaphragm. (2790-1, *Tonics,* this section)

Yellow Dock Root
Yellow dock root is a blood purifier, actively affecting liver secretions. (643-1, *Ginseng,* this section)

Yellow Root
Yellow root affects pneumogastric forces and gastric juices of the pyloric end of the stomach. (2790-1, *Tonics,* this section)

Tonics
The readings' compounds or prescriptions already noted in this section might properly be considered tonics, always to be used in conjunction with other therapies. Other tonics, consisting of a number of constituent parts designed to make for balance, will now be considered.

The first is designed to add to vitality with regard to the nervous system, the circulation and the reaction and retractions in the physical forces.

. . .to meet the needs of the conditions. . .rather would we build upon that vital force. . .that exists in the system, adding to the vitality of the body so that the system receives the proper reaction throughout in the vibratory forces of its nervous system, its circulation, its reaction and retractions throughout the physical forces of the body. . .First we would prepare. . .this for the body. . .in the form of a tonic, yet so active in its principles as to set that vital force *necessary* for *resuscitation* of the vitality and vitim(?) [elan vital?] of the system. . .To ½ gallon of rain water, add: (Preferably. . .in their original, or in the herb, state) sarsaparilla root, 1 ounce; wild cherry bark, 1 ounce; yellow dock root, ½ ounce; burdock root, ½ ounce; black snake root, ½ ounce; elder flower, 2 ounces; dog fennel, ¼ ounce; prickly ash bark, ¼ ounce.

Reduce this by simmering (not boiling) to ½ the quantity (1 quart). Then add, after this is strained, the properties of this: Cut 2 drams balsam of tolu in 3 ounces pure grain alcohol and add: sarsaparilla *compound,* ¼ ounce; sassafras oil, 20 drops; mullein oil, 40 drops.

Shake solution together before the dose is taken, and take

[one] teaspoonful 4 times each day. . .*after* the meal. *Eat* the meal. Let the diet be principally...of vegetables, but those that grow *beneath* the ground—all tuberous; and nuts and such. Not too much fruit, though orange juice may be taken liberally. Little of meats save the juice of same.

When the whole quantity of these properties as given. . .[is] taken, then we would give further instructions for this body.

111-1

This reading, 111-1, was given Oct. 18, 1928. Unfortunately this man did not request another till May 20, 1946, by which time Edgar Cayce had passed on.

The next tonic is structured to assist the intestinal tract of [4551] through sparking the liver, gall forces and pancreatic juices to make proper secretions to add to the blood supply.

The conditions as exist through the intestinal tract itself. . . [are] reflexes from this condition. . .in the liver and the action of the gall forces and the pancrean juices as taken into the system to act on the blood supply that is needed for the body.

To bring about an equilibrium within this body and to produce within the body those properties...necessary to bring a balance of force in the body. . .[Directions for medicinal properties follow and then:] prepare a tonic for this body, in this: black haw bark, two ounces; dogwood bark, two ounces; prickly ash bark, two ounces; yellow dock root, two ounces; elder flower, four ounces.

This would be put in one gallon of water, rain water, reduced by simmering, not boiling, to one quart. Strain, and while still warm add to this four ounces of sugar, with four ounces of grain alcohol, and three drams of balsam of tolu—this would be all put together. . .The dose would be a tablespoonful four times a day.

This is not to be taken till after the medicine properties have been well cared for in the system. . .   4551-1

The following tonic prescription also takes blood supply into account. [1019] suffered from disturbing conditions, including a poor circulation which was unable to supply proper nutriment to all parts of the body. Suggestions were made for osteopathic adjustments and manipulations, the use of the Radio-active Appliance, diet and ingestion of this compound.

To 2 ounces of strained honey add 4 ounces of distilled water. Allow to come to a boil. This would be the carrier. Then to this add: essence of wild ginseng, ½ ounce; essence of wild ginger,

¼ ounce; tincture of stillingia, ¼ ounce; essence of Indian turnip, 10 minims; tolu (cut in 1 ounce of alcohol), 3 drams.

Shake the solution before taking. The dose would be half a teaspoonful before each meal and before retiring.

. . .The honey as a carrier is [to create] a normal reaction to the gastric juices of the stomach, the intestines throughout.

Stimulation from the wild ginseng is to the gastric flow but acts primarily upon the glands of the gastric flow for an activity to the thyroid, to the ducts and glands within the liver area itself as stimulated by the Indian turnip, also the ginger, that will work directly with the gastric flow in the liver's activity, as well as the stillingia, which in this combination makes for an activity to the kidneys for purifying or cleansing same, thus building or purifying the blood supply and adding to the gastric flow.

These, in combination with the *quantity* of the alcohol as a preservative, with the activity of the balsam of tolu in same, will make for activities of a general stimulation. . .   1019-1

The following tonic compound was recommended for [3810], a man approximately 60 years old, who was suffering from toxemia due to retention of bacilli in his blood stream and to improper elimination, which allowed poisons to be taken up and distributed to capillary and emunctory forces. The optic nerve had become affected, and this had resulted in partial blindness. The tonic was to clear out the poisons in the system.

. . .to create the correct vibration necessary to restore the vibration that would give sight again to the body even better than one of its age, we would first eliminate from the system those poisons that produce the condition in the body. . .Then we would create the vibratory force necessary to give the equilibrium of forces in the body. We would take this into the system first: sarsaparilla root, 2 ounces; yellow dock root, 2 ounces; burdock root, 2 ounces; black haw bark, 2 ounces; prickly ash bark, 2 ounces; elder flower, 4 ounces.

This would all be placed into one gallon of rain water, reduced by simmering—not boiling—to one quart. While still warm add to this: four ounces of grain alcohol with three drams of balsam of tolu. . .

The dose of this will be a tablespoonful four times a day. While this is being taken into the system we would give heat sufficient to the body to get the effect of these forces through the whole circulation. . .blood force, lymphatic and capillary. . .

So the body becomes as it were steeped or seeped in these medicinal properties that we are giving into the body. . .

This will reduce the body in weight, and while this is being given to the body the diet should be very little. . .only those properties carrying. . .much of green vegetable matter especially—no meats. . .the sweats will be kept up as long as the medicinal properties hold out. . .for four ounces. . .[The vibration that will be necessary after this has been given to the body] will be to the fourth dorsal and the whole length of the cervicals. . .By electrically driven vibratory forces to create the proper incentive to these portions of the body. . .

We will find that within nine weeks we will have this body so the sight will be returned in its proper form.   3810-1

The next tonic seems to be initial therapy for a person who needed a real overhaul.

Then, in the *beginning* of applications that will aid the physical body, for any permanent relief, there must be *changes* made in the attitude the body holds towards individuals, self, and life; yet these *may* be changed in the *variations* as may be brought about to the physical functioning body. Then, *aiding* these, we will have the basis to work on. . .

Then for the better elements at the present time, these we would give as internal applications for the system, use those in equal quantities of gold seal or life everlasting, and of ginseng in the wild state, and Indian turnip, and that of snake root and elder flower—an ounce each, to thirty-two ounces of distilled water, reduced by simmering (not boiling) to half the quantity. Then add to this: tincture of stillingia, ¼ ounce; syrup of ipecac, 40 minims; oil of sassafras, 10 minims.

Cut 2 drams balsam of tolu in 2 ounces grain alcohol. Shake solution together before the dosage is taken, and the dose would be [a] half teaspoonful every four hours. The activities of these properties with the system—in those of the herbs as given: The life everlasting is for that tendency of the creation in system of those elements. . .that create a high vibration in the blood supply, both as to the respiratory and heart's action; while that in ginseng for the activity of the glands in the system as are affected by the subjugation or depressions of the body, as in a general manner. The Indian turnip acting as a stimuli [stimulus] to the functioning of the distresses in the assimilations in the duodenum; while. . .the elder flower [acts on]. . .the vibratory forces as changed in the whole of the mesenteric system, aided by. . .[the combination] of the stillingia and sassafras as the *clarifier* of the blood stream. . .
[with a] tendency. . .[toward] the allaying of nerve pressure. The alcohol. . .[a stimulus] and carrier, as is the tolu for the digestive system.

232

When this has been given for at least ten days, we would then begin with. . .the ultraviolet ray. . .Then we would give the further instructions for these corrections, after *these* have been given for ten days. . .   5664-1

This last tonic was designed to stimulate a body in which no great amount of change was immediately needed.

To relieve the condition for this body we would keep those forces for the system much as we have at the present time. We would only take those of a stimulation to the body to give the correct vibration through the system with the air and water... as in this: To one gallon of rain water we would add: 4 ounces wild cherry bark, preferably from the north side of the tree; 2 ounces yellow root; 2 ounces red root; 1 ounce prickly ash bark; 1 ounce elder flower.

Reduce this by simmering, not boiling, to one quart, strain, while warm add: 2 drams balm of Gilead, 6 ounces grain alcohol.

The dose with this would be [a] teaspoonful four times each day before meals. The effect. . .on the system is to give. . . stimulation to the organs and to the eliminating forces in the system, as in this:

The active principle from the wild cherry bark with the other ingredients is a stimulation of the lungs, throat and bronchials and those organs above the diaphragm.

The yellow root is for the pneumogastric forces and gastric juices of the pyloric end of the stomach itself.

The red root is a stimulus for the secretions given by the pancrean forces and the spleen in its functioning from the blood cell forces as desʋroyed there.

The prickly ash bark is for the blood supply as acted upon in the emunctory forces of the liver itself proper.

The elder flower is [for] the functioning of the organs of the pelvis with the action of the kidneys, with the stimulation from the alcohol and balm of Gilead in these organs. . .

Q-3. What time is required to bring this body to normal if the treatment as given is followed?

A-3. Sixty to ninety days. . .   2790-1

A Cough Medicine and Expectorant

The following combination was advised for [243] as a general healing agent, which would also function as a cough medicine and expectorant.

As a cough medicine, an expectorant, and for a healing

through the whole system, prepare: Put 2 ounces of strained pure honey in 2 ounces of water and let come to a boil. Skim off the refuse, then add 1 ounce of grain alcohol. To this as the carrier, then, add in the order named: syrup of wild cherry bark, 1 ounce; syrup of horehound, ½ ounce; syrup of rhubarb, ½ ounce; elixir of wild ginger, ½ ounce.

Shake well the solution before the dose is taken, which would be about a teaspoonful and this may be taken as close together as every hour. It will allay the cough, *heal* those disturbing forces through the bronchi and larynx, and make for better conditions through the eliminations. [Other directions follow.]   243-29

Inhalants

Of the various inhalants presented in the readings, a few have been selected as being of somewhat general application.

Apple Brandy

The apple brandy inhalant is a particularly effective one. According to Dr. William A. McGarey it was recommended for nearly every case of tuberculosis.[39] The following references give details of this therapy.

For a 36-year-old woman with tuberculosis:

Use the inhalations two or three times a day from the apple brandy. Put half a gallon or a gallon of the brandy in a container at least twice the size or [encompassing] twice the... space used by the brandy; that is in a charred oak container— if it's a gallon of brandy, use a two-gallon container; if it's half a gallon of brandy, use a gallon container. Preferably when it is put in, close the bung where it is put in with an oak or bung stopper. Then in the top, or one end of the container, the keg, bore a hole a quarter of an inch. Insert a metal tube— preferably of silver or nickel, or copper. This would extend an inch or inch and a half into the container, and two or three inches above same. This then would be kept tightly corked, either with a screw cap or cork. Keep close to heat, but not heating necessarily; so that evaporation takes place. Only inhale the gas that arises *from* the brandy distilling, as it were, itself, or throwing off the fumes. Shake a little if there is not sufficient gas when the second or third inhalation is taken. This may be inhaled directly from the tube, or a rubber tube may be attached—but do not lose the gas! This *is* effective, efficient.   1560-1

[39]William A. McGarey, M.D., "Notes from the Medical Research Bulletin," *The A.R.E. Journal,* March, 1975, pg. 82.

Another reading takes into account the desirability of a vent to avoid undue vacuum during inhalation and gives further options for the material of the tube. It also emphasizes that *pure* apple brandy is to be used.

Prepare a charred oak keg, about a gallon and a half to two gallon keg. If a gallon and a half, put in same three-fourths gallon of pure apple brandy.

This keg should be so prepared that there would be two small openings in one end. One would act only as a vent when inhaling the fumes of the evaporated brandy into the throat and lungs from the other opening, which would be prepared with a small tube—either of rubber or metal, or glass—that will not touch the brandy, but open into the vacuum above same, so that the fumes from the brandy may be inhaled two or three times a day. This should be kept where it will evaporate more quickly than ordinarily; not so much heat as to cause too great an evaporation, but where there is sufficient to create something more than the ordinary evaporation. Keep the vents tightly corked when not in use.   2978-1

The effect of the inhalations is explored in the following extract.

Inhale these fumes 2 or 3 times a day. In the beginning, do not inhale too much. Do inhale it, do not swallow it. While it will not hurt to swallow it, it is not as helpful to the body. The gas will not only act as an antiseptic, but will, with the properties that should be increased in the body, aid the change in the circulation, aiding these chemicals in their proper proportion to the body assimilation and the body activity, or the whole of the digestive forces, and eliminate the cause of infection in the lungs proper, and we will find it will gradually heal those areas where at present there are openings, though not a great deal of live tubercle, but the adhesions. . .are the more irritating for deep breathing.   5097-1

This treatment, which is so effective for restoring the lungs of those with tuberculosis can naturally be used for other severe conditions as well.

Edgar Cayce: Yes. . .these are rather serious disturbances for this body. From cold and congestion and lack of vitality, there is a great deal of inflammation in the pleura or that area of the capsule of the lungs. Because of this irritation there is an accumulation from lymph circulation or a formation of quantities of fluid. These are causing adherences or lesions or

adhesions in portions of the lung.

These will require rest in the open, though this should be not too much in the sun but not entirely out of the sun. When there are the great accumulations, of course, these should be drained, but we should begin with the use of packs about the body, especially as a jacket which should be made with mud baths, which may be put about the body, as to prevent this adherence of the pleura to either the walls of the lung or the cavities or the area of the body-structure itself. This, as we find, should be made with antiphlogistine or the California mud, medicated. . .[Directions follow for other therapy.]

We would for the healing of same use the brandy keg which has been described, how that this is a charred container, at least a gallon and a half or two gallon. Into this put a gallon of apple brandy and have this where it is kept warm to produce [a] quantity of the gas forming, and only the gas should be inhaled, at least twice a day. . .[Directions follow for other therapy.] 5374-1

Combinations for Asthma, Bronchitis, Catarrh, Hay Fever, Sinusitis

For a complaint of asthma, bronchitis and gall bladder trouble:

. . .many of these [functioning organs] suffer under the stress and strain of the condition existent. The head, neck, throat and lungs *offer*. . .the greater distress. At the same time, the greater improvement may come to the body through these very same conditions, for with the assistance of the system to produce the proper reflexes through the activity of a purified blood supply, the carbon may be added to system in such a manner as to bring resuscitation to the functioning of the system, and aid the whole body in its ability to recuperate. Also there must be considered the abilities of the system to bring about the collaboration of the eliminating systems in their proper order and distribution, for to produce—in a condition as existent in this body, [4252], an overtaxation to one portion of the system through the non-cooperation of the rest of the eliminating system would be to only *centralize* the condition in some one portion of the functioning organs in elimination. Either, then, the lower hepatic circulation, liver and kidneys, lungs, or. . .the digestive system, would be the sufferer, without this proper coordination being brought about. . .[so that] the condition would be assisted or *eliminated* from the body.

In the functioning of the organs, then, these must be kept

...in the way of cooperation, or collaboration, or cooperating in the *proper* manner of elimination. Through the respiratory system must come the proper amount. Through the alimentary canal must come the proper amount. Through that of the distribution through the hepatic circulation—the liver in its function, both as excretory and secretive, must be kept in balance...eliminating through the kidneys, and through these portions of the system, should be kept in balance.

To add, then, for this body, that vibration as will bring about the resuscitation of the forces in the body, we would *begin* with these—though there will be found that it will be necessary for a change from time to time to bring about the normal forces for this body.

Begin first, then, using these as inhalants for the body. These should be prepared, then, in this manner, and *used* in the manner as is outlined.

First there should be that of pure apple brandy, as would be kept in a *charred* container—not of any other but a *charred* container, at least two quarts of same in a container twice the size of the quantity, and so arrange that this being kept near a fire will produce fumes above same, and same may be inhaled into the throat, bronchials and lungs, at least twice each day— not a solution, only that gas as is thrown off by evaporation from same. This will act as a healer for the lungs, the throat, the larynx, and the whole system. Also a. . .[stimulus] for the blood supply as will be carried into the system by this being inhaled.

Then we would use *this* as an inhalant. . .whenever there is the necessity of reducing the irritation...produced in throat by . . .the improper relation of the sympathetic and cerebrospinal nerve system, from the 4th and 5th dorsal, 4th, 3rd, 2nd cervical, to the throat—in attempt of the system to throw off through these portions of the body. This will act only as a *cleanser,* and as the form of the active forces in preventing the spread of infection from conditions that should be *eliminated* from the body: To 4 ounces of at least 85% alcohol, add: eucalyptol, 22 minims; benzoin, 5 minims; rectified oil of turp, 5 minims; rectified creosote, 8 minims; Canadian balsam, 10 minims; tincture tolu in solution, ¼ minim.

Keep this in a glass corked container at least twice the size of the amount of solution. Do not shake solution until ready to be inhaled. Inhale both through nostril and through the mouth.

To cleanse the nostril region, where there has been infection in the soft tissue of face, nose, antrum, and other portions of this part of body, pour a portion of this solution in hot boiling water and cover head, inhaling same in the nostril—not through mouth, but in the nostril.

When shaken cold, inhale in mouth *and* nostril—but to *cleanse* the nostril *heat* in boiling water; for each of these properties are thrown off at a *different* heat, and it is necessary that head be covered to receive benefit from same.

4252-1

For the asthmatic condition, have those properties made into an inhalant, as this: To 4 ounces of pure grain alcohol (not 85%, but pure *grain* alcohol—that's a 190%, or 190 proof), add: eucalyptol, or oil of same, 20 minims; benzosol, 10 minims; oil of turp, or rectified oil of turp, 5 minims; tolu in solution, 40 minims; benzoin, tincture of, 5 minims.

Keep in a container at least twice the size, or an 8 ounce bottle with a glass cork. Shake solution together and inhale deep into the lungs and bronchi two or three times each day.

5682-1

The inhalant should be kept up, but we would renew the properties as taken and give them in this manner and form at the present time: To 4 ounces of grain alcohol, we would add 15 minims, eucalyptus oil; 5 minims, benzosol; 10 minims, balsam of white pine or white pine oil.

This is to be inhaled into the bronchials or mouth and into the system three to four times each day or when necessary to prevent the tickling sensation or the spasmodic condition occurring at times in the bronchials.

304-3

Q-1. Can anything be done to relieve the nasal catarrh?
A-1. Do these [therapies] which have been indicated. Use the inhalant which may be outlined for the body in this: Prepare a large mouth bottle. Put two vents into the opening of the bottle in which solution is put. Leave a two-ounce space, at least, above solution in container. Add the following ingredients in the order named: pure grain alcohol, 4 ounces; oil of eucalyptus, 20 drops; rectified oil of turp, 5 drops; tincture of benzoin, 15 drops; oil of pine needles, 10 drops; tolu in solution, 5 drops.

Shake the solution, then removing the cork from vents, inhale deeply into the nasal passages—not too much in the beginning, just once or twice. Then inhale into the throat.

3480-2

Among other directions for hay fever therapy:

Then, use through the latter portion of August and September, this as a combination: Prepare in the manner indicated, putting together the ingredients only in the order named. First we would prepare a bottle with a large mouth, two vents through the cork and these vents capable of being corked themselves with a small cork. Neither of the vents is to enter the solution, so use a six ounce container. In this container put four ounces of grain alcohol (at least 90 proof), then add in the order named: oil of eucalyptus, 20 minims; rectified oil of turp, 5 minims; compound tincture of benzoin, 15 minims; oil of pine needles, 10 minims; tolu in solution, 10 minims.

When this is to be used, shake the solution together, remove the corks from the vent, inhale deep[ly] through the nostril so ...[the fumes will] enter the nasal passages, also...the upper and back portions of throat, both passages. Shake between each deep inhalation.   5347-1

As we find, most conditions physically are very good throughout this body. There are tendencies and inclinations, the correction of which may relieve the body from some anxieties which arise in the experience at times, as well as make for greater abilities in the mental and spiritual activities which may be part of the experience of the entity.

There are periods when there are those aggravating headaches, which arise apparently from something disagreeing with the digestion. These are only part of the sources or causes, for...when there are sudden changes in atmospheric pressures, there are periods when the body apparently tends to take cold easily, and the soft tissue in the face and throat gives trouble. These are partially the greater source of the disturbing areas.

For, with this sinus disorder, there is then a form of catarrhal reaction. This forms in the circulation that which tends to produce a greater amount of acidity throughout the system. This acidity causes those inclinations for cold and for the congestion in the liver and the kidneys. Naturally with these congestions, we have a variation in the circulation between lungs, heart, liver and kidneys...there is no organic disturbance in lungs, heart, liver or kidneys, and yet with these tendencies for the increase in the circulation, and for the attempt to eliminate the congestion produced by this superacidity, all may show some reflex conditions and may, without ...these disturbances [being relieved] later cause distress.

In meeting the needs, then, of the conditions in the present: First, we would have prepared an inhalant. Take at least a 6 to 8 ounce container, preferably a large mouth bottle. Prepare this so there are 2 vents in the cork of the bottle, which may themselves be corked, so that neither of these vents extends into the solution. For only the fumes or gases, which are formed by the combination of that which will be placed in same, are to be inhaled into the nostril; and the effect is...

through this gas from same to the antrum, throat and the soft tissue of the face and head. Put, then, into the container first, 4 ounces of pure grain alcohol. Then add, in the order named: oil of eucalyptus, 30 minims; rectified oil of turpentine, 10 minims; compound tincture of benzoin, 20 minims; oil of pine needles, 5 minims; tolu in solution, 15 minims.

These will be suspended in the alcohol. Shaking [the combination] together and then removing both of the small corks, inhale deeply into the nostril. This will also go into the trachea and bronchi, and it will relieve those tensions, acting as not only an antiseptic, but as an allaying of the inflammation which tends to affect also the soft tissue, and those tendencies towards the conditions indicated. Do this 2 or 3 times each day.

For the disturbance which already exists by absorption from mucus and circulation, as parts of discharge or drippings through the throat to the stomach, have at least 3 to 5 to 10 (would be well) hydrotherapy treatments. These may be put far apart in the latter portion of the treatments. These would be given, not with dry heat, to form the activities of the superficial circulation, but a fume bath with witch hazel in same. Not too much of this, only just sufficient so that perspiration begins in all pores of the body. Then have a shower, and then a massage with equal portions of olive oil and peanut oil. [Other directions follow.]   5147-1

Applications Through the Skin

Massage Oils

The readings tell us that massage can be a preventative as well as a curative measure for the body.

For the hydrotherapy and massage are preventive as well as curative measures. For the cleansing of the system allows the body-forces themselves to function normally, and thus eliminate poisons, congestions and conditions that would become acute throughout the body.   257-254

The reason for massage is clearly stated.

The massage is very well, but we would do this the more often. . .As long as there is an opportunity of it producing the effect to all areas of the better activity to the organs of the body. The "why" of the massage should be considered: Inactivity causes many of those portions along the spine from which impulses are received to the various organs to be lax, or taut, or to allow some to receive greater impulse than others.

240

The massage aids the ganglia to receive impulse from nerve forces as it aids circulation through the various portions of the organism.   2456-4

The method of massage, areas covered, etc., depend on the particular condition, as illustrated by the following selections.

When it is necessary or better to massage in other directions, we will indicate it. Here we have the tendency. . .for a flow toward the head. Keep it in that way in which there is a flowing away from the head. If you were to dam a stream, would you sometimes attempt to knock it away so the water would clear a little bit? Not much you wouldn't, if you wanted to prevent it from flowing back! This is just a practical condition that exists in the law of nature itself. Massage away from the head as we have given. There are areas, as outlined, where the massage may be in a circular motion. It may be all of the circular nature if it will be kept away from the head always.   3117-2

Massage applications are excellent for each body, and well for this one. . .once in ten days or once in two weeks. This should be sufficient with regular activities that the body has... Swedish massage. . .is for the superficial circulation, to keep attunement. . .between the superficial circulation or the lymph and the exterior portion with the activities of the body. These treatments should not be hurried, and there should be given sufficient period for the reaction to the body.   1158-11

The readings were sometimes specific as to just who should do the massage—in some cases one professional or another, occasionally a member of the family. Dr. Harold J. Reilly, who worked with Edgar Cayce readings for many years and was founder-director of the Reilly Health Institute in Rockefeller Center, has assembled directions for some simple massage techniques to be used at home. We refer the reader to the comprehensive health-care volume authored by Dr. Reilly and Ms. Brod.[40]

For further discussion of massage techniques the reader is referred to an excellent article by Mary Alice Duncan, P.T., a practicing physical therapist with extensive training and many years of professional experience.[41]

---

[40]Harold J. Reilly, D.Ph.T., D.S., and Ruth Hagy Brod, *The Edgar Cayce Handbook for Health Through Drugless Therapy,* Jove Publications, Inc., New York City, 1977, pp. 257-294.
[41]Mary Alice Duncan, P.T., "Physiotherapy in the Edgar Cayce Readings, The Concept of Wholeness," *An Edgar Cayce Health Anthology,* A.R.E. Press, 1979, pp. 21-33.

In this article Duncan notes the implication in the readings that oils used in massage are absorbed by the skin and act as food for underlying structures. For maximum results it would, therefore, seem best to work with the cold-pressed oils found in health stores.

Peanut Oil

The readings frequently advised the use of peanut oil, combinations of peanut and olive oils and combinations of peanut and olive oils with lanolin added. Lanolin seemed to be a specific for itching and skin irritation.

Massage with peanut oil—yes, the lowly peanut oil has in its combination that which will aid in creating in the superficial circulation, and in the superficial structural forces, as well as in the skin and blood, those influences that make more pliable the skin, muscles, nerves and tendons, that go to make up the assistance to structural portions of the body. Its absorption and its radiation through the body will also strengthen the activities of the structural body itself. 2968-1

Q-21. Should I resume peanut oil rubs?
A-21. There is nothing better. These may be given by any good masseuse. If they are taken once a week, it is not too often. For, they do supply energies to the body. . .Those who would take a peanut oil rub each week need never fear arthritis. 1158-31

To improve skin condition of face, back, scalp and hair:

At least once a week, after a good thorough workout of body in exercise following the bath afterward, massage the back, the face, the body, the limbs with pure peanut oil. Then this will add to the beauty. . .And the oil rubs once a week, ye will never have rheumatism nor those concurrent conditions from stalemate in liver and kidney activities. 1206-13

Then for the supplying of better energies to the body, especially in the superficial circulation:
About twice each week almost bathe in olive oil or peanut oil; especially peanut oil—in the joints, the neck, across the clavicle, across all the areas of the spine, the rib and the frontal area to the pit of the stomach, across the stomach and especially in the diaphragm area; then across the hips and the lower portion of the back and across the sacral area and then the limbs themselves. Massage these by dipping the fingers in

242

the oil. Do not sponge off immediately. Do this just before retiring, wipe off with tissue, and then bathe off in the morning. . .if these are kept consistently, we will not only build strength but supply the better circulation throughout the whole body.   1688-7

For foot discomfort:

As for the limbs—each evening, or at least three to four evenings a week, soak the feet and the limbs to the knees in a fluid made from boiling old coffee grounds. It is the tannic acid in this that is helpful, which can be better obtained from boiling the old grounds (but not soured). . .Following such a foot bath, massage peanut oil thoroughly into the knee and under the knee, through the area from the knee to the foot, and especially the bursa [bursae] of the feet. . .This done consistently will relieve these tensions.   243-33

Peanut Oil and Olive Oil

Of evenings, when prepared for the night's rest, massage the body *thoroughly* with an equal combination of olive oil and peanut oil. This would include the head, or the sides of the face and neck, across the chest, across the abdomen, as well as down the spine and the limbs. . .   2140-1

Massage deeply and heavily along the cerebrospinal system, from the base of the brain to the end of the spine, on either side of the spine with an equal combination of olive oil and peanut oil. This does not mean just rubbing it on, but massaging it into the system in a circular motion; finding each segment. . .along the cerebrospinal system.   2302-1

For prostatitis:

After the massage, each time, we find it would be well to massage the affected area—that is, of course, across the small of the back and extending all the way over the prostate area. . . and on either side of the limbs—with an equal combination of olive oil and peanut oil. Massage in all the body will absorb. Do this after the manipulations are given, each time.   1539-4

Q-5. What causes excessive dryness or peeling of skin on bottoms of feet?
A-5. Poor circulation. Hence the needs for the massage and oil rubs [of peanut oil and olive oil in equal parts], which should include the limbs—of course—and especially the feet, with

adjustments in the muscular forces and bursa [bursae] of the feet.   1770-5

Peanut Oil, Olive Oil and Lanolin

For making or keeping a good complexion...for the skin, the hands, arms and body as well—we would prepare a compound to use as a massage by (self) at least once or twice each week. To six ounces of peanut oil, add olive oil, two ounces; rosewater, two ounces; lanolin, dissolved, one tablespoonful. This would be used after a tepid bath in which the body has remained for at least fifteen to twenty minutes; giving the body then [during the bath] a thorough rub with any good soap—to stimulate the body-forces...Sweetheart or any good castile soap, or Ivory, may be used for such.

Afterwards, after shaking it well, massage with this solution. Of course, this [amount] will be sufficient for many times. Shake well and pour [some] in an open saucer or the like, dipping fingers in same. Begin with the face, neck, shoulders, arms; and then the whole body would be massaged thoroughly with the solution; especially in [the area of] the limbs, in the areas that would come across the hips, across the body, across the diaphragm...Not only [will this] keep a stimulating [effect] with the other treatments...indicated [hydrotherapy, massage and osteopathy] taken occasionally, and give the body a good base for the stimulating of the superficial circulation; but [also the solution] will aid in keeping the body beautiful; that is, [so] as to [be free from] any blemish of any nature.   1968-7

Peanut oil, 2 ounces; olive oil, 2 ounces; lanolin (liquified), 1 teaspoon. Shake this solution and massage thoroughly into the lumbar and sacral areas, and especially along limbs... under the knee, in the foot, especially in the bursa of the heel and the front under the toes or in the instep.   3232-1

Olive Oil

Yes, we have the body [of an 11-year-old boy] and those anxieties of the mother respecting this body and the developing of the hindrance in the locomotion...

In the general physical condition...there is a deficiency of calcium...This may be best materially aided by the supplying of this element in the foods...

But without the use of a regular massage *and* an oil or food value to those affected portions, this would not be so well.

Hence...we would use alternately a massage one evening

with olive oil and the next with cocoa butter; doing this for five to ten minutes, a rub from the hip and sacral area all the way to the toe, especially on the limb that is hindered in development—massaging all that the body will absorb. To be sure, sponge off the body first with hot water, so that the skin will absorb the properties more readily. After the body has been thoroughly massaged and has absorbed all it will, then rub off with a soft tissue. . .Each time before the application the body may be sponged with hot water, or hot applications may be wrapped about the body to open the pores. [Directions for other treatment follow.]   1785-1

Olive Oil in Combination

For the exterior forces, [a breaking out] as upon the hands and outer portions of the body, keep these bathed so they do not dry or crack, with sweet oil. This is a combination. . .of olive oil and preparations that are healing, with a little of glycerine in same. . .Or there may be made a combination of glycerine, camphor and olive oil, but just the sweet oil for the present.   1005-16

To relieve much of the scar tissue on the left limb we would use sweet oil combined with camphorated oil [in] equal parts. Massage this each day for 3 to 6 months and we would reduce the most of this.   487-15

Q-5. *Are the scars on the legs or stomach detrimental in any way to the proper functioning of the body?*
A-5. Little or no hindrance. These may be aided in being removed by sufficient time, precaution and persistence in the activity; by the massage over those portions of small quantities at a time of tincture of myrrh and olive oil, and camphorated oil. These would be massaged at different times to be sure; one, one day and the other the second day from same . . .In preparing the olive oil and tincture of myrrh, heat the oil and add the myrrh—equal portions, only preparing such a quantity as would be used at each application. The camphorated oil may be obtained in quantity. Only massage such quantities as the cuticle and epidermis will absorb. This will require, to be sure, a long period but remember the whole surface may be entirely changed if this is done persistently and consistently. In the massaging, do not massage so roughly as to produce irritation. The properties are to be absorbed. Do not merely pat the solution on, and do not use tufts of cotton or other properties to dab it on—dip the fingertips into the solution, and it won't hurt the fingers either—it'll be good for

them! and massage into affected portions.

. . .the therapeutic value of the properties given to the skin itself is as follows: As given, as known and held by the ancients more than the present modes of medication, olive oil— properly prepared (hence pure olive oil should always be used)—is one of the most effective agents for stimulating muscular activity, or mucous membrane activity, that may be applied to a body. Olive oil, then, combined with the tincture of myrrh will be very effective; for the tincture of myrrh acts with the pores of the skin in such a manner as to strike in, causing the circulation to be carried to affected parts where tissue has been in the nature of folds—or scar tissue, produced from superficial activity from the active forces in the body itself, in making for coagulation in any portion of the system, whether external or internal. . .The camphorated oil is merely the same basic force [olive oil] to which. . .[have] been added properties of camphor in more or less its raw or original state, [rather] than [in] the spirits of same. Such activity in the epidermis is not only to produce soothing to affected areas but to stimulate the circulation in such effectual ways and manners as to combine with the other properties in bringing what will be determined, in the course of two to two and a half years, a new skin! 440-3

For a 54-year-old man, suffering from asthenia and inability to assimilate food properly:

. . .the greater help would come from the massage following, at least every other day, a hydrotherapy treatment which would be given with fume baths or a cabinet or an open container in which there would be a pint of water and in this two teaspoonsful of witch hazel. Let this boil. No other heat, but the fumes from this which may settle over the body. Then have a thorough massage and rubdown using equal portions of olive oil, tincture of myrrh and compound tincture of benzoin. These should be massaged in and along the cerebrospinal system, especially, always away from the head. 5372-1

For a 45-year-old man with incoordination of the nervous system:

In the *mornings*, thoroughly massage the whole of the cerebrospinal. . .*after* the massaging thoroughly with that of cold applications. . .[rubbing] into the centers along the spine, equal parts tincture of myrrh and olive oil. *Heat* the oil, not to boiling, but nearly so, and add the myrrh. About a tablespoonful of each should be used. . .at each application. 5467-1

For a 6-year-old boy with cerebral palsy:

Well that the body, each evening, be rubbed *thoroughly* with those forces as may be found in an ointment—which acts as a lubricant for the whole system. These may be alternated between cocoa butter and olive oil, or olive oil and myrrh and then cocoa butter. These will make for bettered condition for the body's rest and for the activities of the extremities—as well as centers along the cerebrospinal system...this would also be helpful for this body, were the spine rubbed very thoroughly, not in the ordinary treatment as of manipulation, but a more coarseness, so that we will stimulate the nerve ends as they function through the muscular portion of the body.   5568-6

Each day, in the evening, to bring better rest, we would massage over the *whole* body—that is, beginning over the base of the brain to the tips of the toes—equal parts of olive oil and tincture of myrrh and sassafras oil. Massage this gently into the system, so that the capillary circulation picks up—in its internal reaction—from such gentle massaging.   133-2

The activity of the olive oil is as *food* that may be absorbed by the lymph and emunctories of the system, provided the pores and the exterior portions of the body have been relaxed or opened before this is massaged into the system. The activity of the properties as go *with* same, the myrrh and...sassafras oil ...add to the *strength* of the muscular tissue, of the sinew along the system, [so] as to carry—the one stimulating the muscular forces, the other carrying to the cartilaginous forces, and to every nerve fiber itself, that of strength and activity. 5423-1

While there still remains weakness (and at times this will cause distress...especially [to] the nerve along the sciatic... along the inside) . . .the massage occasionally of the mullein and the olive oil with myrrh. . .will keep the conditions in a nearer normal way and manner.   275-8

Q-3. What can I do to cure callous or bunion on my left foot?
A-3....an application morning and evening—not bound on, but massaged thoroughly; and this means not just dabbing on and leaving same, but take three to five minutes of massaging. First, for five to ten days, use common baking soda wet or saturated with spirits of camphor. Then, after this has been used until the soreness is removed, use equal parts of olive oil and tincture of myrrh, and it'll be like [a] baby's foot! Massage each of those into the portion where there is the disturbance.
          574-1

Various Oils in Combination

For blindness:

. . .we would compound a specific rub to be used *after* the fume baths—now. To 2 ounces of Russian white oil, or Nujol, as the base, add—in the order named: cedar wood oil, ½ ounce; pine needle oil, ½ ounce; peanut oil, 1 ounce; sassafras root oil, ¼ ounce; oil of mustard, 20 drops. These, to be sure, will tend to separate; but before using shake well together, pouring a small quantity in a saucer. Dip the fingers into same and massage along the spine from about the middle of the back *upward* to the base of the brain. Then massage in a circular motion on each side of the spine, each segment and along each side, *downward* to the central portion of the spine. . .This will stimulate the activities of the optic forces, and we should soon begin to see some light. . .*This* as given is a special rub. . .and is only to the 9th dorsal or from the 9th dorsal to the base of the brain; while the other [peanut and olive oil massage] is over most of the body. . .as a stimulation to the whole of the perspiratory system.   2302-3

For glaucoma:

Do have each day a thorough massage with a combination of oils which we will indicate. This need not be professionally given, but *should* be given thoroughly; not something to be gotten through with, but take care and precaution. This would be especially from the base of the brain, or 1st cervical, to the 9th dorsal along the spinal system. The oils would be combined in this manner: To 4 ounces of Russian white oil, or Usoline, as the base, add—in the order named: peanut oil, 1 ounce; oil of cedar wood, ½ ounce; oil of sassafras root, ¼ ounce, lanolin (dissolved), ¼ ounce. Shake these together thoroughly before being poured into an open container, in which the fingers may be dipped to massage along the spine. This would be especially at the base of the brain, at the lower portion of the cervicals and on the upper dorsals—these areas especially; just what the body will absorb. Preferably do this of evening when ready to retire.   630-3

. . .a small portion of the following compound massaged into . . .[the feet, ankle, limb and hip] will be most beneficial: To 4 ounces of Russian white oil, add: witch hazel, 2 ounces; rub alcohol, 1 ounce (not wood but *rub* alcohol compound); oil of sassafras, 3 to 5 minims.

Shake this together. Only use a small portion of same at the time. Begin with the hips and rub down.

This would be good for anyone that stands on the feet much, or whose feet pain, or ankle or knees or tendons.   555-5

Q-4. Please give me something that will ease my back.

A-4. This is a very good specific: To 1 ounce of olive oil, add: Russian white oil, 2 ounces; witch hazel, ½ ounce; tincture of benzoin, ½ ounce; oil of sassafras, 20 minims; coal oil, 6 ounces. It'll be necessary to shake this together, for it will tend to separate; but a small quantity massaged in the cerebro-spinal system or over sprains, joints, swellings, bruises, will *take out* the inflammation or pain!   326-5

Castor Oil

Q-5. What causes the little place on this eyelid and what will remove it?

A-5. Cyst as from breaking of cellular forces. Mássage with the pure castor oil.   1424-4

Q-3. What treatment would remove the mole on my chest, or is this advisable?

A-3. . . .The massage with castor oil twice each day; not rubbing hard, but *gentle* massage around and over the place. And it will be removed.   573-1

Q-1. Should moles on the back be removed? If so, by whom and what method?

A-1. . . .these are not to be disturbed to the extent of material or outside influence.

The massaging. . .with just the castor oil will prevent growth. . .[Persistence with massaging] will remove same entirely.   678-2

Q-1. What should be done for the small mole or soft growth on left side of back, just below the shoulder blade, that gets irritated at times and is painful?

A-1. Use a small quantity of castor oil with a little soda mixed in same. This will make it sore for a day or two, then it will disappear.

Q-2. Just rub it on?

A-2. Just rub it on, two or three days apart, for two or three times.   4033-2

Q-14. The small growth on the first finger of my right hand is still there. Should anything further be done?

A-14. This may be massaged with pure castor oil and be removed. . .

Q-15. *How often?*

A-15. About twice a day; before retiring and when arising.

261-10

Q-4. *What is the best way to remove warts?*

A-4. This one on the right knee is gradually leaving. Put equal portions of castor oil and soda on the finger tip, massage this, it'll make it sore but it'll take it away also. 308-13

Other Massage Solutions
Camphor and Soda

Q-8. *What caused growth on foot, and what should be used if it repeats itself?*

A-8. This was from irritation; and that best for the reduction of same. . .would be a massage with baking soda which has been dampened with spirits of camphor. This will be good for anyone having calloused places or any attendant growths on feet; for it will remove them entirely! 276-4

Ipsab

Formula for Ipsab, the principal ingredient of which is prickly ash bark, called by the Indians "toothache bark":

To 6 ounces of distilled water, add 2 ounces of prickly ash bark. Reduce by simmering (not boiling) to 2 ounces. Strain and add powdered common salt until we have a very thin paste. Rinse or rub gums with this once every 2 days until this trouble in the mouth and gums has subsided. 4436-2

For problems involving the gums and teeth:

We would use the same (Ipsab) not upon cotton, for this body, but upon the finger use it and massage; not only the gums where the teeth are but where they are not! And we will find that the stimulation to the activities of the throat itself, to the salivary glands, to even the tonsil area, will be materially aided by the activity of the combination of the calcium with the iodine in same, as well as the antiseptics that arise from the vegetable forces in same as combined with sodium chloride. 569-23

Note reading excerpt 314-2 in the section "Ingestion of Food, Air and Water Containing Mineral Forces," under *Iodine*, that iodine as well as calcium is needed for the formation of healthy teeth.

Use Ipsab to keep *these [teeth] clear from the tartar* and [to stop the bleeding from the gums]. 257-13

Q-1. What can I do about pyorrhea condition in my teeth?
A-1. Use Ipsab regularly each day and rinse mouth out when it is finished with Glyco-Thymoline. 5121-1

The receding gums and those tendencies towards pyorrhea would be allayed by the consistent use of Ipsab as a massage for the teeth and gums. 3696-1

Locally, we would use the compound known as Ipsab to massage the gums. This will *purify* and make for such a condition as to assist in correcting the trouble where there has been the softening of the teeth themselves—or the enamel on same. 1026-1

Q-23. What causes the gray film on teeth?
A-23. The chemical balance in the system and the throw-off or discharge from breath in the lungs. This [the breath] is a source from which drosses are relieved from the system, and thus passing through the teeth produce [evidences of] same on the teeth. Keeping such cleansed with an equal combination of soda and salt at least three to four times a week will cleanse these (teeth) of this disturbance. The use of Ipsab as a wash for mouth and gums will further aid in keeping these conditions cleansed; and use any good dentifrice once or twice a day.
457-11

For a discussion of this formula the reader is referred to an article by Tom Johnson and Carol A. Baraff.[42]

Vinegar and Salt

We would begin with the corrections in the limb and knee, and. . .these will respond. There must be those precautions that sufficient time is given for the healing; and when this is accomplished (but not too soon) use a massage—massage very thoroughly; keeping the salt and vinegar on same, not only as a poultice but as a rub. When this has healed, then gradually—

---

[42]Tom Johnson and Carol A. Baraff, "Ipsab—An Herbal Remedy for Gum Problems," *An Edgar Cayce Health Anthology*, A.R.E. Press, 1979, pp. 91-93.

when the poultice and the rubs are used—the body may work the knee again. 438-3

. . .occasionally massage the knee and hip with a saturated solution of vinegar and salt; *pure* apple vinegar, not synthetic—nor that containing too much of raw acetic acid. 275-15

In the area of the knee, where ligaments have been torn, use about twice each week this combination: moisten table salt (preferably iodized salt) with pure apple vinegar, not having [it] too liquid, but that it may be gently massaged into the knee-cap, [and] the end of the ligaments. While this will hurt a few times at first, if this is kept up each day for quite a while we will get better results here. 3336-1

The ligaments about the knee we would massage well with almost a saturated solution of pure apple vinegar and common table salt, preferably the very heavy salt [rather] than that carrying too much of chal [chalk?] or ingredients to prevent the sticking. We. . .prefer the baser or common salt for this purpose. . . 304-3

Packs

Under *Massage Oils* we referred to the implication in the readings that substances applied to the skin are absorbed by it and act in conjunction with underlying structures. This same implication is found with regard to products constituting packs, pastes, ointments and washes.

Castor Oil Packs

The pack most widely used as a result of advice in the readings is the castor oil pack. Dr. William A. McGarey has treated it at length in his book *Edgar Cayce and the Palma Christi,* to which the reader is referred.[43]

A brief discussion of these packs will be included here.

According to the readings, under optimum conditions spirit or the higher intelligence directs the total activities of a person. In these circumstances the direction is enhanced by the use of oil, which is normally found in the body. The readings indicate that the oil helps the mind forces to better coordinate different parts of the body and to bring the spirit into closer communication with the body. This process is compared to the lubricating

---

[43]William A. McGarey, M.D., *Edgar Cayce and the Palma Christi,* A.R.E. Press, 1970.

effect of oil on machinery. An agent has to apply the oil, which helps the parts of the machinery to work together. Just so does spirit use the oil to help keep the body functioning properly. When the body is malfunctioning, application of oil under precise conditions can help it resume normal operation.

This was an interbetween emotion, or—as indicated—a partial psychic experience. Consider that which takes place from the use of the oil pack and its influence upon the body, and something of the emotion experienced may be partially understood.

Oil is that which constitutes, in a form, the nature of activity between the functionings of the organs of the system as related to activity. Much in the same manner as [oil would act] upon an inanimate object—it acts as a limbering agent or allowing movement, motion, as may be had by the attempt to move a hinge, a wrench, a center, or that movement of an inanimate machinery motion. This is the same effect had upon that which is now animated by spirit. This movement, then, was the reflection of the abilities of the spirit of *animate* activity as controlled through the emotions of mind, or the activity of mind between spirit *and* matter. This was a vision...

1523-15

Thus there should be, then, the realization that organs and their functionings have become aware, or conscious, of their activity, their function within the system.   1523-8

Castor oil packs are generally applied to the abdominal area. The readings suggest that they stimulate the lacteals or lymphatic vessels in the villi (or loops) of the small intestine. These approximately five million villi provide an absorbing surface of some ten square meters.[44]

A pack designed for this area may be prepared as follows: Fold a soft white flannel cloth into two or three thicknesses. Finished measurements should run 8 inches by 10 inches to 12 inches. Saturate this cloth with castor oil, place it in a covered enamel pan that has no breaks in it or a covered pyrex dish; warm this in the oven for a few minutes. Meanwhile the area of the bed where the person will take the pack, should be protected by a piece of plastic, covered in turn by a piece of old sheeting for comfort. The person should lie on his back there, place the

[44]George O'Malley, D.O., in collaboration with Peter Rudnikoff, D.O., "Castor Oil Pack Therapy—A Report," *The Searchlight,* May 1961, pg. 1.

253

hot pack over the abdomen in the area of the liver and gall bladder so that it extends down over the caecum (right lower quadrant of the abdomen) and appendix,[45] then put another protective plastic over the pack and top this with a heating pad, adjusted to keep the area hot but not uncomfortable. The pack should be left on from one to one and a half hours. Afterwards the skin of the area may be cleansed with a solution of two teaspoons of baking soda to a quart of water.[46]

The pack may be kept for future use, preferably in a closed plastic container in the refrigerator. It can be reused a number of times but only by the same person and only over a limited period. When it is reused, additional oil should be added to replace that dissipated in the prior application.

Castor oil packs are given in a series, broken by intervals of rest. The number in the series varies with particular needs. It is often desirable to follow up with small doses of olive oil. See references below. Also note in them that the type of pack just outlined was recommended to alleviate gallstones and liver and gastrointestinal difficulties.

For gallstones:

Have at least three to four thicknesses of old flannel saturated thoroughly with castor oil, then apply an electric heating pad. Let this get just about as warm as the body can well stand—cover with oil cloth to prevent soiling of linen. Keep this on every afternoon or evening for an hour. Then sponge off [the oil on the body] with soda water. Do this at least seven days without breaking. One hour each day, same hour each day. After and during those periods take small doses of olive oil, two, three times each day. These [small doses of olive oil] should not be so severe as to cause strain, but be careful after about the 3rd or 4th day to observe the stool, and there should be indications of the gall ducts being emptied and [there] should be gravel. . .and. . .some stones. 5186-1

For cholecystitis and gastroduodenitis:

. . .lack of assimilation and digestion for the system. . .castor oil packs. Take these each evening for three days in succession, and then the large dose of olive oil. Leave off three to four days, then take another series. Continue in this manner until the condition has entirely cleared. Then leave off three to four

[45]*Ibid.*, pg. 2.
[46]McGarey, pg. 132.

weeks; then [repeat]. . .regularly—in series—even though there is not the severe pain.   294-199

Have sufficient periods of the castor oil packs. To be sure, they are disagreeable, but they will break up lesions as no other administrations will. The best time to take these is the evening. . .These should be given in series, applied for an hour each evening for two or three evenings *before* each osteopathic adjustment is to be made. . .Keep these up until this coldness and the lesion in the right side. . . [are] removed—which is just a hand's breadth below the point of the rib, or over that area of the ducts.   2153-4

We would increase the activity of the liver in its functioning, so as to bring about a better assimilation. We would increase this activity through that of counterirritation externally, using. . .the castor oil packs for same. . .   18-2

Castor oil packs may also be applied to other areas of the body. The size of the folded flannel is tailored to the size of the area. In those that are markedly curved, such as the neck, a hot water bag may be substituted for the heating pad. Also for neck coverage it seems desirable to leave on the heat for a half hour only.

Grape Packs
    See *Grapefruit Juice and Grapes* and *Grapes* under the section "Fruits."

Mullein Stupes
    For mullein stupes see section "Plant Products for Healing, Oral Applications," *Mullein*.

Potato Packs
    Potato packs or poultices were recommended in the readings for different eye conditions. Dr. William A. McGarey points out that they were seldom suggested for cataracts but were recommended for blepharitis or stye and that they are usually effective in treating this latter condition.
    Dr. McGarey goes on to explain that the potato, used in the way outlined in the following excerpt, produces an enzyme which encourages lymphatic flow through the eye and its supporting structures. Such flow results in better elimination of any buildup of material from the interior of the eye.[47]

---

[47]William A. McGarey, M.D., "Notes from the Medical Research Bulletin," *The A.R.E. Journal,* May 1977, pp. 133-134.

Each three hours (during the waking day. . .) there should be a dressing placed on the eye (with it closed. . .) of scraped Irish potato (old—not new. . .). This scraped very fine and placed over same, making a cake or covering of same about one-half inch thick.   20-1

Other readings call for different schedules for the application.

Also, through the pressures indicated in the areas about the upper dorsals, inflammation is caused to the eyes, or optic forces themselves, so that the inflammation in the lids and the granular condition appearing upon the ball of the eye come from a nerve exhaustion. . .[Directions for therapy follow.]
At least twice a day, for an hour, apply to the eyes the scraped Irish potato—not the new or this year's crop, but the old Irish potato. This would be put right on the eyelid (with the eye closed, of course), and then bound on for about half an hour to an hour. Afterwards the eyes would be cleansed with a weak cleansing solution for the eyes, that is antiseptic; this about the proportions used for washing a baby's eyes. . .   1963-1

Q-4. What should be done for granulated eyelids?
A-4. Use a weak solution of boracic acid. About twice each week use those [poultices] of scraped Irish potato, bound of an evening over the eye.   409-22

For local condition, inflammation, in eyes, use scraped (old) Irish potato in evenings, that the inflammation may be drawn from the eye, cleansing with a mild antiseptic of mornings. . .
Q-1. How long of evenings should the Irish potato be kept on the eyes?
A-1. While it sleeps, while resting. Cleanse in morning.
1005-1

Pastes, Solutions and Liquids for Application to the Skin

Camphor

Q-1. What caused, and may anything be done to eliminate the red spot on my nose?
A-1. This is from a broken cell. Do not irritate too much, or this may turn to mole or wart—which would be a disfiguration to the body.
We would keep a little camphor, or camphor-ice on same of evenings.   288-51

These. . .[ingrown toenails] would respond to the dampening

of baking soda with spirits of camphor and putting a small quantity of same on cotton, or alone, under the tip of the nail, close to the irritated place. This will remove the condition if used daily—or nightly. 1770-4

For trembling of right leg and foot—caused by "calculous places. . .from improper shoes, and from irritation":

Bathe the limb from the knee down with warm olive oil. Then apply the saturated solution of spirits of camphor, with bicarbonate of soda. Even spread it on, as a very thin layer... bandaging this with a *thin* cloth. . .about the limb and foot. . . Let this remain over the evening, or night. . . 3776-13

Castor Oil and Soda

Q-6. How can [1179] get rid of her warts?
A-6. Apply a paste of baking soda with castor oil. Mix together and apply of evenings. Just the proportions so it makes almost a *gum;* not as dough but more as gum. . .A pinch between the fingers with three to four drops in the palm of the hand, and this worked together and then placed on—bound on. It may make for irritation after the second or third application, but leave it off for one evening and then apply the next— and it [the wart] will be disappearing! 1179-3

For the conditions of toes and nails, use baking soda moistened with castor oil. Put this under the points or edges where ingrown toenails give disturbance. This may make. . . [the area] sore for one time, but rub off with spirits of camphor. These may make for roughening but it will rid the body of those tendencies of ingrown toenails. 5104-1

Mustard
For aching and burning feet:

. . .well if the feet and limbs be bathed in very warm water, to increase the circulation in this portion of the system, putting mustard in the water when same is done. . . 3776-9

For colds and grippe:

Keep the feet bathed well with mustard water; this extending to the knees, even to the hips—even sitz baths of the mustard water would be well if not made too heavy. . .rather sponge off across the small of the back, down the limbs and then bathe the bottoms of the feet with a combination of equal parts of mutton suet, spirits of turpentine, spirits of camphor and tincture of benzoin. Heat these each time before the combination is applied, not to boiling but so they may be stirred thoroughly together. Massage into the bottoms of the feet and under the knees, back of the neck, across the face, especially the upper antrums and just under the eyes or around those portions of the body. We will find these will help materially. Do this two, three times a day.   1005-15

Plantain
For skin rash:

...we would first apply a local application for the hands, that would be combined by an ointment prepared at least every other day. Take a cup of cut plantain; the tender leaves, not the heavy. Some of the seed would also be well at this season. Then add to same an equal amount of top fresh cream (do not pack) in a cup or glass or whatever container this is measured in. Stir this together and let it come to a boil. Then apply over the hands and wrist where there are those irritations. Cover this for the night and then take off of morning, cleanse with an antiseptic (. . .any mild antiseptic). . .in a few days these conditions will disappear from the hands and wrist, if better circulation and elimination. . .[are] set up between the liver and the kidneys and the stimulating of the alimentary canal...
                5161-1

For the abrasions, or where there is the effect of centralizing of conditions of poisons. . .use a poultice of bruised plantain leaves—prepared in this manner:
Bruise very thoroughly the plantain leaves, using one ounce with two ounces oil of butterfat or very thick fresh cream. Boil together. When cold, apply as an ointment to the place. . .it will soon leave. . .   631-3

First, we would give [the suggestion] that there be prepared an ointment from the leaves of young plaintain, at this particular season of the year [July], growing in the vicinity where this body lives [Kentucky]. Yes, it is this herb, that you desire oft to get rid of, in the yard, garden or walk. Do not use the seed, so much, in the ointment. Gather the tender leaves, about the quantity that may be crammed, not too tightly, into a pint cup. Then put this into a quart enamel container (with an enamel or glass top) and add one pint of sweet cream, poured off the top of milk.
Cook this until it is rather thick. Do not allow to burn.
Then use it as an ointment over the areas where these

258

protuberances gather at times—for they do vary. They become as warts or moles that become infected and sore and run. This ointment will tend to dry same. 3121-1

. . .it might become. . .a growth that would be detrimental. Could be turned into that of malignant nature, but not at present. *Not* to be removed! Use rather that of the gentle massage around and across the muscle and tissue that lead to the glands of the breast, from the intercostal, exterior and interior nerve centers, those as come from 5th, 6th dorsal, coming around each side of the body and about the breast itself, with those properties found in Iodex one evening; then the next evening use a combination of oil of butterfat with. . . plantain, mixed one to twenty.

Q-3. One of plantain to twenty of the butterfat?

A-3. These cooked together, or mixed together—using the leaf with the property itself. . . 325-20

Tar Soap
  For dandruff:

Q-5. Is there any special treatment recommended for dandruff and can it be entirely cured?

A-5. . . .this may entirely cure same: To 4 ounces of same [pure water] add 20 minims of 85% alcohol, with that of the oil of pine, 2 minims. This should be rubbed thoroughly into the scalp, so there is the proper reaction. . .Then, with this still damp. . .massage thoroughly into the scalp [a] small quantity of white vaseline. Then wash the head thoroughly with. . .a tar soap. Do this about once each week. It will disappear. 261-2

Vinegar
  For sunburn:

There is no better than plain, pure apple vinegar!
Of course, the use of any of the detergents or oils; the sun tan oil, or Unguentine or any of these applications would be very well. But if proper precautions are taken, there is none much better than the pure apple vinegar. 601-22

Witch hazel

Q-13. What will stop the condition that occurs between the toes occasionally?

A-13. Use occasionally witch hazel in its full strength to reduce this [itching]. Bathe—when feet are bathed, and bathe them often—in *salt* water. 903-16

The author wishes to note here that the Edgar Cayce readings include many other formulas and directions for use of plant products. From the total number, she has chosen ones that seemed especially interesting and informative.

The Culture of Plants

The values given by the readings as stemming from the use of various plants and plant products are obviously based on the assumption that these plants are raised under beneficent, if not optimum, conditions. This is made clear in the following.

[With reference to diet]. . .eggplants at times—parts of those depend upon where the vegetation is grown, as to the character of forces that are carried in same.   1000-2

What is the most acceptable way to raise plants so that beneficent conditions exist? The first point to be considered is what sort of nourishment to provide to enrich an impoverished soil or to replace those elements utilized by the plants as they attain full growth.

The readings advise against the chemical way in this excerpt which tells of a person who is careful to avoid it, knowing full well what a hold it can gain on an individual's thinking and also knowing it is something to avoid.

In the. . .[life] before this. . .in the land known as the Poseidian, or a portion of the old Atlantean. In this period the entity found much of those that pertained to the mysteries of nature, in the application of unseen forces, in the usages of same for man's indwelling and man's physical dwelling. Hence much that. . .brings to the varied consciousnesses of an entity, does the entity often dwell upon; being mindful that those that are of the chemical or chemical combines in the present, do not gain a hold that may not easily be set aside.
                                                                    1741-1

It is possible that in the Atlantean sojourn [1741] saw the damage to fertile farming land which would appear to have occurred from just such chemical practice.

In the latter portion of same [Atlantean culture]. . .as *cities* were builded, more and more rare became those abilities to call upon. . .the forces in nature to supply the needs. . .of bodily adornment, or. . .the needs to supply the replenishing of the wasting away of the physical being; or hunger arose, and with the determination to set again in motion, we find there—in those latter periods, ten thousand seven hundred years before the Prince of Peace came [10,700 B.C.]—again was the bringing into forces that to tempt, as it were, nature—in its storehouse—of replenishing the things—that of the *wasting* away in the mountains, then into the valleys, then into the sea itself, and the fast disintegration of the lands, as well as of the peoples—save those that had escaped into those distant lands.

364-4

So what should we use to enrich the soil for the plants we grow? Chicken manure and composted material, say the readings.

Q-12. May information be given through this channel on the proper methods of farming which would insure the production of products of the best possible food value and balanced content?
A-12. If there is to be insured the producing of the character of fertilization needed, or the making of proper fertilizer—none exceeds, of course, the value of chicken fertilizer, especially for some vegetables. Hence this should be used in rather an abundance, not excessively but in large measures; as well as that produced by the methods of adding such as lime and potash with portions of the soil, or portions of vegetable matter or refuse of vines or grasses in certain characters of vegetation—but always mixed with the droppings of the chicken—for this is the better of *any* that may be had for vegetables!

470-35

It should be noted that the character of some chicken manure today may be different from that found in Edgar Cayce's time due to additives given the birds in their feed. Manure from naturally raised chickens would seem to be closest to that the readings recommended.

"Muck" is a valuable medium for producing superior plants.

. . .in the way and manner as life and life's development spiritually are being presented through that of the lily. . .in the seemingly uncouth and uncomely herb in the muck, the root puts forth itself to obtain from this muck that which the entity sees burst forth in its beauty and fragrance.

137-63

What stronger endorsement could there be for organic farming?

Natural farming methods are known to produce sturdy crops. Since insects prefer weaker growth, insect control should not pose any real problem to the organic farmer. That the insects have a proper place in nature's world and perform a very necessary task in ridding it of weak, and therefore undesirable, growth is borne out by the following.

One capable of seeing beauty depicted in all expressions of nature, whether the bug about its lowly activity of cleansing the conditions about man or the beauty of song in music. . .
539-2

The following excerpt tells us that under the farming methods used just prior to Edgar Cayce's time (which *were* organic), produce was superior in quality to what we generally know today and pests were fewer in number than those today.

Consider the days of old. . .When there were the families that produced upon the farm, how much better not only were the lives of those individuals but the character of the product—and there were not half so many pests to deal with!   470-35

Pruning is advocated by the readings as a help in maintaining strong, healthy plants.

Have not the weaklings in the flock or the unhealthy plants been made sturdy in their relationships of beauty in nature, by purging, pruning and making for those advancements again and again?   262-81

The need of all living things for sunshine and water has been emphasized in the prior volume, *The Hidden Laws of Earth,* in the sections "The Sun" and "Water." After the plant has been supplied with sunshine and water and pruned if necessary, there is still something else needed. The readings tell us that vigor may be established by a person blessing a nut and that it will continue on into the life of a strong, healthy tree.

And the entity, with the very words or the blessings in planting even a nut, may insure the next generation a nut-bearing tree! The entity with its very abilities of the magnetic forces within self, may circle one with its hands and it'll bear no more fruit, though it may be bearing nuts in the present.
These are indications, then, of how the entity may use the energies or vibrations, even of the body, constructively or

destructively. Do not use these for self in either direction. For, as just indicated, if you plant one, be sure it is for the next generation and not for this one. It is others ye must think of, as should every soul. "Others, Lord, others—that I may know Thee the better."   3657-1

The effect of such a blessing has been amply demonstrated by the experimental work of the Reverend Franklin Loehr, which is recorded in detail in his book *The Power of Prayer on Plants.*[48]

The readings go even further in telling us that the characteristics of the gardener or farmer affect the growth of the plants.

To be sure, there is a great deal in the theories that are propagated by some groups, that what is in the vegetables and fruits has much to do with the character. If the man who raises and cares for them does it with love, it makes all the difference! Don't think a grouchy man can ever raise a headed cabbage or a tomato that will agree as well as those raised by a man who laughs and tells a good joke, though it may be smutty! 470-35

In summation, in order to raise healthy plants, one needs to give them the natural nutrients and the care they require, to have a relationship with them which blesses them and, last but not least, to epitomize in oneself those same values one wishes to see in one's plants.

---

[48] Rev. Franklin Loehr, *The Power of Prayer on Plants,* Doubleday & Co., Inc., Garden City, N.Y., 1959.

THE ANIMAL KINGDOM

All of the animals which developed on the earth have not remained. We are told that an ice age eliminated many of great size.

. . .among those who. . .gathered to rid the earth of the enormous animals which overran the earth, but ice. . .nature, God, changed the poles and the animals were destroyed, though man attempted it. . .   5249-1

Let us review the information we have previously gained on those with us today.

In the chapter "The Three Kingdoms" we learned that whereas plants represent the one-purpose life, animals represent the two-purpose life. It appears that the one-purpose life involves the first dimension, time, and the two-purpose life the first and second dimensions, time and space. In other words, animals' lives follow cycles of time and the creatures move around in space. We also learned that animals have group consciousness. The three-purpose or human life apparently involves the three dimensions of time, space and patience. Mind is the dividing factor between man and the lesser kingdoms.

Animals' Minds and Senses

Just what is mind in both man and animal?

Mind is the active force in an animate object; that is the spark, or image of the Maker. Mind is the factor that is in direct

264

opposition. . .[to] will. Mind is that control of, being the spark of the Maker, the *will,* the individual when we reach the plane of man. Mind is the factor governing the contention, or the interlying space, if you please, between the physical to the soul, and the soul to the spirit forces within the individual or animate forces. We have the manifestation of this within the lowest order of animal creation. These are developed as the mind is developed, both by the action of all of the senses of the body, as we have them developed in man. *Mind* is that which reasons the impressions from the senses, as they manifest before the individual. 3744-1

Now how does the animal's mind differ from that of man? The animal does not have a subconscious mind or the higher elements of mind and of matter. Its mind is involved with only the continuation of the species and food. It does have sense and remembrance.

. . .the animal seeks only gratifying of self, the preservation of life, the satisfying of appetites. 2072-8

Q-3. Do animals have the faculty of mind known as subconscious?
A-3. No. The mind of the animal is as pertaining to the conditions that would bring the continuation of species and of foods, and in that manner all in the animal kingdom; pertaining then, mind and spirit; man reaching that development wherein the soul becomes the individual that may become the companion, and One with the Creator.
Q-4. An animal has sense, remembrance, and the higher animals obey orders. How?
A-4. Just as has been given. . .man and mind subdue the earth in every element. . .all manner of animal in the earth, in the air, under the sea, has been tamed of man, yet the man himself has not reached that wherein he may perfectly control himself, save making the will One with the Creator, as man makes the will of the animal one with his. The control then in trained animals being the projection. . .[from] man. The trained mind of those in natural state, the element as given, spirit and mind, the specie[s] keeps life.
Q-5. Explain the difference between experience as in an animal and experience. . .in man, as related to mind.
A-5. In animal is that as appertains to the consciousness of the animal mind, with spirit. . .in man, that. . .of consciousness correlated with man's development, or the higher elements of mind and of matter. Hence man developed, becomes lord and master over [the] animal kingdom. Man degraded becomes the

companion, the equal with the beast, or the beastly man. Then we would find this illustrated as in this: Experience to man gives the understanding through the subconscious obtaining the remembrance. The animal [can draw on] the animal forces [only] as would be found in this: Fire to man is ever dread, to an animal only by sense of smell does it know the difference. The experience does not lead it away.   900-31

We have just noted that by projecting himself man can train animals. It is easy to see that this can result in the performance of circus animals or household pets. Does it account for the phenomena of the Elberfeld horses?

In the period before World War I, Von Osten, a retired teacher, living in the Prussian town of Elberfeld, became certain that some animals could reason and talk like man. He worked with a Russian stallion named "Kluge Hans" (Clever Hans) until he claimed that the horse knew the days of the week, was acquainted with music to some extent and could tell time by a clock, read simple words and solve mathematical problems.

After Von Osten's death, Clever Hans was further educated by Karl Krall, a wealthy manufacturer of Elberfeld, who also enrolled two Arab stallions, a Shetland pony and a baby elephant in this school. The elephant did not respond and was dropped. The Arab stallions soon surpassed Clever Hans.

The horses were taught sums by the use of ninepins. They communicated arithmetical results by tapping with the right foot for units and the left one for tens. The corresponding numerals were then chalked on a board. They progressed from an apparent understanding of these to that of mathematical signs and later reading and spelling.

Numerous scientists came to examine the horses in action. They could find no trickery. When dealing with mathematics the horses were far ahead of the humans in calculation time and resembled modern electronic computers. They related incidents with their tapping which proved to be true. Krall and a Dr. Scholler tried to teach Muhamed to speak, but this proved fruitless. Muhamed explained that it was impossible for him to do so. The many conversations are recorded in Krall's *Thinking Animals*. The onset of World War I put an end to the horses' education.

The examining scientists had by 1914 produced one hundred and sixty-two monographs and treatises on the subject of the horses, which are available for study today at the British

Museum and in other famous archives. Some attributed to the horses a fantastic gift of their own. Others charged the results to telepathy, claiming the animals reflected the intelligence of those examining them. Still others suggested the horses were possessed by a reasoning mind superior to their own minds. In 1955 Dr. William Mackenzie, of Genoa University, President of the Italian Society of Parapsychology and author of many works on physics, psychology and biology, who had examined the horses carefully in 1913, was questioned about them again. He persisted in this last explanation, that they had functioned as "mediums."[49]

The Elberfeld horses do, indeed, pose a problem. Was man's projection in training animals involved here? Or were these phenomena psychic ones? We recall we learned:

Hence we see from the lowest to the highest the manifestations of psychic phenomena in the material world. Hence we have the psychic phenomena of the lower animal kingdom, of the mineral kingdom, of the plant kingdom, of the animal kingdom as advanced, and as then becomes the man's condition, position. **900-19**

If psychic phenomena were exhibited here, from whence did the information come which the horses brought through? Perhaps some day there may be an answer.

Now, let us return to the senses possessed by animals. Fearing is one.

. . .add fearing to the sense of animal senses. **900-47**

In the section "Odors" we learned that there is no greater influence in a physical body, man or animal, than the effect of odors on the olfactory nerves. It was also pointed out there how acute this sense is in animals of the dog or cat families. In the concluding discussion in this section a 1977 report was cited that man's sense of smell is one thousand times less sensitive than that of dogs, and dogs' one thousand times less sensitive than that of insects.

Just as an animal's sense of smell may be more acute than a man's, may not some other senses be more developed, also? It is a matter of record that various animals have become uneasy and fled from the scene of an impending earthquake some

---

[49]A.S. Jarman, "Unsolved Animal Mysteries," *Tomorrow*, Spring 1960, pp. 65-72.

hours in advance of the event. Out of numerous incidents we note the following. At the time of the Yellowstone quake in August 1959, waterfowl usually frequenting Lake Hegben, deserted it about twelve hours in advance of the disturbance.[50] At the time of the great Alaska quake in 1964, cattle on Kodiak Island left their low grazing ground in advance of their usual time and with their owner were safe when the event occurred.[51]

More recently Chinese scientists have been studying animal behavior, hoping to develop instruments to predict earthquakes. Reports of 2,093 cases of unusual animal behavior before a 1976 quake in Tangshan Province have been collected, according to a report in the U.S. Geological Survey's *Earthquake Information Bulletin*. The creatures involved included goats, cats, dogs, pigs, chickens, rats and fish. The Chinese have identified 58 varieties of domestic and wild animals exhibiting unusual behavior before quake tremors.[52]

What is the sensitivity which informs these animals in advance of a quake that all is not as usual? Dr. Carl Schleicher, President of Mankind Research Unlimited in Washington, D.C., tells us that the stresses and strains preceding earthquakes result in changes in the earth's magnetic fields. Such magnetic changes recreated in the laboratory have caused animals and one plant to respond in a fashion similar to that exhibited by animals before an actual quake.[53]

L.M. Hasbrouck, a forecaster of earthquakes, has attributed the animals' behavior to changing patterns of potential in the earth's "field" which induce field-force disturbances, coinciding among other things with the bigger earthquakes. He believes that everything in life—suns, atoms, galaxies, man, animals (including birds)—have a response and react on time to these field-force changes.[54]

These explanations certainly tie in with the statement occurring again and again in the readings that all life is one.

For all life is one, all force is one. . .   136-78

. . .each and every atom in the universe has its relative

[50]L.M. Hasbrouck, "More About Earthquakes: II," *American Mercury*, Jan. 1960, pp. 120-121.
[51]Myrtle E. Sheffer, "Bovine Seismographs?" *Fate*, Oct. 1969, pg. 75.
[52]"Animals Sense Coming Quakes," *The Virginian-Pilot*, Norfolk, Va., Jan. 6, 1979.
[53]Mark C. Blazek, "Nature's Earthquake Alarms," *Fate*, Oct. 1977, pg. 59.
[54]Hasbrouck, *ibid*.

Whatever the sense which detects coming quakes, it is certainly more acute in animals.

What are some other characteristics of animals? An animal—at least a dog—does have understanding, within, of course, the limits previously mentioned or in respect to food and continuation of the species.

Because the dog doesn't talk, people think he doesn't understand.   **552-2**

An animal does not set a routine for itself in respect to regular meals.

Do. . .animals have regular meals? Man's the only one that sets a routine for himself! unless man sets it for the animal and won't let him!   **849-23**

An animal is indeed unable to talk, as Muhamed indicated.

. . .for speech is the highest vibration that is reached in the animal kingdom, and in that respect man in his evolution is above. . .other creatures in the creation.   **294-11**

The Reincarnation of Animals

Although we learned in "The Three Kingdoms" that animals have a group consciousness, they are still individuals. A person may be associated today with an animal he knew in a former life. The story of Mona, a little dog belonging to Mrs. [268] is illuminating. [268] had been of the Roman nobility during the early persecutions of the Christians and had watched these persecutions. Her husband in the present life [280] had been a gladiator who fought in the arena. He had eventually been converted to the Christian beliefs.

. . .in that land now known as the Roman, during that period when there were the persecutions of the peoples for their belief in a new thought, or those thoughts that came with the peoples then called the Nazarites or Nazarenes. The entity then was among those who in *mental* activity warred against these peoples, for the entity was then of the nobility of the land; of the household of Pompeathiolus, and joined in with those who watched often in the persecutions of the peoples.

The entity lost through this experience; yet in the latter portion gained much from that which had been brought over, through the application of self to the tenets within the mental abilities of the entity.   268-3

. . .in that land now known as the Roman, when there were those destructions by the people in power of those that adhered to a thought, a way, a change that was being brought by the adherence to a particular line of thought. The entity was then among the soldiery of the period. . .Then, the entity finally threw itself, as it were, into the defense of those that made for the following of those from the foreign land. . .

The entity then was an individual of striking appearance in the physical. In the present there is seen the reverential awe that is often experienced by the entity when there is the exhibition or activities of an individual with unusual strength in the physical or in the mental. . .   280-1

Mrs. [268] was told that she had known her little dog Mona as a "lion" at that time. [280] was told that Mona was the lioness with which he had fought.

Q-6. [Where and how have I been formerly associated with] My little dog, Mona?
  A-6. In the same experience.
  Q-7. In the Roman?
  A-7. The Roman.
  Q-8. Was she a dog then?
  A-8. A lion!   268-3

Q-3. What relation is he to the little dog Mona?
  A-3. He fought with the body in the Roman experience.
  Q-4. What was Mona then?
  A-4. The lioness that fought with the entity and with those that destroyed many that the entity was then seeking to aid.
                                                                            280-1

An 11-year-old niece of [268] was told that whether Mona would be a dog in the future depended on the environ and surroundings. A 14-year-old nephew was not encouraged to try to secure a life reading for the dog.

Q-18. [In what previous lives have I been associated with the following:] Aunt [268]'s little dog Mona?
  A-18. Rome.
  Q-20. Will Mona always be a dog?

A-20. That depends upon the environ and the surroundings. No. 405-1

Q-12. Could a life reading be obtained through these sources for Aunt [268]'s little dog Mona?
A-12. May be. As to *what* it may be is different! It may not be understood, unless you learn dog language! 406-1

It is interesting to note that Mrs. [268] was today inclined to the study of relationships between the various kingdoms, as they exist in actuality. Doubtless she, as well as her husband, was learning to have a different viewpoint toward an animal, whether lion or dog.

At present there are the particular influences that make the abilities of the entity in relationships to those of other kingdoms, and the study in those relationships; as the animal, the mineral and the vegetable kingdoms are all of interest to the entity, and their activities or associations. . .one with another are of particular interest; yet in the rite or the rote of these little interest is found. Their material activity. . .in association one with another is of particular interest to the entity in the present. 268-3

Another reading reference concerning Mona ties in with the role of spirit in animals. [1318], a Viennese female who was a teacher of the occult, was informed that the attraction existing between her and the dog came from the high vibratory forces of both of them.

Q-7. What association in the past have I had with Mrs. [268]'s present little dog, Mona?
A-7. We do not find same.
Q-8. Why has little Mona been so attracted to me?
A-8. The vibratory forces of the high vibrations of each.
1318-1

We have learned previously that, lacking the subconscious, animals do not have access to past lives but that they do have memory. Was it the memory of a smell, or just what, that prompted one animal's attempt to uncover a treasure buried by a former human companion, at that time Governor of Roanoke Island in the days of early settlement?

There have been the indications with an animal that was a portion of the entity's experience during that period in the

271

attempt of the animal to uncover those things as pertained to same.

These indicate a place. . .that it should be.   853-7

We saw that [268]'s nephew was not encouraged by the readings to try to secure a life reading on Mona. A letter from [4525], a cousin of Edgar Cayce, asking whether he would read for a little cocker spaniel, elicited the following reply from the seer in his conscious state.

"No, have had many requests for such readings as you asked for—but have never undertaken such; there seems always so much to be done to try and help our fellow man, seem never to have had time for such." (4525-1)

Transmigration of animal to man is clearly denied in the ensuing passages.

This is not intended to indicate that there is transmigration or transmutation of the soul from animal to human. . .2464-2

Q-7. *Has my soul-entity experienced transmigration through minor plant and animal kingdoms?*
A-7. Those kingdoms are of the universal soul-consciousness. Each soul entity was created, or began in the *beginning* with the Father.   1641-1

Man's Role Toward Animals

What should be the relationship between man and animals? It should not be too close. Man should maintain the proper perspective and remember that although both are one in spirit, man may be a co-creator with God and an animal cannot be.

In the influences of likes and dislikes in the entity, here we find these become very decided all of a sudden—and as much of a sudden they change. This is a characterization of those whose influences are under Neptune or Cancer, with the days in that period, in that *sphere* in which the entity finds expression, or entering in, coming in, near the dog days. Then, as to animals and their relationships—these are held too close to as of one. All *force* and all *power* is of one source, as is life—but the *associations* of each are individual, and should be classified so *by* the entity in its *study* of the relationships of animal matter, celestial matter, material matter. In *spirit* one, but all flesh is not of one flesh—as some are given a cosmic influence only and others the ability to become one with the creative energy itself, in its *cleansing* of itself to be one in its relationships. 1910-1

It is made clear in the readings that man should exercise supervision over the animal kingdom. This was brought out in the chapter, "The Three Kingdoms." How this supervision should be exercised is apparent in the story of Valtui, an Arabian princess, living around 10,500 B.C., who tamed the animal kingdom by music and love.

Then in the name Valtui, the entity was in the associations of the king's or leader's household. . .

The entity's activities in the sojourn had to do with the domestication and use of the wild animal life and also those that later became the servants with and of man in his activity; and brought about much that had to do with the raising of the horse from the smaller or pigmy animal to the charging steed; that had to do with the using of the wolve[s] and the wild things for the closer companionship to man. . .

The entity, then, as would be termed in years, was 22 years of age when she assumed the rule of the peoples whom her associate or uncle *left* and entered into Egypt.

. . .The entity then began the activity of inducing her followers to use the varied associations for the development of not only a greater social activity but a greater commercial activity, as would be termed today, in relation to the animal kingdom about them to be used as a benefit to the peoples. . .

As may be rightly gathered from that given concerning this entity, this soul in its unconscious use of life. . .gave to man. . . that [which] has been the aid, the help, the companion throughout the years, the ages since.

. . .In the conscious use of these same influences. . .directed by those that had found. . .the relationship between the Creative influence and the creature and its brother, the creature and its Maker, the entity so applied self as to bring harmony into the *kingdom* over which the entity ruled. Not as ruled by might, rather by love. Hence the instruments used were of the reed or flute, that is known in the present, and made the hearts of many merry; not as of those that would gratify the satisfying of carnal forces, but rather that as awakened within each those abilities for the expressing of—in its physical body—the music of the spirit in its activity in and through the body. So in the present, as the experiences of self. . .go to make up its abilities to quell within the breast of many a tortured soul or many a tortured body that wars within itself with the spirit that is willing and the flesh is weak with its own desires, that

as. . .may be given by the entity in word or by the music will
bring something to each of the vision that came to those that
were under the entity's supervision or kingdom in that sojourn
. . .this entity in its beauty of experience in manifesting. . .life
brought also. . .the humblest. . .animal [the horse] to represent
in man's life its closest companion and the burden bearer with
the women that the entity aided in freeing from many of their
burdens.   276-6

Note that in this account man is referred to as the animal's
brother.

In another reading it was brought out that today [276] should
use musical instruments of the reed type and that the sound of
these resembles closely the voices of the bird or animal
kingdom. We might say that [276] in taming the animal
kingdom communicated with it in its own language.

Q-4. How should entity minister through the music spheres?
A-4. These. . .would have the better outlet on those of the
reed instruments; for these. . .appertain the closer to *nature* in
the imitation of the voices or the expressions of the animal, or
the bird kingdom, or hence would have a stronger appeal for
the entity, and *allow* an expression that might not be found in
the stringed instruments.   276-3

In a later life, [276] was safe from attack by any wild beast.

. . .in that land now known as the Roman, and during that
period when there were the ministering and teaching of those
peoples that came up from Judea. The entity was among those
who accepted those teachings, and coming in contact with
those of that period, taught by the lessons of, the experiences
of self and others in the contacts of this new peace, yet
suffering in body, by privation—yet able in mind to control
those beasts, both of the field and of the dens and lairs that the
body was placed in; the body bore same, gaining—gaining—oft
the liberation for the teachings again through these *strange*
abilities in this particular period; being among those who
journeyed again to the Grecian land for the teaching of the
peoples, as the entity was carried away from same.   276-2

*Q-11. Give date of incarnation as Phoebia and describe
strange abilities of entity in that period, also as to control of
those beasts of the field, dens, and lairs?*
A-11. This. . .was during those periods when man was called
upon oft to defend self against the beasts of the fields, in dens,

in lairs, in arenas; and the entity through its own development—as had been attained or gained during that period—
showed forth the ability to walk with the denizen of the forest
without being afraid, also to walk among those in the arena
without fear; and *no harm came* to the entity through their
activity, but from those that made themselves lower than the
beasts; for, as has been given, all may be tamed, but the tongue
hath no man tamed! In that day, then, during the first century,
as is counted in the present. 276-3

[276] was told that in the present incarnation her duty toward
animals was to have affection for them, control them and bring
to the attention of owners how animals can be of help to man.

*Q-10. Just where does body's duty lie towards animals in
this incarnation?*
A-10. The ability to control and to show that close affection
that may exist between the human mind, as controlling
through the manners in which the entity is efficient, and to
bring to the attention of others how animals—in their various
spheres—are dependent upon their owners, or those who
contact same, as to what *their* activities may be to the benefit
of man; for, as was given in the beginning, "Be ye fruitful;
multiply, and *subdue* the earth." Make all that was made,
making that—then—as an ensample of, or *completing* as it
were—the promise that is given to man, that he may be one
with, one of, the *Creative* Forces in the universe, by the
manner in which he may use those various abilities through
his experiences in a material world; and as all of earth's
creation is a form or manifestation of the love as is shown
forth to those beings that may be one-with the Creator, so may
the love that may be seen between those of the lower order, or
those in their development in a material plane, so may this
entity show to others, to the animal kingdom, that as has been
received, as may be given by self, by the entity, in *their* behalf.
276-3

[276] asked whether the soul consciousness of any of her
animals in the life as Valtui had incarnated in her present dog,
Peggy. The answer could be taken to indicate that a household
pet is likely to incarnate again with a loving owner.

*Q-16. Was the soul-consciousness of [my dog,] Peggy present
in this room, in any of my animals then?*
A-16. Yes.
Q-17. Which one?

Other reading references emphasize affection for and control of animals.

> ...the particular interests that arise from that sojourn of the entity [as an emissary to Persia and Arabia] may be seen manifested innately in the interest in animal—dog, horse and the like, that make for a peculiar influence in the experience of the entity; and the abilities of the entity to train, teach or to control this nature is in the entity's *innate* activity from that sojourn.   594-1

> Thus the greater necessity for the entity's activities to be in environs where there are the opportunities for the expressing of sympathy, to be in the position where the entity will have others depending upon the entity, and where there is required the activity of the entity for expressing that bond of sympathy that may bring the greater beauty—as with horses, dogs, birds, flowers; any of those things where there are the needs for that love, sympathy, understanding to be expressed by the entity for the bringing out...of the better points, the better activities of...[those] dependent upon the entity...   1367-1

In calling attention to birds (a part of the animal kingdom) John James Audubon contributed greatly to his fellow man.

> The entity then was among those peoples that found a haven there [Louisiana], and brought to those lands in the latter experience the joys of many, and builded for much that has given joy and peace to the minds and hearts of many who have loved God's little folk in the bird kingdom.
> Then, in the name Audubon...   410-2

Animals as Lessons to Man

Although man is entrusted with the supervision of the animal kingdom, the various species in it serve as lessons to him.

> ...as a soul, as a developing body then sees in the creatures, in the various kingdoms as *they* care for their young, as they are selective in their mating, as they are mindful of the influences and environs, learn from these nature's lessons or God's expression to the children of men; that He indeed is in His holy temple and is *mindful* of man's estate—if *man* minds

the *laws* of nature, of God. For love is law, love is God.

1248-1

Marital fidelity may be learned from the goose.

Q-3. Should divorces be encouraged?
A-3. This depends upon first the education of the body. Once united, once understood that the relationships are to be as one, less and less is there the necessity of such conditions. Man may learn a great deal from a study of the goose in this direction. Once it has mated, *never* is there a mating with any other—either the male or female, no matter how soon the destruction of the mate may occur—unless *forced* by *man's* intervention... Just as indicated in all of the animals. . .in their *natural* state these are in the forms as their *names* indicate and from these man may learn many lessons; which *was* attempted in the beginning.

826-6

The interpretation of one of Edgar Cayce's dreams explains that the name of every animal or bird is based on some peculiarity of its group, which actually represents a particular phase of man's development in the earth or the mind consciousness of some particular element.

Gertrude Cayce: You will have before you the body and the enquiring mind of Edgar Cayce present in this room and the dreams this body had on the dates which I will give you. You will give the interpretation and lesson to be gained from each of these, as I read same to you.

Edgar Cayce: Yes, we have the body, the enquiring mind, Edgar Cayce. This we have had before.

The dreams. . .come to the entity. . .through one of those channels as has been presented: that is, the conscious visions, or conscious conditions made applicable to the consciousness of an entity, through the process of the subjugation of the conscious body-mind by sleep.

Ready for dream.

Q-1. Saturday morning, 12/4/26. I dreamed I had an enclosure in which. . .[were] all manners of birds, beasts and fowl, with a large, high wire fence around this. I noted especially there was a bear, goat, sheep, deer, goose, fox, wolf and dog. The dog was one I knew. I was feeding, and realized that it took different feed for the various kinds of fowl and beast that were there, but at the time I was feeding shelled corn. A few grains went through the fence, and I saw the goose and the wolf go through the fence, but I couldn't understand how they went through, so I stooped down trying to see how they went out and then came back in after getting the few grains. While stooping I heard and saw a commotion among all the animals and birds. It seemed as a warning cry, each in its own language was trying to tell me I was in danger. I realized it was the bear behind me, but I thought bear doesn't do anything but scratch and hug one to death. I glanced over my left shoulder, and realized the bear was sitting behind me, on its haunches, with its forearms or paws outstretched. The dog, the goat, and the deer sprang to scare the bear away. In a flash I wondered if the bear meant harm or did he mean to caress me. I woke up shaking.

A-1. In this there is presented a vision of far meaning to the entity, when properly understood, and many various phases of the entity's endeavors are visioned in the presentation of this to the entity.

The enclosure is as that condition hedged about by the entity's field of endeavor to be of assistance, aid, help, to others, and in the same there is seen all manner of beast and fowl and birds. Some especially are noted.

For, as seen, each animal, each bird, each fowl, has been so named for some peculiarity of that individual beast, bird or fowl, and in this manner represents some particular phase of man's development in the earth's plane, or that consciousness of some particular element or personality that is manifested in mind.

Not that man develops from the animal, or the animal develops from the man, but. . .all beast, all birds, all fowls, were made for man's use and sustenance. Hence [each] must supply, in name, manner, position in life, in its phase of living, in its habits, in its conditions, associations and relations, some element [that] is necessary for man's development.

In this phase, and in this light, then, we find the entity, the individual, supplying that food for the development, physically and mentally, for these different phases of mankind, in mankind's personality. And all are seen represented, as seen by the consciousness of the individual that various phases of the vegetable or animal world [are] necessary for the full and complete development of the animal, beast, bird or fowl that is to be sustained.

As seen in the casting of corn, or that which is the necessity to supply certain phases of the development of animal, or of the fowl kingdom; and as some grains pass through the enclosure; or as. . .some words. . .spoken by the entity are as casting pearls before swine, or go beyond reach. Yet. . .two—which represent different phases of man's consciousness, or man's personality, or. . .man's individuality in the earth plane—the goose, the wolf, are even able—though [it was] cast beyond their reach—to reach same. How this is understood, or how this is reached. . .[is] that which troubles the entity. And as the entity stoops to see, to understand how these animals or fowl pass in and out, or gain access to the knowledge, or gain a portion of the knowledge that is received by that cast, there appears the heavier beast that to others. . .that is, those about it—would appear to do harm.

. . .the character of the beast itself. . .presents a phase of a development to the entity regarding certain individuals, or a certain class, rather than individual personages—of a class that would act in such a manner as this beast does regarding the information, or the truths or the lessons being cast before these for their sustenance. As seen in the manner of the beast— represented by the bear: that one who would under certain circumstances be very destructive, under other phases of its consciousness playful, and as caressing and as loving and as tender and as protective to the best interests of the individual in every way, as [much so as] would any of those who come to the individual's assistance.

Yet, as seen when there is the fear of destructive forces, there are especially three characters that rise to the defense of the truth. One in the form of the dog (which represents a certain nature, character, or disposition of an individual— which may not always be trusted), [another] in the deer, (which represents another form). . .other[s] in the fox and wolf. . .some that would save for self, yet would be destructive to all. Some that are. . .[as one] protecting that which it loves, that it may destroy itself. . .The characteristics, the elements, the conditions.

This is a beautiful lesson, to be studied hard, and much may be gained therefrom. For it will be found the basis of something that may be used as a lesson to many.   294-87

There is a sidelight as to how karmic conditions may not only cancel out an animal's usefulness as a lesson but also bring about an unfortunate environment for both person and animal. In this case it is best that the animal be removed from the situation.

Q-7. What causes him to be frightened when near the family dog? Should we dispose of the dog, or try to overcome his fear?
A-7. This is part of a karmic condition. As we find it would be well to get rid of the dog, for this creates not only a very unfortunate environment for the body, but for the dog also—as to its usefulness.   2963-4

To attain the most desirable relationship with animals it is best to remember the following:

. . .Life as it manifests, whether in the grass, the rose, the tree, the dog, the cat, the bird, the animal, *is* a manifestation of that ye worship as God.   1367-1

Animal Products for Food

In the first chapter of this book we learned that the three-purpose development or human life absorbs the two-purpose animal life, which becomes one with it. Could this have a bearing on the use of animal products for food?

The readings remind us that an endorsement of the use of certain types of meat appears in the Bible.

Q-5. Is meat conducive to age [aging]?
A-5. Not necessarily. [If] one thinks so, it is! Wasn't there given. . .in the beginning, to those first of Promise, "Of the fruit of the field ye shall eat"? Again there is found when there is given to man the activities in knowing good and evil, that the beast of the field of certain natures, that made of certain vibrations, brought certain vibrations from within the same system.   900-465

Various individuals were told in the readings that they needed particular meat products for health. (See section "Ingestion of Food, Air and Water Containing Mineral Forces.") The following excerpts serve to clarify the issue.

Meats of certain characters are necessary in the body building forces in this system and should not be wholly abstained from in the present. Spiritualize those influences, those activities, rather than abstaining.   295-10

But to attempt, where the bloodstream—where the body building forces or the nature's warriors within self have been builded for generations, those that have required the stability or stamina of meat—to relieve self of same entirely is to take from the revivifying influences of that body. For, spirituality by the flesh is as the spiritual life in its essence, a growth.
                                    443-6

Q-14. Why were meat and fish and milk prescribed in the reading, as I use no meat, now, and dislike shellfish?
A-14. It wouldn't be bad if you would use it! And the

influences of same, in the *character* or *nature* that is *purified,* for this body *would* be better, as we have found and given, to build the proper activity for the system.   1703-2

Most Valuable Portions of Meat

It is not the flesh of animals that is of the greatest food value. Rather it is the juices. These are blood and nerve tissue building.

Not meats, except as for strength, and that would be the juices rather than the meat proper.   2198-1

Q-5. What is a nerve building diet?
A-5. Those of the celery, radish, those of the *green* vegetables, in tomatoes. Those of the active forces in these are the nerve building, with those of the *juices*—but not the flesh—of animal.   255-3

Let the diet, while these treatments are being administered, be those of blood and nerve tissue building properties—but of the alkaline reaction in the system. Hence those of the juices of fruits, of nuts and the like, are the *principal* foods. Juices of *beef* may be taken, but not the flesh. This should be extracted by heating, but not added in, other than the juices as prepared in proper seasoning.   4252-1

Liver, tripe (part of the stomach of cattle and hogs) and pig knuckle also are body and blood building. (578-5) Gristle, pig's feet and souse (pickled pig's heads, ears and feet) are among the best sources of calcium. (1158-31) Calcium may also be obtained from chewing the bony parts of fowl (neck, head, wings, feet, etc.), prepared so that the juice may be chewed out of them (3076-1), and from the broths of fowl, made from the neck, feet, back or the like, cooked for a long time. (1885-1) For exact excerpts see section "Ingestion of Food, Air and Water Containing Mineral Forces," *Calcium.*
Brains, too, may be eaten for blood building.

Occasionally we would add those of the blood building, once or twice a week. The pig knuckles, tripe and calf liver, or those of *brains* and the like.   275-24

Preparation of Meat

The readings admonished that meat should not be fried—

rather, boiled, baked, broiled, roasted or prepared in Patapar paper or a steam cooker.

Beware of all fried foods. No fried potatoes, fried meats, fried steaks, fried fish or anything of that nature. 926-1

The meats. . .would be fish or shellfish or lamb, and occasionally wild game or fowl. However, none of these should ever be fried. 3823-2

Q-1. Is fish bad for this body?
A-1. There may be occasions when this can be taken, but not that that's fried. Boiled or baked, or broiled, would be well—but *not* fried! 348-15

. . .those that are boiled, roasted or broiled are much better than any fried meats of *any* kind. 416-6

Even. . .the chicken or fish would be better cooked in the Patapar paper or a steam cooker. 133-4

In fact, cooking of any foods in quantities of grease should be avoided as fats are not easily assimilated.

Beware of white potatoes, fats of any kind, and greases. No meats save fish, fowl or lamb. No fried foods. No white bread. Not too much of pastries. 2415-2

Keep away from too much greases or too much of any foods cooked in quantities of grease—whether of hog, sheep, beef or fowl! But rather use the *lean* portions and those [meats] that will make for body building forces. . . 303-11

In the diet keep away from fried foods, or large quantities of fats that are not easily assimilated. 1684-1

Souse, unpickled, however, may be fried in batter.
For a person with upset stomach, general debilitation, etc.:

Take beef juice often, also pig's feet or souse (not pickled). Use this when possible, but not too much of the fat portions. The souse, though, should be fried in batter. 3469-1

Varieties of Meat

Wild Game
We noted in the section "Ingestion of Food, Air and Water Containing Mineral Forces" under *Iron* that [4834] was

advised to eat wild game, nothing that had been killed with blood in it, and that it was pointed out here that wild game eats from nature, tame game what it is fed. (4834-1) According to the reference following, wild game, if properly prepared, is the choicest meat of all.

Q-1. Is it all right for me to eat rabbit and squirrel, baked or stewed?
A-1. Any wild game is preferable. . .to other meats, if these are prepared properly.
Rabbit—be sure the tendon in both left legs is removed, or that as might cause a fever. It is what is called at times the wolve in the rabbit. While prepared in some ways this would be excellent for some [specific] disturbances in a body, it is never well for this to be eaten in a hare. Squirrel—of course, it is not the same in this. This stewed, or well cooked, is really . . .preferable for the body, of course—but rabbit is well if that part indicated is removed.   2514-4

Wild game was recommended along with other meats.

Evenings—rather the whole vegetables, but combine same at times with the meats that are *only* of the mutton or lamb or fish or fowl or wild game.   831-1

Pork

Except for a little crisp bacon occasionally it is best not to eat the flesh of pigs. The dross it makes in the body functioning causes a fungus to develop, which may crystallize muscles and nerves, causing acute pain.

No raw meat, and very little ever of hog meat. Only bacon. Do not use bacon or fats in cooking the vegetables. . .303-11

The meats taken would be preferably fish, fowl and lamb...Breakfast bacon, crisp, may be taken occasionally.
                              1710-4

Here, in the condition of this body, we have a result of the absorption of certain character of foods.
The character it makes in the body-functioning causes a fungi [fungus] that produces in the system a crystallization of the muscles and nerves in portions of the body.
These results have been apparent in the pelvic organs, the whole lumbar-sacral area, portions of the sciatic nerves, the knees and feet—all of these are giving distress.

These distresses began as acute pain, rheumatic or neuritic. They are closer to neuritic-arthritic reactions. This is pork—the effect of same.

Q-3. *What had the body been eating that it should not?*

A-3. Meats, in the form of hog meat.   294-95

Note, however, the use of pig knuckles, pig's feet and souse under "Most Valuable Portions of Meat." Excerpts following tell us that pig's feet contain vitamins, hormones and gluten as well as calcium and recommend hog tripe as blood building and hog kidneys and tripe as an aid in keeping down uremia and uremic reaction.

. . .there should be the more efficient supply and more quantities of the vitamins B and B-1 and D. These, through the food supply, would be the better means for obtaining helpful directions for the body forces.

These vitamins would be found supplied best by having at least twice a week the pig's feet, well cooked and well jellied—using the gristle portions especially, or mostly.   556-18

. . .blood-building foods; as pig's feet and the like. These carry the hormones and the gluten that supplies in the assimilating system the better body building.   1519-4

Q-12. *Could any other tonic be substituted for the Ventriculin?*

A-12. . . .blood puddings, or liver or pig's feet or tripe. . .These will be much slower; they will not carry as much of the iron, but *more* of those things in some forms that will be more easily assimilated. . .these are the juices of these very portions of the animal fat (in the Ventriculin) that are assimilated by the system; and if these are used in their regular state, of course, this should supply then at least one meal each day from either tripe, liver, pig's feet or the like. . .and when the pig's feet, eat *only* the gristle force, not fat!

Q-13. *How would they be prepared?*

A-13. Roast.   556-4

. . .pig's feet. . .would be very well, especially because of the needed activities for the muscular force and because of the gluten that forms from same.   849-37

. . .the hog tripe—not *pickled,* but. . .nicely prepared, and *not* fried. This will add and build *blood,* and build it quickly.

1377-5

No hog meat of *any* kind unless it is the tripe or the liver or the kidneys—these are very good in keeping a balance and. . . aid in keeping down uremia or uremic reaction from a taxed system.   658-15

Beef

Beef is recommended for occasional use in a well-balanced diet.

Evenings: Fruits, as cooked apples; potatoes, tomatoes, fish, fowl, lamb, and occasionally beef, but not too much. Keep these as the main part of a well-balanced diet.   1523-17

Rare steak and beef juice are good for cold and congestion.

First, be mindful of the diet. Keep away from too great quantity of starches. Build with beef juices. And once or twice or three times a week a good rare steak—not too great a quantity but this regularly, as well as the beef juice—will make for strength.

Take the beef juice especially before the evening meal, or after resting a few minutes when returning from labors.
                                                                243-29

Beef juice is recommended as a valuable adjunct in body building. It gives strength and vitality.

Beef juice is *not* beef broth. Directions for preparing beef juice follow:

Pure beef juice, not broth, prepared in this manner: Take a pound to a pound and a half, preferably round steak. . .no fatty or skin portions. Dice this into half-inch cubes. . .Put same in a glass jar without water in same. Put the jar into a boiler or container with water coming about half or three-fourths toward the top of the jar. . .Put a cloth in the container to prevent the jar from cracking. Do not seal the jar tight, but cover the top. Let this boil (the water with the jar in same) for three to four hours.

Then strain off the juice, and the refuse may be pressed somewhat. It will be found that the meat or flesh itself will be worthless. Place the juice in a cool place, but do not keep too long; never longer than three days. Hence the quantity made up at the time depends upon how much or how often the body will take this. It should be taken two to three times a day, but not more than a tablespoonful at the time—and this sipped very slowly. Of course, this is to be seasoned to suit the taste of

the body. Well, too, that whole wheat or Ry-Krisp crackers. . .
be taken with same to make it more palatable.   1343-2

Beef juice should be taken regularly as a medicine, a
teaspoonful four times a day at least, but when taken it should
be sipped, not just taken. . .[in] a gulp.   5374-1

We would use the beef juice as a tonic, as a medicine; not
merely as the diet but to be taken several times each day, but
not more than a teaspoonful at a time—and this sipped very
slowly.   2140-1

Beef juice would be excellent for the body taken as medicine,
or as doses—teaspoonful at a time, or as improvement is
shown, tablespoonful at a time may be taken.   5522-1

Q-5. What quantity of beef juice to be taken daily?
A-5. At least two tablespoonsful, but no fat in same. A
tablespoonful is almost equal to a pound of meat; . . .[you would
be taking] two pounds of meat a day; and that's right smart for
a man that isn't active!   1424-2

Also once a day it will be most beneficial to take beef juice as
a tonic; not so much the beef itself but beef juice; followed with
a red wine. Do not mix these, but take both about the same
time. Take about a teaspoonful of the beef juice, but spend
about five minutes in sipping that much. Then take an ounce of
red wine, with a whole wheat cracker.   2535-1

. . .we would use small quantities at a time—but take almost
as medicine—beef juices. . .This is easily assimilated, gives
strength and vitality, and is needed with the vital forces of the
body in the present. Take at least a tablespoonful during a day,
or two tablespoonsful. But not as spoonsful; rather sips of
same. This sipped, in this manner, will work toward producing
the gastric flow through the intestinal system, first in the
salivary reactions to the very nature of the properties
themselves; second with the gastric flow from the upper
portion of the stomach or through the cardiac reaction at the
end of the esophagus that produces the first of the lacteals'
reaction to the gastric flows in the stomach or digestive forces
themselves; thirdly, making for an activity through the
pylorus and the duodenum that becomes stimulating to the
activity of the flows without producing the tendencies for
accumulation of gases.   1100-10

From the above we learn that beef juice, prepared and sipped according to directions, will stimulate the gastric flow through the intestinal system.

We have noted previously that the beef products liver and tripe are useful in blood and body building and brains useful in blood building and that calcium may be obtained from gristle. Also note the following:

The meats should be such as lamb, fowl, fish, or the like. Occasionally the *broiled* steak or liver, or tripe would be well.
808-3

In the diets; keep away from heavy foods. Use those which are body building, such as beef juice, beef broth, liver, fish, lamb; all [these] may be taken, but never fried foods. 5269-1

At least one meal each week (in the meats) should consist of liver or tripe, because of the blood purifying that these make for the body.
826-1

For a 36-year-old tubercular woman:

Have liver often, and this the rarer the better; taken at least two or three times a week.
1560-1

Then, have especially those foods that carry more of the calcium and the vitamins A, D, B-1 and other B complexes. Hence we would have plenty of liver. . .
2679-1

. . .blood building foods; as the whole wheat, beef juices, broiled liver, pigs' feet and the like. These carry the hormones and the gluten that supplies in the assimilating system the better body building.
1519-4

. . .at least once each week—tripe, liver, cod liver, fish liver, pig liver, calf liver—any of these.
3842-1

. . .if we are rather patient we will find the blood itself being built up—with the *diets* that will make for blood building forces. Not too much at the time, but plenty of. . .liver juice made in the same way and manner as the beef juice—this will be strengthening to the body.
632-3

Those of the tripe. . .that carry the *glucose,* that make for a change in the blood supply, that aid to build up.
421-2

The diets. . .along those lines that make for nerve *building*. . .

Little or no meats. . .though those that will add for nerve forces, as tripe, brains, kidneys, liver, spleen, or such, these will be beneficial to the body in small quantities.   3747-1

In the evening. . .the meat juices. . .that will supply more gluten. . .Brains and such. . .   501-2

Beef marrow also was recommended, to be obtained from vegetable soup.

Have the marrow of beef, or such, as a part of the diet; [eat such foods] as the vegetable soups that are rich in the beef carrying the marrow of the bone, and the like. . .and *eat the marrow!*   1523-8

See the section on "Vegetables" for the uses of gelatin (powdered beef bone) in vegetable salads and as an adjunct to vegetable juice for drinking. See section "Fruits, Grains, Beans and Nuts" under *Preparation of Fruits* for gelatin combined with fruits for desserts. Additional endorsements of gelatin follow.

. . .a great deal of any form of desserts carrying quantities of gelatin. Any of the gelatin products, though they may carry sugar at times, these are to be had oft in the diet.   2520-2

Gelatin may be prepared with any of the vegetables—as in the salads for the noon meal—or with. . .milk and cream dishes. These would be well for the body.   3224-2

Junket, even those principles as from gelatin and the like are to be desired, if they agree with the body or if the appetite will take portions of same.   1885-1

Lamb
In the *Individual Reference File* of extracts from the readings, compiled for the use of A.R.E. members, we find this statement: " 'Fish, fowl and lamb, never fried' is a phrase which appears in hundreds of the readings given by Edgar Cayce. . ." ("Diet—Meat") It seems unnecessary to include more than a few of the recommendations for the three.

Q-3. Please outline the proper diet, suggesting things to avoid.
A-3. Avoid too much of the heavy meats not well cooked. Eat plenty of vegetables of all characters. The meats taken would

be preferably fish, fowl, and lamb; others *not* so often. Breakfast bacon, crisp, may be taken occasionally. 1710-4

. . .a little of the meats such as lamb, fish, fowl—these are preferable. 840-1

. . .fish, fowl, or lamb perferably, as the meats or their combinations. 275-45

Fish, fowl and lamb. . .supply elements needed for brain, muscle and nerve building. 4008-1

Fowl

The information in the preceding section is applicable here also. For references to obtaining calcium by chewing the bony parts of fowls and/or eating broth prepared from same, see "Ingestion of Food, Air and Water Containing Mineral Forces," *Calcium.*

A few more excerpts will be given on the subject.

It would be very well to take foods to supplement [the present diet], especially foods from which the body may assimilate larger quantities of calcium, such as fish, chicken especially prepared in a way where the bones may be eaten. The feet and neck of the chicken are worth a lot more than the breast, although the breast is more palatable. Chewing the bones will be worth more to the body in strengthening and in the eliminations. These should be broiled or stewed, but do keep the lid on so that the boiling will not carry off that which is best to be taken. 5069-1

When there is a great deal of fowl—that is, of chicken, goose, duck, turkey or the like, and the bony pieces or broths of same are taken—it is not so necessary for great quantities of Calcios. 808-15

For a 36-year-old tubercular woman:

Eat all of the chicken that is possible—*every day,* but do not fry same! or merely roast. Rather it would be broiled or baked, or cooked in its own juices inside the oven. 1560-1

. . .especially those foods that carry more of the calcium and of the vitamins A, D, B-1 and other B complexes. Hence we would have plenty of. . .fowl. . . 2679-1

For tendencies to arthritis:

Do not eat. . .the fat of. . .the fowl. . .fats work a hardship upon the kidneys as well as upon the upper hepatic circulation, and tend to make the stress greater.   1888-1

Fish and Seafood Products

See the section "Ingestion of Food, Air and Water Containing Mineral Forces" for excerpts on and discussion of the use of fish and seafood in the diet. A few other references will now be added.

Fish or shellfish. . .prepared in varied manners; though never too much of these fried. Rather have them broiled, boiled, baked, stewed, scalloped or the like.   2517-1

. . .seafoods may be prepared in stews, soups or in whatever manner is most satisfactory to the body.   3134-1

Even. . .the fish would be better cooked in the Patapar paper or a steam cooker.   133-4

Q-3. Please suggest foods to stress. . .
A-3. . . .there should be the stressing of those that are nerve building; such as. . .fish, especially seafood—not freshwater fish.   4033-1

. . .and of the larger varieties—(fish) that carry a great quantity of those properties for body and blood building.
                    1973-1

When eating canned salmon eat the bony portion; don't take it out, as it will aid with the oil in same, to supply elements necessary for the body building forces.   2890-3

. . .meats. . .that carry the sinew. . .that is wild game or fish.
                    3972-1

. . .preferably those of wild game or fowl or fish. . .those that carry the sinew and vital forces. . .   4810-1

The vitamins necessary in the system, and especially vitamin E—whose activity in the system is for reproduction of the activity through every gland of the body itself, or those forces that are from silicon, iron, gold, or the activities from phosphorus—as of shellfish. Especially clams, oysters, more than any of the others—unless it is lobster. These are well to be taken two or three times each week; but these should be boiled.
                    1048-4

. . .foods that are easily assimilated; plenty of fish, both canned and fresh.   3267-1

Little fish, or any carrying iodine (as any of the shellfish) may be used in moderation. Do not mix same, however, with milk. The action of these would be detrimental to the system.
4789-1

Sardines in oil, *never* in mustard, may be used sparingly.
1001-1

Plenty of oysters that carry the greater part of iron, and as little of copper or manganese as possible.   4164-1

Q-3. What foods contain gold, silicon and phosphorus?
A-3. . . .These are contained more in those of the. . .varieties that are given as same. . .Oysters. . .   1000-2

The oyster or clam should be taken raw as much as possible; while [having] the others [shrimp, lobster, etc.] prepared through roasting or boiling [broiling?] with the [use of] butter, would be better than [having them] prepared in other manners.   275-24

Q-1. What effect has alcohol when you eat raw oysters?
A-1. It produces a chemical reaction that is bad for *most* stomachs. Oysters should never be taken with whiskey.
2853-1

. . .beware of some combinations—especially of shellfish of *any* nature with alcoholic influences for the system near the same time.   1293-2

Especially conch soup would be well for this particular body. These may be obtained, even though rare. . .[on] the southern and eastern coast of Florida.   5010-1

Also there may be obtained from the turtle egg those influences for longevity that may be created in certain cellular forces in the body.   659-1

. . .the cod liver oil would be a beneficial condition in keeping away cold.   1490-1

Well that as much of. . .cod liver oil as is easily assimilated be taken. Be governed as to the quantity. . .as to how same is assimilated—for [this] is detrimental when not being assimilated by the system, for it acts as an irritant to the gastric and to the juices of the intestines and digestion, when not assimilated. 4874-3

...the halibut [oil] rather than the cod liver [oil] for this body. 1179-3

. . .plenty of the shellfish—or fish proper. These are good, whether in the dried or in the fresh. The fresh carry more of that vitamin as makes for stamina in the vital forces of reproduction of *every* form *of* life in the system. Remember, this is for good and bad influences or bacilli as may be in [the] body! Hence, these should be carefully selected, and be *very* fresh and not from polluted waters. 501-1

Most people are familiar with the need for the greatest freshness in all fish and seafood products. That they should also come from unpolluted waters cannot be stressed too greatly. In Edgar Cayce's time pollution was slight compared to what it is today. How much more do we need to inquire now into the origin of all fish and seafood that we eat!

Dairy Products

Cow's Milk and Buttermilk
For [275] raw milk, if certified, was said to be preferable.

...milk. . .*preferably* the raw milk *if* certified milk! 275-24

Give all the cool fresh milk that may be taken. Be sure that it is from tested kine or cows, however. 1324-1

The type of food the cows eat may, however, render the raw milk unacceptable.

...raw milk—provided it is from cows that don't eat certain characters of food. If they eat dry food, it is well, if they eat certain types of weeds or grass grown this time of year [January], it won't be so good for the body. 2752-3

Raw milk is rich in calcium.

There should be those precautions that there be plenty of calcium in the system for developing of bone and muscle tissue. Most of this, of course, may be had from raw milk. 540-7

The pasteurization of milk should be properly performed.

Q-3. Is the raw milk I am taking now well, or is pasteurized milk better?
A-3. Pasteurized milk is. . .preferable, provided it is pasteurized properly. The raw milk as taken in the present is *not bad,* but there are some surroundings about its source that are not so good. 340-31

Although there is material producing worms to a limited extent in all intestines, milk with bacillus in it may cause them to increase rapidly. However, addition of raw, green foods to the diet can eliminate the sources.

Q-4. How did the trouble of pinworms originate. . .?
A-4. Milk! You see, in every individual there is within the intestinal tract that matter which produces a form of intestinal worm. This is in everyone. But with a particular diet where the milk has any bacillus, it will gradually cause these to increase, and they oftentimes develop or multiply rapidly; and then they may disappear, *if* there is taken raw, green food!
Q-5. Would you change the kind of milk she drinks?
A-5. It isn't so much the change in the kind of milk that is needed. Either add the raw, green foods as indicated, or give those properties as would eliminate the sources of same [the pinworms]. But it is better, if it is practical, to induce the body to eat lettuce and celery and carrots, even a small amount. One leaf of lettuce will destroy a thousand worms! 2015-10

For most individuals irradiated or dried milk is more healthful than fresh.

Q-3. Can milk and dairy products be included in diet?
A-3. Milk products may be gradually added, but for the body yet it is much preferable to use dry milks or malted milks rather than raw milk. There is so easily an overstressing upon milk, by many; for there are many products much more healthful than milk. So few milks are free from tubercle; so few are free from those influences that cause a great deal more irritation than help—unless irradiated or dried milk is used. These as a whole are much more healthful to most individuals than raw milk. 480-42

It seems pertinent to note here that calcium lactate tablets are procurable in health stores today.
Milk is recommended for use in the readings as body

building. It is stimulating to the lymph system. It does not produce mucus as some suppose.

The diet should be more body building; that is, less acid foods and more of the alkaline-reacting will be the better in these directions. Milk and all its products should be a portion of the body's diet now.   480-19

...use those foods that are rich in the vitamins that make for a stimulation to a lymph circulation.

First we would have...the rich vitamins from the milk that is dried, or milk and egg, milk with bread that would be crumbled in same. Have these as a great portion of the diet.   1137-1

Q-15. . . .milk, I find, makes more mucus, the basis for catarrh.

A-15. This if taken properly is *not* the basis of mucus. If this is thy experience, then there are other conditions producing same. For milk, whether it is the dry or the pasteurized or raw, is near to the perfect combination of forces for. . .human consumption.   1703-2

Orange juice and milk should be taken at opposite ends of the day.

Orange juice and milk are helpful, but these should be taken at opposite ends of the day; not together.   274-9

Raw milk should preferably not be taken with raw vegetables.

Q-1. Should I take milk at the meal when I am taking raw vegetables?

A-1. Milk may be taken; preferably not raw milk. That is, rather milk that has been prepared, or milk that has been heated sufficiently for the curdling of certain food forces—the caseins that are hard upon the system.   1158-1

Milk should be chewed two or three times before it goes into the stomach.

Bolting food or swallowing it by the use of liquids produces more colds than *any one* activity of a diet! Even milk should be *chewed* two or three times before taken into the stomach itself, for this makes for the proper assimilation of the lacteal activity in the system; and when acted upon by the gastric flow of the hydrochlorics in the duodenum area, it is better assimilated and gives more value in the whole of the body.

808-3

An overwrought person should drink water or buttermilk instead of sweet milk.

Especially. . .[for] this body there should not be food taken when the body is overwrought in any manner. . .[because] of high-strung conditions or. . .wrath, or. . .depression of any nature. . .Preferably take water or buttermilk—*never* sweet milk under such conditions.   243-7

Buttermilk of the Bulgarian kind, commonly known as yogurt in this country, does not tend to produce gas.

Q-9. Is buttermilk good?
A-9. This depends upon the manner in which it is made. This would tend to produce gas if it is the ordinary kind. But that *made* by the use of the Bulgarian tablets is good, in moderation, not too much.   404-6

Bulgarian buttermilk and fresh milk warm with animal heat both contain phosphorus.

The phosphorus forming foods. . .[include] plenty of milk—the Bulgarian the better, or the fresh milk that is warm with the animal heat which carries more of the phosphorus and more of those activities that are less constipating, or acting more with the lacteals and the ducts of the liver, the kidneys, and the bowels themselves.   560-2

The milk warm with animal heat adds fat to the system and is helpful to the action of the chyle (a modification of lymph occurring in the lacteals).

Milk should be taken into the system preferably warm with animal heat which will add fatty portions in the system and will produce better forces in the chyle.   4466-1

Yogurt acts as a cleanser through the colon and intestines.

Use yogurt in the evening meal. . .This is to act as a cleanser for the alimentary canal, as well as a better balance for the fermenting and the eliminations of poisons from the system.   1762-1

Also we would add yogurt in the diet as an active cleanser through the colon and intestinal system. This would be most beneficial, not only purifying the alimentary canal but adding the vital forces necessary to enable those portions of the system to function in the nearer normal manner.   1542-1

Milk—this in some manners is tabu for the body, yet in others is excellent...the Bulgarian milk, or...the buttermilk would be the *better* for the system. This is acid in the reaction, to be sure, in *some* cases. Not so here! For the bacilli...created in system through same will produce effects such that we will have a cleansed colon by the use of same.   5525-1

Yogurt can build up vitality.

...for the creating of the proper conditions in the digestive system, the Bulgarian milk or *buttermilk,* properly handled. *Preferably*...the Bulgarian would be the better, this adding sufficient of the lactic and lacteals for the system for the proper stimulation through the lacteal ducts...[to] the lachrymal system, or of the changing into the new forces for the blood supply.   142-5

Then for the strengthening of the body, for the gradual building up of the vitality, use yogurt.   5210-1

Yogurt tablets, comprising honeycomb with milk, may be used instead of the more fluid yogurt.

The character of milks taken would be varied; not that carrying too much curd nor yet too much of any of those properties that produce too great a quantity of activity in the intestinal tract. Here we find that the tablets as of honeycomb with milk would be well, as prepared by the Kellogg Institute— in that termed yogurt, but the *former* and not the latter preparation would be much better you see—in the tablets. These would be taken about one or two a day.   643-1

Some people were advised to take buttermilk with no specification that it be Bulgarian. In light of the following reference specifying the buttermilk as churned milk, it would seem that both yogurt and churned buttermilk were advised at different times.

...if preferable, change entirely and use only buttermilk, or churned milk...or clabber, which would be preferable...
556-3

Buttermilk has a germicidal effect.

Any form of yeast or a yogurt for the body will be well. Of course, this is a portion of that as will be had from buttermilk. It is those germicidal influences in same that will be effective upon the intestinal system.   538-57

Homogenized Milk

The following reference points out that for one person, a pregnant woman, homogenized milk was preferable to non-homogenized.

Q-9. Does the homogenized Vitamin D milk have greater advantages or disadvantages for this body during pregnancy?
A-9. It's advantageous.
Q-10. How much should be taken?
A-10. That to satisfy the body's appetite.
Q-11. Is there no possibility that the milk will produce dangerous fat making delivery difficult?
A-11. Not if other conditions, that have been indicated for the body, are kept intact.
Q-12. Would milk have the tendency to make the baby larger which in turn would make a Caesarean necessary for this body?
A-12. Not necessarily.   457-12

Goat's Milk and Mare's Milk

Goat's milk and mare's milk were advised in the readings for some people. It would seem that the goat's milk was easier for these particular persons to digest because of the kind of curds it forms in the stomach.

Goat's milk or mare's milk may be taken by the body in small quantities, *provided* same *agrees* with the body. . .for this will agree in small quantity, yet if too much is crowded into the system, the system will *not* be able to handle same.   5714-2

Q-5. Did this body have whooping cough, or was the cough caused from bad milk?
A-5. Whooping cough. . .Those manipulations and those conditions accorded for the body's eliminations have kept the body well, and the germ—or that producing whooping cough, as yet, has not been *entirely* eliminated from the system. The effects of same are greatly diminished. . .Hence goat's milk and modified Mellin's Food the better for the body.   5520-1

Q-1. How much milk should he drink each day [for general debilitation]?

A-1. This should be goat's milk or mare's milk...These would be...preferable to...raw milk and...may be taken...in *smaller* quantities and often...   4320-3

In the character of *milks*—this will not always agree with the system, for curds would be produced from same that would be bad. Then, these may be altered by the *character* of the milk at times as may be taken...the goat's milk...may be used occasionally. This with the cereals, or with the foods, or with the first morning foods.   5545-1

Ice Cream
Ice cream was advised for some persons. However, the boiled milk in it made it unsuitable for an adult man, [461], with anemia.

Not too great a quantity of sweets at any period, as desserts; though ice cream, ices or the like may be taken in moderation.
                                                            480-13

Ice cream...or such may be given, that the body will take, and will give strength to the body.   2299-13

Noons...take dried milk, not raw milk—and especially not that which has been boiled. Hence ice cream is *not* so good.
                                                            461-1

Butter
Butter should be used as a seasoning for vegetables if any seasoning *is* to be used.
For a person with gastritis:

...no greases, no fats should be taken. Of course, butter may be taken. And the vegetables should be prepared preferably with butter if any seasoning is to be used.   3033-1

Butterfat or dairy products are recommended when a little fat may be needed for digestion.

Q-7. *What causes nerve pain below shoulder blades on right side of spine?*
A-7. This is a part of those disturbances from the digestive forces. A little fat here needs to be taken; especially as from butterfat or dairy products.   1770-7

Cheese
Cream cheese and cheddar cheese are recommended—in moderation.

Do be consistent with the diets—keeping away from. . .too [many] starches—for instance, spaghetti and cheese; though cheese may be taken in moderation if it is a cream or cheddar cheese. 459-11

All cheese should be taken in moderation.

A great deal of fats will. . .be hard on the body, as indicated by the lack of ability for digesting greases in the present. Butterfats and cheeses and such are well to be taken in moderation. 1409-9

Cheese combined with proteins sometimes upsets digestion.

Cheeses at times with proteins. . .produce improper fermentation. 1158-3

Eggs

Eggs in the diet may be helpful in preserving the teeth.

Q-10. Suggest diet beneficial to preserving teeth.
A-10. Eggs. . .these are particularly given to preserving the teeth; or anything that carries quantities of calcium or aids to the thyroid in its production would be beneficial—so it is not overbalanced. . . 1523-3

For some persons a daily egg yolk was advised; for others the use of eggs, whole or yolks, was to be intermittent. If eggs are coddled, they do not contain the extra amount of acid usually formed by the white (when cooked?). However, for some persons the albumin of the white is important.

Methods of cooking eggs are also given in the following excerpts.

For help in building up a 10-year-old boy's system:

. . .If some good whole grain cereal is taken. . .combined with the yolk of an egg each day [this] should supply sufficient [help] and be much better assimilated by the body than. . .[food] reinforced from vitamins. 2780-2

Q-1. Would it be advisable to eat all the following items daily . . .First, egg yolks?
A-1. These are good taken about twice or three times a week, but not every day, to be sure.
Q-2. How much?

A-2. Whether half a dozen, dozen, one or two! Whatever is the desire or the need for the body! Depends on how much is to be added with it when it is taken!   1158-21

Q-1. Are eggs good for the body?
A-1. Not too much of same, and *only* the yolk—this either hardboiled or cooked in this manner: Put in *boiling* water, taking it off the stove and letting it stay in the water for five minutes—then eat the yolk principally.   1657-2

For a five-month-old baby:

The yolk of an egg would be well to be taken once or twice a week, though half a yolk or the like should be sufficient for one meal—but if he takes more, it will be very well. Prepare same in this manner: Let the water come to a hard boil, then drop an egg in and immediately set the water off the heat; and when it is possible to take the egg out with the hand (without a spoon), then it is ready to give to the child—but *only* the yolk. . .This is the manner of preparation, and is what we would call a *coddled* egg. . .   1788-6

Eggs may be taken, but use more of the yolk than of the white and they should be prepared either in the form of soft-scrambled or coddled.   924-1

As to the diet: Have plenty of eggs, but not the white of the eggs. This may be taken in spirita frumenti with milk about once a day, making what is called eggnog.   5097-1

Q-1. Should I avoid eggs?
A-1. This depends upon supply of other elements. There are some elements in eggs not found in other foods—ordinarily, sulphur. The whites, however, do occasionally cause certain elements to be bad for the body. These we would take occasionally, not necessarily avoiding same.   5399-1

Egg yolks are very well. . .may be taken as a part of the morning meal. Especially is this well if they are cooked hard, then mashed or eaten with those things that make it more palatable. The sulphur here is especially desirable as also the elements that aid in digestion.   1206-9

Q-3. Should egg whites still be eliminated from my diet? If so, why?
A-3. Egg white, unless it is prepared in the form of a coddled egg, makes for a formation of acid by the extra amount of those

qualities that we find in same. With the changes that are wrought, it would be very good to use the whole egg—provided it is coddled or soft-scrambled. 567-8

Q-42. Whole eggs or yolks?
A-42. Whole eggs about once or twice a week, yolks about three times each week. In most instances, it is best that they *not* be taken raw. If taken raw, take them *with* something else; as in orange juice or beer or the like. 1158-31

Eggs may be taken, provided they are not too hard nor yet too soft when prepared. Or better still, take them entirely raw, with milk or stimulants that would make or cause same to assimilate with system. 1713-16

For a 36-year-old woman with tuberculosis:

Take *eggs, raw*—if they can be taken. And if the body can assimilate same, take the *whole* egg; for the albumin of the white—while it may be severe at one time, it is necessary at other times. And these may be taken in *beer* if so desired, or in a little whiskey—but take the whole egg. This once or twice a day will be found to be *most* helpful. 1560-1

Do not eat fried foods of any kind, *ever,* [1586]; especially not fried eggs. 1586-1

Honey

Honey is valuable in producing proper fermentation in the digestive processes and is, therefore, body building. One person was advised to take it on bread two or three times a week. Another was told that if sugar and candy were eliminated, half an ounce to two ounces of honey with the honeycomb might be ingested daily.

Q-13. What type of sweets may be eaten by the body?
A-13. Honey, especially in the honeycomb; or preserves made with *beet* rather than cane sugar. Not too great a quantity of any of these, of course, but the forces in sweets... [which] make for the proper activity through the action of the gastric flows *are* as necessary as body building; for these become body building in making for the proper fermentation (if it may be called so) in the digestive activities. Hence two or three times a week the honey upon the bread or the food values would furnish that necessary in the whole system. 808-3

Q-1. Why does sugar in any form hurt my teeth?
A-1. If it hurts the teeth, leave it off! The drainages of the system, or from the system, are of such natures that this is the same as a *combustion* (and a great deal of it mental!). So, leave it off! Use honey in the honeycomb; not that which carries glucose or the like (and the type of candy that has been used also, but leave it off).

Q-2. How much honey may be taken each day?
A-2. Half an ounce to two ounces would not be too great a quantity. But only that in the honeycomb, *with* the honeycomb.   440-17

Honey in the honeycomb was advised for a number of people.

Q-4. Is it best for me to have any sweets?
A-4. Any sweets would be only honey *with* the honeycomb.
                                             1512-2

It is best to have the honey and honeycomb from sweet clover, buckwheat and similar sources. It is important that the comb be made from the clover and buckwheat.

First, as for the diet, let those be little of sweets, save as would be found in honey and honeycomb of the better nature. That is, as that produced by sweet clover, buckwheat, or such natures.   85-1

As regarding the honey and honeycomb...a portion of this is of that same cellular nature. Small quantities may be taken with impunity, yet the greater portion of same *should* be *comb* made from clover and buckwheat, rather than from flower or herb...see that the honeycomb as used is from the apiary that has this annex to same for the care of the bee making same.
                                             953-21

Honey was preferable to cane sugar for [1206] and [849].

When sweets are taken, we find that honey or maple sugar, or candies made with beet sugar, are preferable to cane sugar.
                                             1206-11

Q-8. What sweets may be taken, or are best for the body?
A-8. Honey, or those made with honey. Not cane sugars, *not* cakes, *not* pies! These should be taken very, *very* seldom!
                                             849-54

The value of milk and honey together is emphasized in a

reading for a man (today a dentist) who had been the first dentist for the Children of Israel when they settled around Shiloh. This selection shows the connection between strength of character and strength of the skeletal structure.

As in the teeth, so in the mind, the vibrations, the products of the land are different. Those so oft described, with which the land flowed, to which the entity went, are too seldom a part of the diet of those who would be healed of those [debilitating?] tendencies in their youth—milk and honey.   3211-2

A teaspoon or less of honey stirred into a glassful or cupful of warm or hot milk, taken in the evening, may be helpful for arthritis, neuritis or insomnia.

Be mindful that not too much coffee or tea is taken. Take at least a glassful of milk each day, preferably at the evening meal. Even if this is warm (not hot but warm), so as to dissolve half a teaspoonful of honey in same, it would be all the better [for arthritis, neuritis].   2816-1

For insomnia:

Also when the osteopathic treatments are begun, but not until then (for the system should be cleansed thoroughly first, by the taking of the two rounds of the properties indicated), we would begin taking each evening before retiring about a cupful of heated milk (raw milk, preferably), in which there would be stirred a level teaspoonful of pure honey. Do not boil the milk, but just let it come to the heating point, and then stir in the honey.   2057-1

Q-3. What will help the body sleep better?
A-3. Eliminating the poisons and the tensions, or "buzz" as it were upon the nerve system. . .will naturally make for easier sleep.
In the beginning of these, if there is the tendency for sleeplessness, or insomnia, stir a teaspoonful of pure honey in a glass of *hot* milk and drink same.   2050-1

Honey and milk should be taken as a nightcap, as it were. Stir or dissolve a full teaspoonful of strained honey into a glass or tumbler of heated milk. Taking this about twenty to thirty minutes before retiring will be found to be most helpful, most beneficial [for hypertension].   1539-1

Considerations Concerning the Eating
of Meat and Vegetables

There can be considerable variation in the dietary requirements of various individuals. The author will not attempt to
cover the ramifications in this book. A considerable amount of
advice from the readings has been included here previously in
the descriptions of the values of different food items.

Alkalinity and Acidity

The excerpts which follow show the importance of establishing a balance between acid-producing and alkaline-producing
foods in a normal diet and cite some advantages of alkalinity.

Q-5. What foods are acid-forming for this body?
A-5. All of those that are combining fats with sugars.
Starches naturally are inclined for acid reaction. But a normal
diet is about twenty percent acid to eighty percent alkaline-
producing.   1523-3

*Q-15. What causes colds? Can you give me a formula or
method of preventing. . .or curing them?*
A-15. Keep the body alkaline! Cold germs do not live in an
alkaline system! They do breed in any acid or excess of acids of
any character left in the system.   1947-4

. . .keep nearer to the alkaline-reacting foods and these will
overcome toxic forces. . .Have a great deal of the stimulations
from the whole wheat, citrus fruits and vegetables that are
green and raw. Not too much of the meats. Nor raw apples; or if
raw apples are taken. . .[Directions follow as to 3-day apple
diet.]   820-2

A person of sedentary life needs alkaline-reacting foods.

. . .in all bodies, the less activities there are in physical
exercise or manual activity, the greater should be the alkaline-
reacting foods taken. *Energies* or activities may burn acids,
but those who lead the sedentary life or the non-active life
can't go on sweets or too much starches. . .these should be well-
balanced.   798-1

Yet remember that too great alkalinity is more harmful than
a little overacidity.

. . .keep a tendency for alkalinity in the diet. This does not necessitate that there should never be any of the acid-forming foods included in the diet; for an overalkalinity is much more harmful than a little tendency occasionally for acidity.

808-3

Combinations of Meats and Other Foods

Note that a great deal of starch should not be eaten with proteins, including meat. The combination of sweets and meats is preferable to that of starches and meats.

Rather it is the combination of foods that makes for disturbance with most physical bodies. . .

. . .avoid combinations where corn, potatoes, rice, spaghetti or the like are taken all at the same meal. . .all of these tend to make for too great a quantity of starch—especially if any meat is taken at such a meal. . .For the activities of the gastric flow of the digestive system. . .[bring] requirements of one reaction in the gastric flow for starch and another for proteins, or for the activities of the carbohydrates as combined with starches of this nature. . .Then, in the combinations, do not eat great quantities of starch with the proteins or meats. If sweets and meats are taken at the same meal, these are preferable to starches [and meats]. Of course, small quantities of breads with sweets are all right, but do not have large quantities of same.

416-9

Meats should not be taken with starches from above the ground; therefore the combination of potatoes and meat is preferable to that of bread and meat.

Meats or the like should not be taken with starches that grow above the ground. There's quite a variation in the reaction in the physical body, especially where intestinal disturbance has caused the greater part of the inflammation through a body. . . Hence potatoes or the peelings of same with meats are. . . preferable to eating bread with meats. . .Hence they may be combined more together.

340-32

In the last analysis a person needs to study and understand the reaction of foods on his/her own system in a continuing manner and eat according to this.

Know that if there is to be taken. . .beef. . .it is *required* that there be taken the acids to *digest* same—and [if] they are not taken, this will be hard upon the system! But if the food values are taken in combinations and in manners that the system will assimilate same, this is. . .preferable.

Q-5. Please explain the reaction of foods on my system.

A-5. It's just been given! Those that required the bodily foods—there are foods that require (as meats) acids for their proper fermentation; while most of the foods. . .of the vegetable forces, especially of the leafy nature, require more of the slow combination of the lacteals' reaction or the greater quantity of the combination of acid and alkaline. Then if foods are taken in quantities that require an alkaline for their digestion, [and] an acid is in the system—this produces improper fermentation. If foods are taken where acid is necessary and it is not being produced by the system, or not taken into the system in synthetic state, then these produce the disturbances. . .See how the combinations of these, then, make for the necessity of watching, experimenting. . .with that which is good today and may be bad tomorrow. For what would be poison for someone, to another may be a cure. This is true in every physical organism. And unless these balances are being cared for properly, they produce disturbances. 1259-2

Everyday Meats vs. Strong Meats

There is a warning against strong meats as contrasted with everyday ones.

As has been given of old, [Daniel 1:5-17]. . .the children of Israel stood with the sons of the heathen, and all ate from the king's table, and that which was taken. . .exercised the imagination of the body in physical desires. . .strong drink, strong meats, condiments that magnify desires with[in] the body. . .this builded as Daniel well understood, not for God's service. . .he chose rather that the everyday, the common things would be given. . .that the bodies, the minds might be. . . more perfect channel[s] for the manifestations of God; for the forces of the Creator are in every force that is made manifest in the earth. 341-31

Flexibility in Diet

Although there is much advice on dietary requirements for individuals, there is also the advice not to be too rigid.

. . .it is well that the body not become as one that couldn't do this, that, or the other; or as a slave to an idea of a set diet.
1568-2

Be careful that there is kept *sufficient* of the roughages in the diet, but *do not* become cranky on the diet question and thus set *in* the imaginative and impulsive system such expectancies as to produce a cogental reaction in the digestive forces of the body. Be precautious, but know that the body *adjusts* itself readily—unless the imaginative or impulsive system prevents it from doing so.   340-31

Then the diet: This should be not so rigid as to appear that you can't do this or you can't do that, but rather let the attitudes be. . .everything that is eaten, as well as every activity. . .purposeful in conception, constructive in nature. Analyze that! Purposeful in activity, constructive in nature!
                                                                            1183-2

The Source of Meat

For today's world another warning can be added. The readings have told us that vegetables vary in food values according to where and how they are grown. There has also been an admonition against eating seafood from polluted waters. It follows that the source of any food and the substances it contains are of great importance. In Edgar Cayce's day there was not an extreme use of pesticides and herbicides in producing foods and of additives in processing them. With changed conditions we all need to be aware of what our food, including meat, consists. The purest, most naturally produced would seem to be the best and to embody that which the readings recommend.

Proper Eating Conditions

No matter what we are eating, some general rules apply to insure its proper digestion.

It is especially necessary to take enough time in both eating and chewing. Plenty of water should be drunk before and after meals. This, also, should be chewed—four to twenty times—so that the saliva may be well mixed with the food or water. An individual should not eat if worried, overtaxed, very tired, very excited, very angry or in some condition which makes it impossible for proper digestion to take place. A person should never take food he finds does not agree with him. He should never eat just to pass the time.

In the matter of the diet for the body—these, we find, are quite varied under circumstances and conditions over which the body often hasn't the control [as a traveling man]. Most of all, train self never to bolt the food. Take *time* to assimilate, masticate, so that *assimilation* is well—and we will find that with these kept, with an *even* balance between those that produce acid and those that make for the alkaline, if well-balanced will digest under most all circumstances. Well to drink *always plenty* of water, before meals and after meals—for. . .when any food value *enters* the stomach, *immediately* the stomach becomes a storehouse, or a medicine chest, that may create all the elements necessary for proper digestion within the system. If this *first* is acted upon by aqua pura, the reactions are more near normal. Well, then, each morning upon first arising, to take a half to three-quarters of a glass of *warm* water; not so hot that it is objectionable, not so tepid that it makes for sickening—but this will clarify the system of poisons. This well especially for this body. Occasionally a pinch of salt should be added to this draught of water. 311-4

Each time you take a mouthful, even if it's water, it should be chewed at least four to twenty times; whether it's water or bread or a carrot, onion, cabbage or what! Each should be chewed so that there is the mastication, and that there is the opportunity for the flow of the gastric forces from the salivary glands [to be] well mixed with same.   3823-3

Be mindful of the diet. . .Take time to eat and to eat the right thing, giving time for digestive forces [to act], before becoming so mentally and bodily active as to upset digestion.   243-23

Never [when] under strain, when very tired, very excited, very mad, should the body take foods in the system. . .And never take any food that the body finds is not agreeing with same. . .   137-30

True, the body should eat—and should eat slowly; yet when worried, overtaxed, or when the body may not make a *business* of the eating. . .[the food] will not digest, as the body sees.   900-393

The Importance of Food
What we think and what we eat—combined together—*make* what we are, physically and mentally.   288-38

An Animal Product for Healing
Mutton Tallow Compound
The mutton tallow compound described below was advised as a treatment for colds and congestion of the throat and upper chest.

Prepare this compound in two solutions. . .melt the mutton

tallow and this would be a separate solution, until the others are added. Do not attempt to mix the tallow in its original state, but melt it. Then—while it is not too hot, but before it congeals—add an equal amount of each of the other ingredients—first the turpentine, then the camphor [spirits of turpentine and spirits of camphor].   2175-2

Massage the glands on the throat and upper portion of the chest, in the hollow of the throat and neck, on the glands of the side, with an equal combination of mutton tallow (melted), spirits of turpentine and spirits of camphor; and. . .[in the] evening put two thicknesses of flannel around same.

This should within twenty-four to forty-eight hours. . . reduce the conditions [for this body].

With the diet. . .take those things that are more of the liquid nature.

Have good eliminations, preferably with either the Castoria or syrup of figs, or any compound that is of senna base.

Do these. . .for the immediate [needs]; and have a good, general, thorough osteopathic treatment to relax the body thoroughly afterwards.   1100-29

DOMINION OVER THE EARTH

We have now explored the three kingdoms of the earth—mineral, plant and animal, seen how wonderfully and beautifully they are constructed and how they interact with one another. The plant utilizes the strength and power of minerals; the animal utilizes the strength and power of plants and minerals; man utilizes the strength and power of all three. For it is man who has dominion over the earth. It was for his needs that "there was made all that was made." (3744-4)

Why was man endowed with all these bounties? That he might use them in perfecting himself into a spiritualized being, able to go on to further realms laid out for his progress back to God, ultimately to be a companion to the Father.

The earth is the Lord's and the fullness thereof. The universe He called into being for purposes that the individual soul, that might be one with Him, would have, does have, those influences for bringing this to pass or to be in the experience of every soul.   1347-1

Let us use these gifts that God has given us in ways to strengthen our minds and bodies. Thus we may be enabled to pursue more effectively our true spiritual purpose. Let us keep our bodies as a sacred trust, for

...thy body is the temple of the living God.   3492-1

BIBLIOGRAPHY

Blazek, Mark C., "Nature's Earthquake Alarms," *Fate,* October, 1977, pg. 59.

Bulfinch, Thomas, *The Age of Fable,* A Mentor Classic, The New American Library, Inc., New York and Toronto, 1962, pp. 336-337.

Carley, Ken, "Lapis Lazuli," *The A.R.E. Journal,* July, 1975, pp. 161-169.

----- "Reflections of a Rockhound," *The A.R.E. Journal,* November, 1973, pp. 229-236.

----- "The Stones of Egypt," *The A.R.E. Journal,* September, 1974, pp. 200-211.

Cayce, *The Edgar Cayce Readings,* as referenced.

Church, W.H., "An Almond a Day," *An Edgar Cayce Health Anthology,* A.R.E. Press, 1979, pp. 62-75.

Clapp, Robert O., "Blessed Ragweed—The Most Hated of Weeds," *An Edgar Cayce Health Anthology,* A.R.E. Press, 1979, pp. 45-51.

----- "The Healing Powers of Saffron Tea," *An Edgar Cayce Health Anthology,* A.R.E. Press, 1979, pp. 52-61.

Crow, W.B., D.Sc., Ph.D., *Precious Stones,* Samuel Weiser, Inc., New York City, 1968, pp. 28, 29, 32, 34, 35.

Cruden, Alexander, *Cruden's Unabridged Concordance to the Old and New Testaments and The Apocrypha,* Baker Book House, Grand Rapids, Mich., 1966, pg. 514.

Duncan, Mary Alice, P.T., "Physiotherapy in the Edgar Cayce Readings, The Concept of Wholeness," *An Edgar Cayce Health Anthology,* A.R.E. Press, 1979, pp. 21-33.

Gibbons, Euell, *Stalking the Healthful Herbs,* David McKay Company, Inc., New York City, 1966, pp. 224, 225, 249.

Hasbrouck, L.M., "More About Earthquakes: II," *American Mercury,* January, 1960, pp. 120-121.

Hopkins, Charity, "Your Nose Knows More Than You Know," *Parade,* January 2, 1977, pg. 10.

Jarman, A.S., "Unsolved Animal Mysteries," *Tomorrow,* Spring, 1960, pp. 65-72.

Johnson, Tom, and Baraff, Carol A., "Ipsab—An Herbal Remedy for Gum Problems," *An Edgar Cayce Health Anthology,* A.R.E. Press, 1979, pp. 91-93.

Krochmal, Arnold and Connie, "Ginseng, Panacea of Five Leaves," *Garden,* September/October, 1978, © 1978 by the New York Botanical Garden, pp. 25-28.

Loehr, Reverend Franklin, *The Power of Prayer on Plants*, Doubleday & Co., Inc., Garden City, N.Y., 1959.

Lucas, Richard, *Nature's Medicines*, Award Books, New York City, ℗ 1966 by Parker Publishing Co., Inc., pp. 40-58, 155, 162, 163.

McGarey, William A., M.D., *Edgar Cayce and the Palma Christi*, A.R.E. Press, 1970.

------ "Notes from the Medical Research Bulletin," *The A.R.E. Journal*, May, 1973, pg. 134.

------ "Notes from the Medical Research Bulletin," *The A.R.E. Journal*, March, 1975, pg. 82.

------ "Notes from the Medical Research Bulletin," *The A.R.E. Journal*, May, 1977, pp. 133-134.

------ "What is Adequate Therapy for the Epileptic?" *An Edgar Cayce Health Anthology*, A.R.E. Press, 1979, pg. 166.

Nichols, Cecil, "An Introduction to Herbs in the Edgar Cayce Readings," *An Edgar Cayce Health Anthology*, A.R.E. Press, 1979, pp. 39-44.

O'Malley, George, D.O., in collaboration with Rudnikoff, Peter, D.O., "Castor Oil Pack Therapy—A Report," *The Searchlight*, May, 1961, pp. 1-2.

Reilly, Harold J., D.Ph.T., D.S., and Brod, Ruth Hagy, *The Edgar Cayce Handbook for Health Through Drugless Therapy*, Jove Publications, Inc., New York City, 1977, pp. 257-294.

Sheffer, Myrtle E., "Bovine Seismographs?", *Fate*, October, 1969, pg. 75.

Time, Chicago, Ill., "To Catch a Thief," Vol. 86, July 30, 1965, pg. 59.

Virginian-Pilot, The, Norfolk, Va., "Animals Sense Coming Quakes," January 6, 1979.

------ "Apple Gas Causes Plant Blossoms," Aug. 11, 1965, pg. 24.

Zim, Herbert S., and Shaffer, Paul R. (Professor of Geology, University of Illinois), *Rocks and Minerals*, Golden Press, Inc., New York City, 1957, pp. 84, 88.

THE WORK OF EDGAR CAYCE TODAY

The Association for Research and Enlightenment, Inc. (A.R.E.®), is a membership organization founded by Edgar Cayce in 1931.

- 14,256 Cayce readings, the largest body of documented psychic information anywhere in the world, are housed in the A.R.E. Library/Conference Center in Virginia Beach, Virginia. These readings have been indexed under 10,000 different topics and are open to the public.

- An attractive package of membership benefits is available for modest yearly dues. Benefits include: a journal and newsletter; lessons for home study; a lending library through the mail, which offers collections of the actual readings as well as one of the world's best parapsychological book collections, names of doctors or health care professionals in your area.

- As an organization on the leading edge in exciting new fields, A.R.E. presents a selection of publications and seminars by prominent authorities in the fields covered, exploring such areas as parapsychology, dreams, meditation, world religions, holistic health, reincarnation and life after death, and personal growth.

- The unique path to personal growth outlined in the Cayce readings is developed through a worldwide program of study groups. These informal groups meet weekly in private homes.

- A.R.E. maintains a visitors' center where a bookstore, exhibits, classes, a movie, and audiovisual presentations introduce inquirers to concepts from the Cayce readings.

- A.R.E. conducts research into the helpfulness of both the medical and nonmedical readings, often giving members the opportunity to participate in the studies.

For more information and a color brochure, write or phone:

A.R.E., Dept. C., P.O. Box 595
Virginia Beach, VA 23451, (804) 428-3588

Discover the wealth of information in the Edgar Cayce readings

Membership Benefits You Receive Each Month

Dreams
Soul Mates
Karma
Earth Changes
Universal Laws
Meditation
Holistic Health
ESP
Astrology
Atlantis
Psychic Development
Numerology
Pyramids
Death and Dying
Auto-Suggestion
Reincarnation
Akashic Records
Planetary Sojourns
Mysticism
Spiritual Healing
And other topics

**EDGAR CAYCE FOUNDATION and
A.R.E. LIBRARY/VISITORS CENTER**
Virginia Beach, Va.
OVER 50 YEARS OF SERVICE